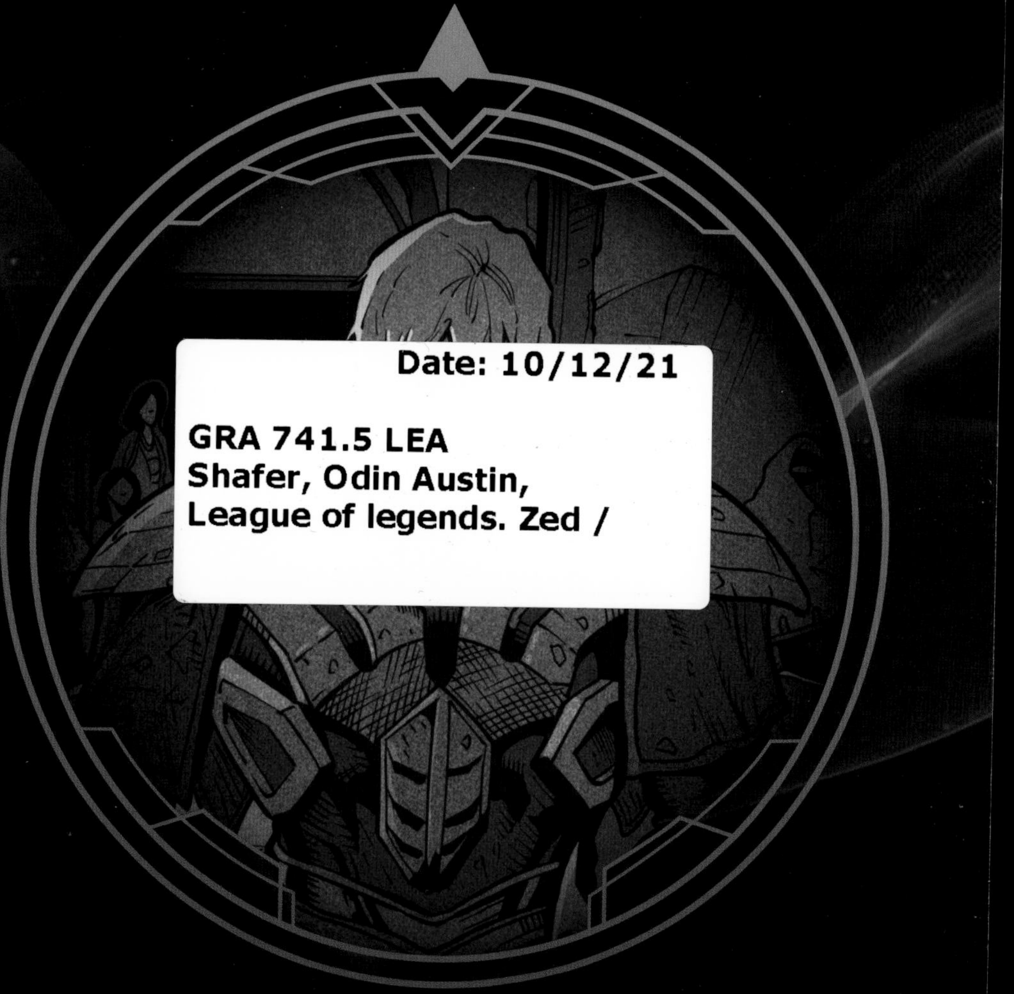

IONIA

Twelve years ago, the empire of Noxus invaded.

Its armies were defeated only after many years, and at great cost.

Shaken by the war, these lands exist now in an uneasy peace.

In these turbulent, changing times, a man who has been called a patriot, a hero, a pariah, and a criminal, finds himself at a crossroads...

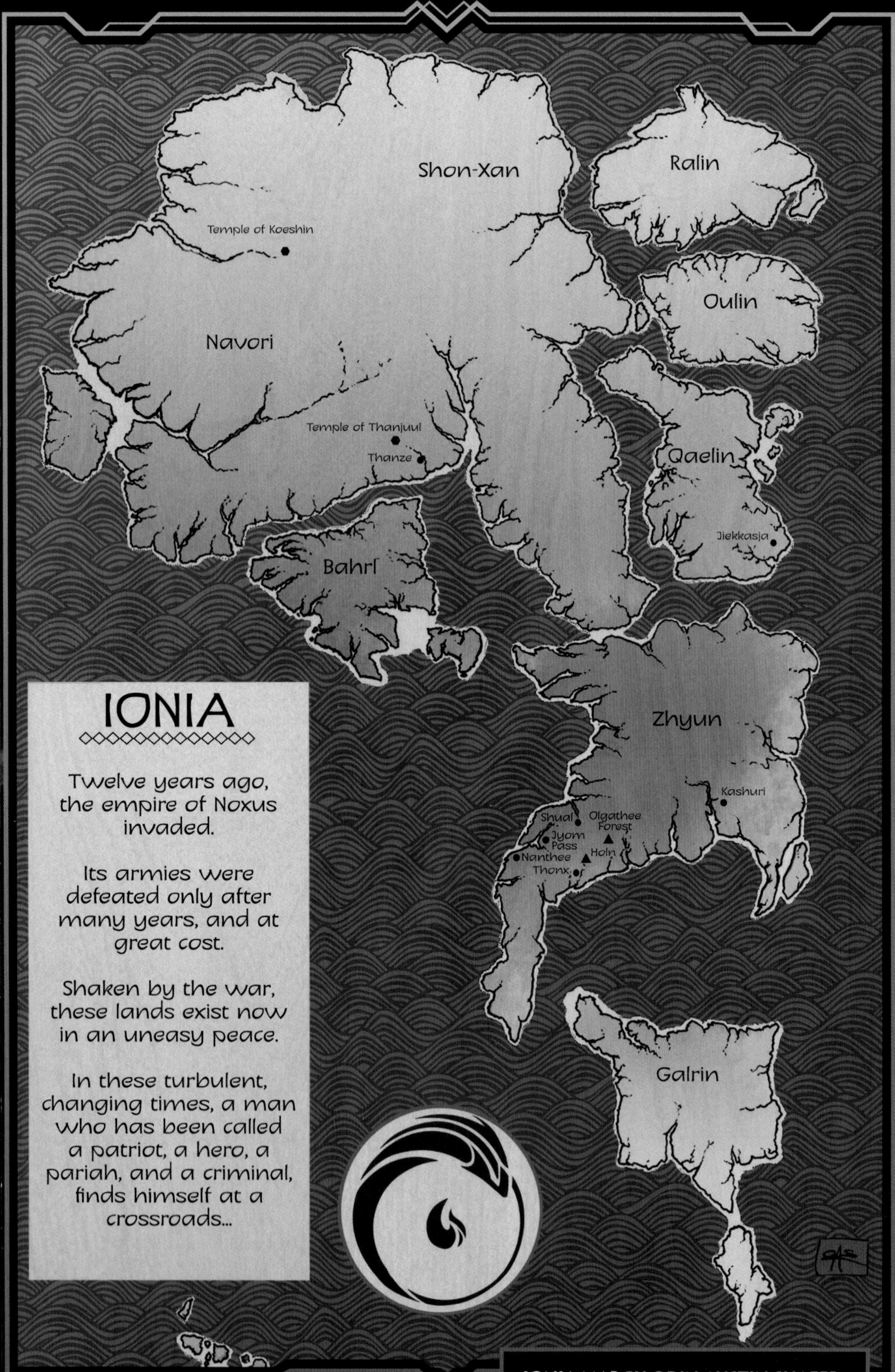
Shon-Xan
Ralin
Oulin
Temple of Koeshin
Navori
Temple of Thanjuul
Thanze
Qaelin
Jiekkasja
Bahrl
Zhyun
Kashuri
Shual
Olgathee Forest
Jyom Pass
Holn
Nanthee
Thonx
Galrin

IONIA MAP BY ODIN AUSTIN SHAFER

LEAGUE OF LEGENDS

ZED ™

ODIN AUSTIN SHAFER
WRITER

EDGAR SALAZAR
PENCILER

LORENZO RUGGIERO
INKER

CHRIS O'HALLORAN
COLORIST

COMICRAFT'S JOHN ROSHELL (#1-2)
& TYLER SMITH (#3-6)
LETTERERS

EDGAR SALAZAR WITH **ANDRES MOSSA** (#1)
& CHRIS O'HALLORAN (#2-6)
COVER ART

MARTIN BIRO
ASSISTANT EDITOR

SHANNON ANDREWS BALLESTEROS
ASSISTANT EDITOR (#6)

MARK BASSO
EDITOR

JOE HOCHSTEIN
ASSOCIATE MANAGING EDITOR,
DIGITAL ASSETS

TIM SMITH 3
MANAGER,
DIGITAL COMICS PRODUCTION

SVEN LARSEN
DIRECTOR, LICENSED
PUBLISHING

MARK ANNUNZIATO
EXECUTIVE DIRECTOR, STRATEGY
& BUSINESS DEVELOPMENT

COLLECTION EDITOR **JENNIFER GRÜNWALD** ♦ ASSISTANT MANAGING EDITOR **MAIA LOY**
ASSISTANT MANAGING EDITOR **LISA MONTALBANO** ♦ EDITOR, SPECIAL PROJECTS **MARK D. BEAZLEY**
VP PRODUCTION & SPECIAL PROJECTS **JEFF YOUNGQUIST** ♦ BOOK DESIGNER **JAY BOWEN**
SVP PRINT, SALES & MARKETING **DAVID GABRIEL** ♦ EDITOR IN CHIEF **C.B. CEBULSKI**

LEAGUE OF LEGENDS: ZED. Contains material originally published in magazine form as LEAGUE OF LEGENDS: ZED (2019) #1-6. First printing 2020. ISBN 978-1-302-91947-4. Published by MARVEL WORLDWIDE, INC., a subsidiary of MARVEL ENTERTAINMENT, LLC. OFFICE OF PUBLICATION: 1290 Avenue of the Americas, New York, NY 10104. ™ & © 2020 Riot Games, Inc. League of Legends and all related logos, characters, names and distinctive likenesses thereof are exclusive property of Riot Games, Inc. All Rights Reserved. No similarity between any of the names, characters, persons, and/or institutions in this magazine with those of any living or dead person or institution is intended, and any such similarity which may exist is purely coincidental. Marvel and its logos are TM Marvel Characters, Inc. **Printed in the U.S.A.** KEVIN FEIGE, Chief Creative Officer; DAN BUCKLEY, President, Marvel Entertainment; JOHN NEE, Publisher; JOE QUESADA, EVP & Creative Director; TOM BREVOORT, SVP of Publishing; DAVID BOGART, Associate Publisher & SVP of Talent Affairs; Publishing & Partnership; DAVID GABRIEL, VP of Print & Digital Publishing; JEFF YOUNGQUIST, VP of Production & Special Projects; DAN CARR, Executive Director of Publishing Technology; ALEX MORALES, Director of Publishing Operations; DAN EDINGTON, Managing Editor; SUSAN CRESPI, Production Manager; STAN LEE, Chairman Emeritus. For information regarding advertising in Marvel Comics or on Marvel.com, please contact Vit DeBellis, Custom Solutions & Integrated Advertising Manager, at vdebellis@marvel.com. For Marvel subscription inquiries, please call 888-511-5480. **Manufactured between 7/29/2020 and 8/25/2020 by LSC COMMUNICATIONS INC., KENDALLVILLE, IN, USA.**
10 9 8 7 6 5 4 3 2 1

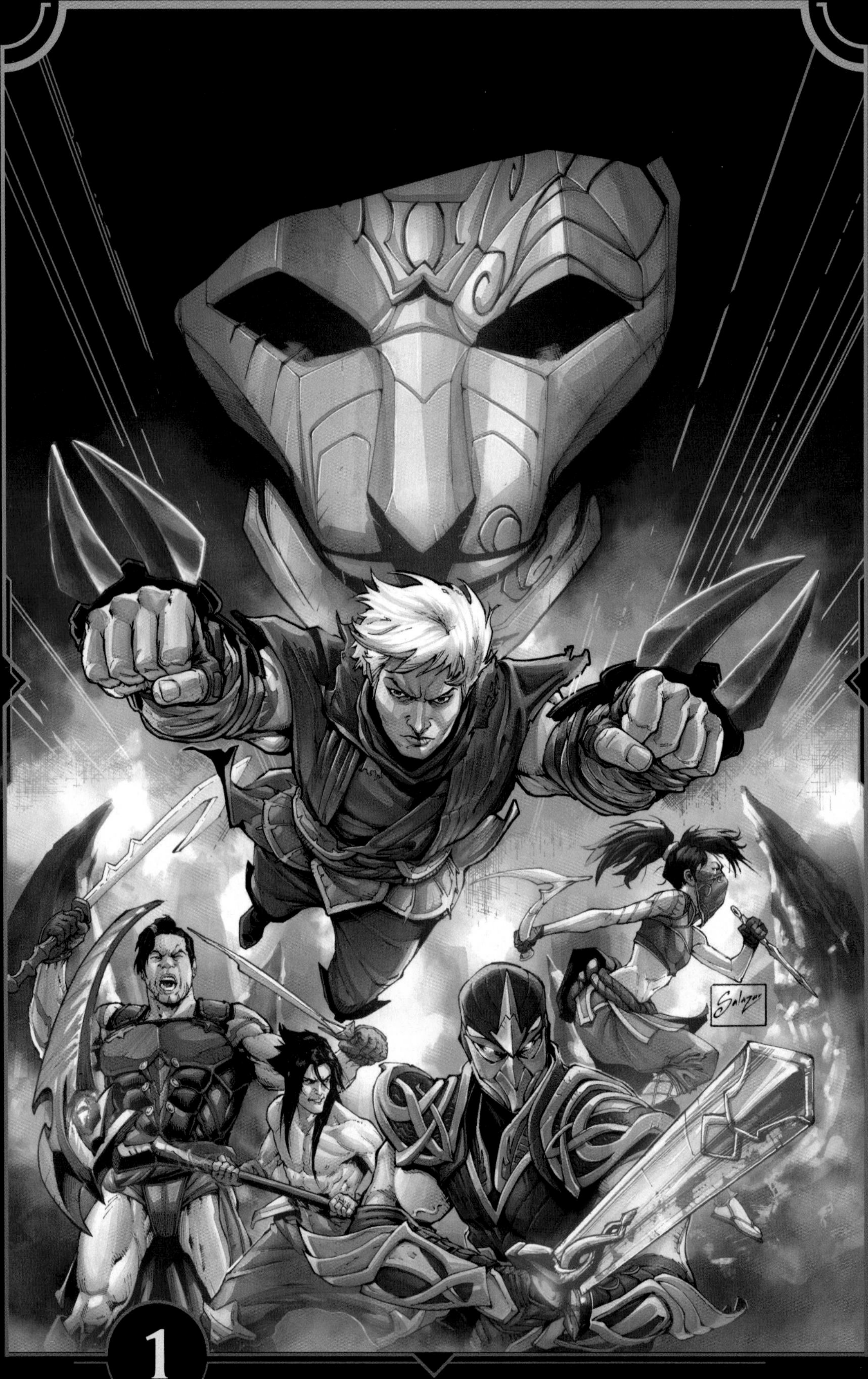
Salazar
1

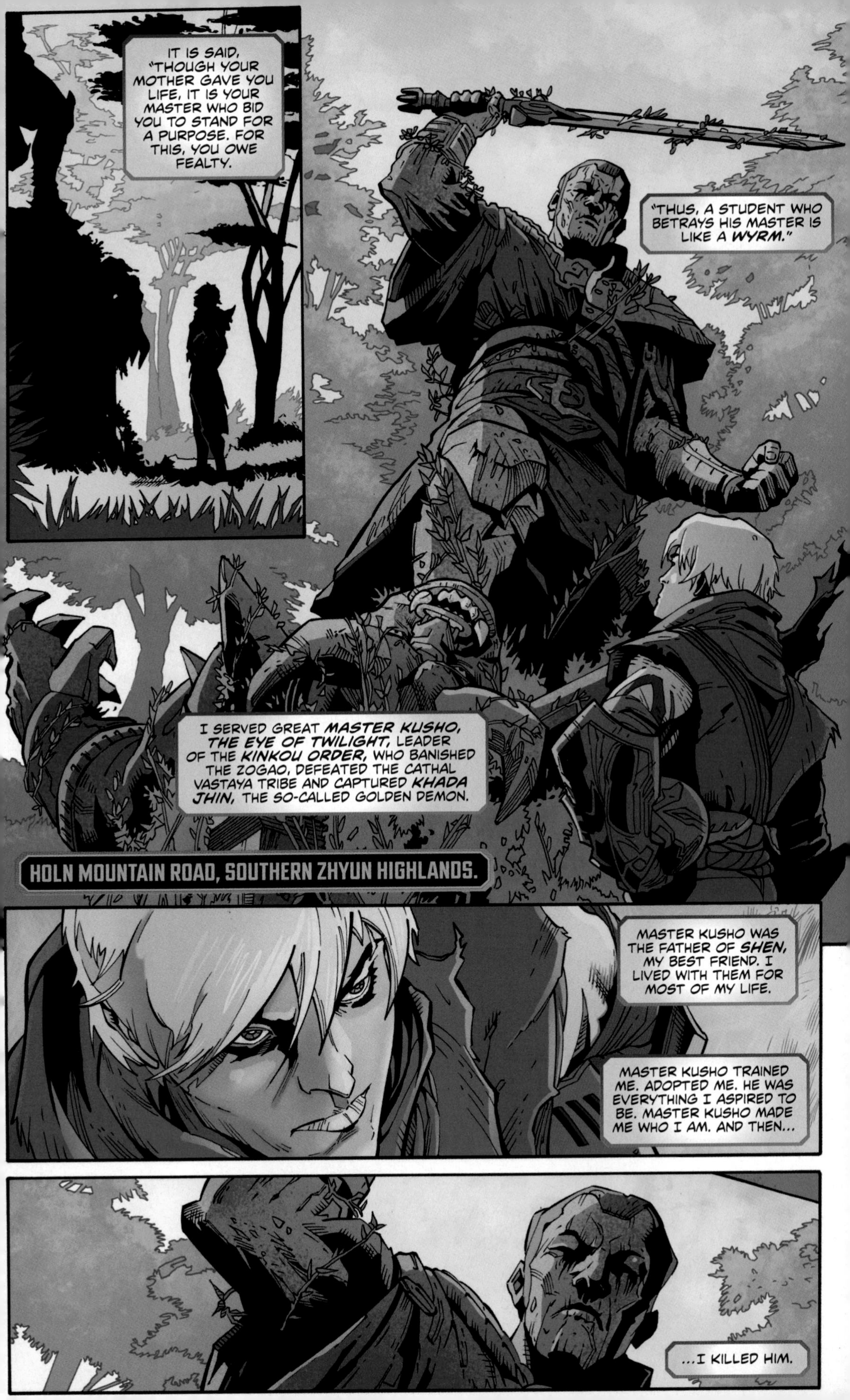
IT IS SAID, "THOUGH YOUR MOTHER GAVE YOU LIFE, IT IS YOUR MASTER WHO BID YOU TO STAND FOR A PURPOSE. FOR THIS, YOU OWE FEALTY.
"THUS, A STUDENT WHO BETRAYS HIS MASTER IS LIKE A WYRM."
I SERVED GREAT MASTER KUSHO, THE EYE OF TWILIGHT, LEADER OF THE KINKOU ORDER, WHO BANISHED THE ZOGAO, DEFEATED THE CATHAL VASTAYA TRIBE AND CAPTURED KHADA JHIN, THE SO-CALLED GOLDEN DEMON.
HOLN MOUNTAIN ROAD, SOUTHERN ZHYUN HIGHLANDS.
MASTER KUSHO WAS THE FATHER OF SHEN, MY BEST FRIEND. I LIVED WITH THEM FOR MOST OF MY LIFE.
MASTER KUSHO TRAINED ME. ADOPTED ME. HE WAS EVERYTHING I ASPIRED TO BE. MASTER KUSHO MADE ME WHO I AM. AND THEN...
...I KILLED HIM.

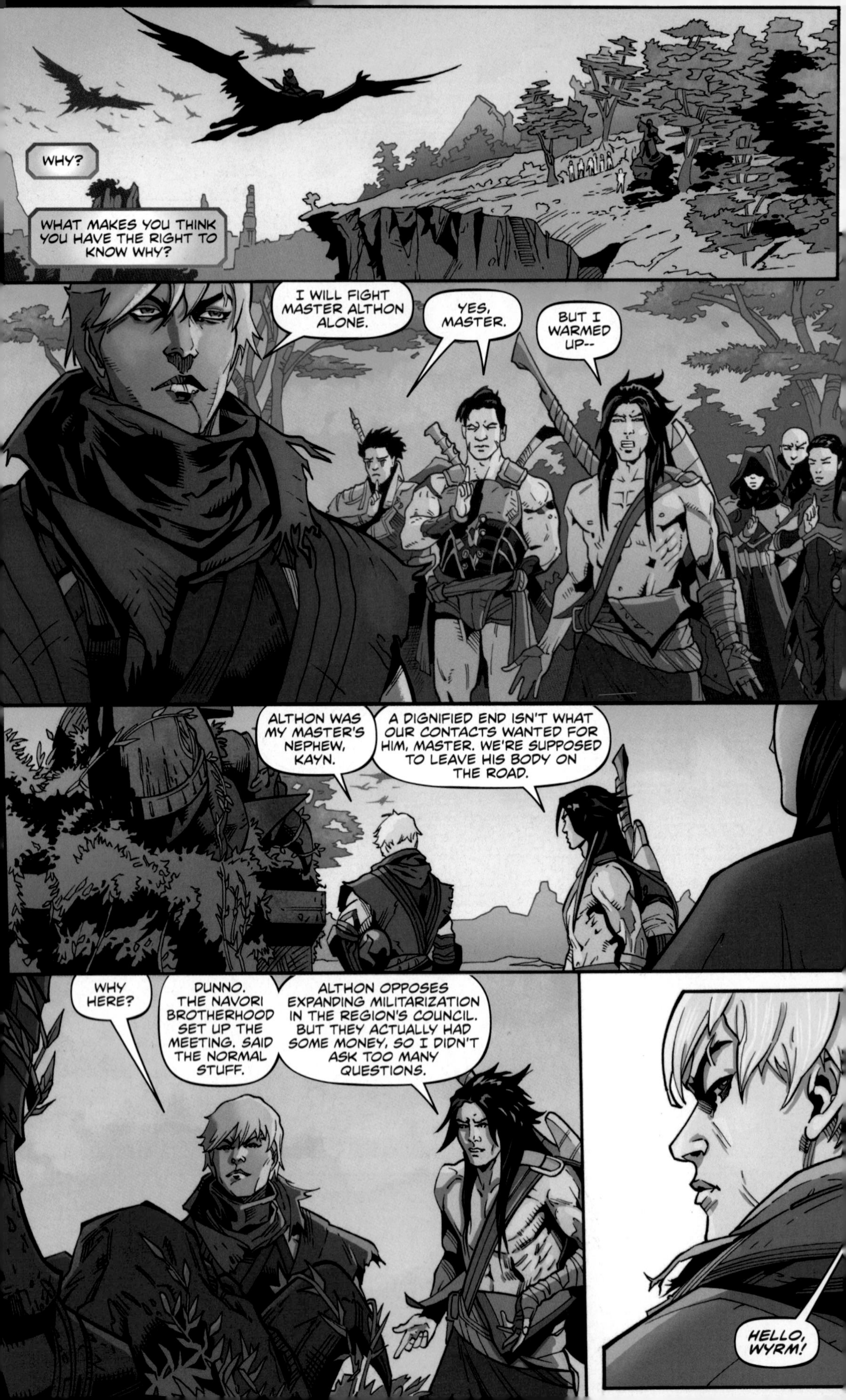
WHY?
WHAT MAKES YOU THINK YOU HAVE THE RIGHT TO KNOW WHY?
I WILL FIGHT MASTER ALTHON ALONE.
YES, MASTER.
BUT I WARMED UP--
ALTHON WAS MY MASTER'S NEPHEW, KAYN.
A DIGNIFIED END ISN'T WHAT OUR CONTACTS WANTED FOR HIM, MASTER. WE'RE SUPPOSED TO LEAVE HIS BODY ON THE ROAD.
WHY HERE?
DUNNO. THE NAVORI BROTHERHOOD SET UP THE MEETING. SAID THE NORMAL STUFF.
ALTHON OPPOSES EXPANDING MILITARIZATION IN THE REGION'S COUNCIL. BUT THEY ACTUALLY HAD SOME MONEY, SO I DIDN'T ASK TOO MANY QUESTIONS.
HELLO, WYRM!

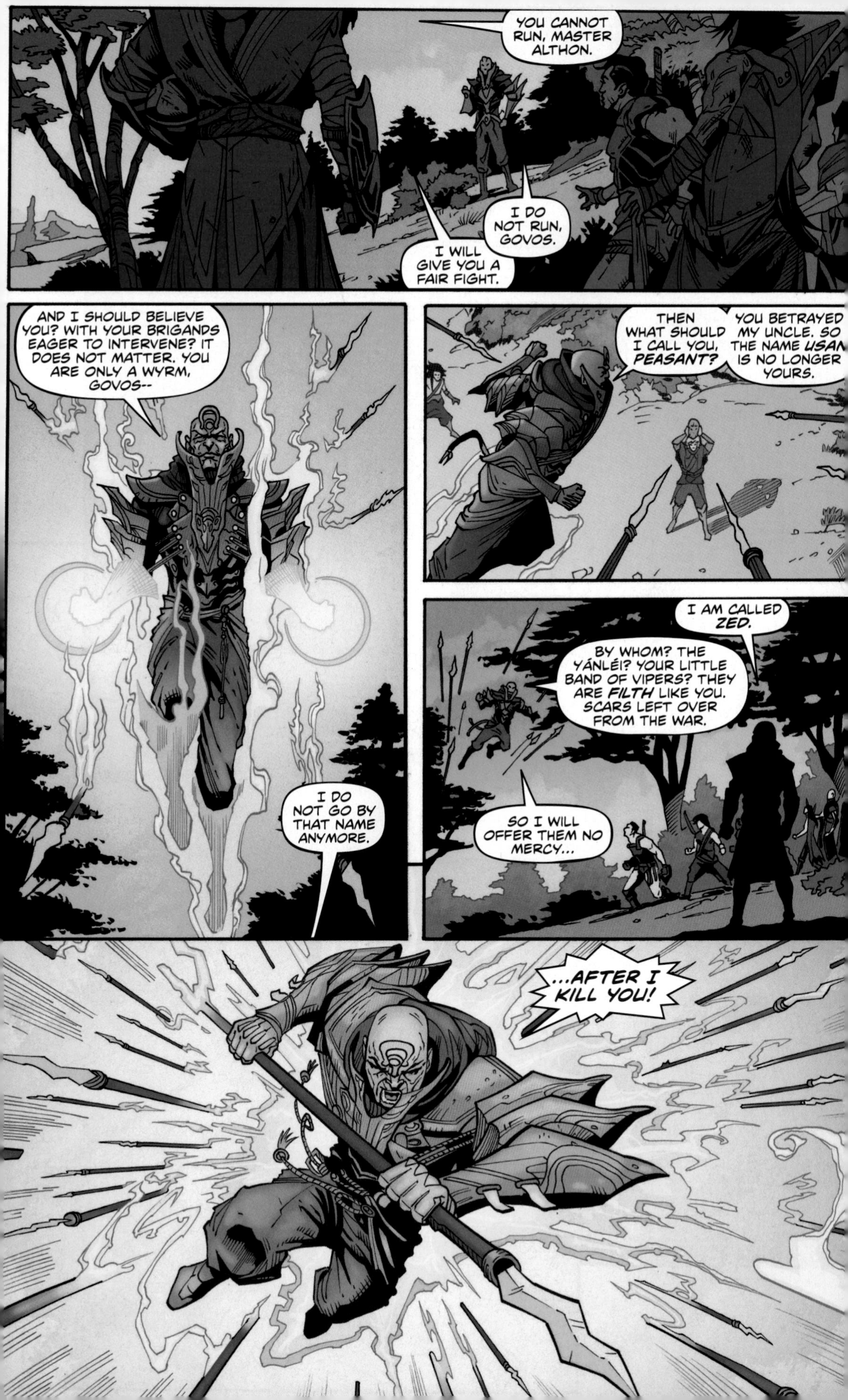
YOU CANNOT RUN, MASTER ALTHON.
I DO NOT RUN, GOVOS.
I WILL GIVE YOU A FAIR FIGHT.
AND I SHOULD BELIEVE YOU? WITH YOUR BRIGANDS EAGER TO INTERVENE? IT DOES NOT MATTER. YOU ARE ONLY A WYRM, GOVOS--
I DO NOT GO BY THAT NAME ANYMORE.
THEN WHAT SHOULD I CALL YOU, PEASANT?
YOU BETRAYED MY UNCLE. SO THE NAME USAN IS NO LONGER YOURS.
I AM CALLED ZED.
BY WHOM? THE YÁNLÉI? YOUR LITTLE BAND OF VIPERS? THEY ARE FILTH LIKE YOU. SCARS LEFT OVER FROM THE WAR.
SO I WILL OFFER THEM NO MERCY...
...AFTER I KILL YOU!

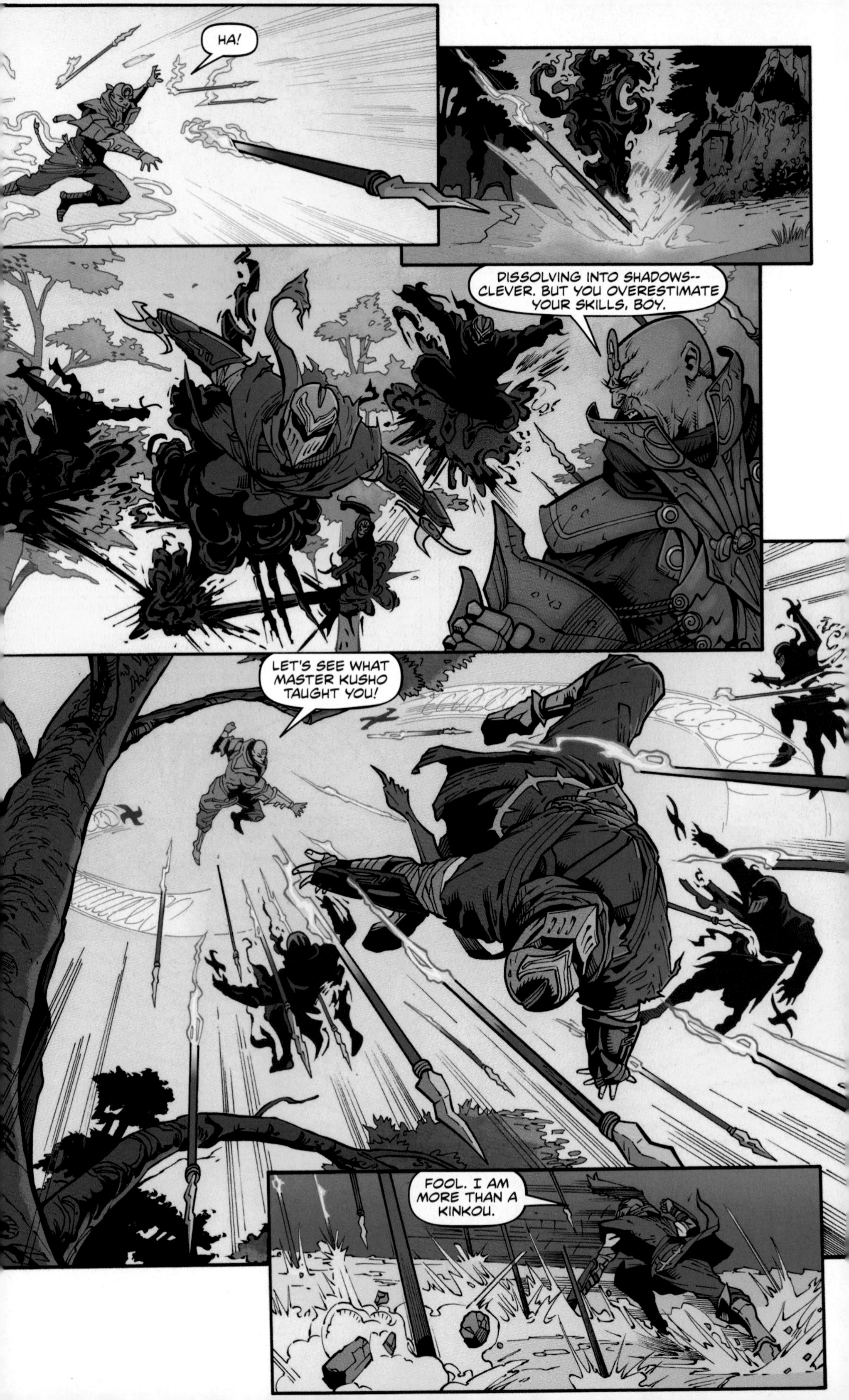
HA!
DISSOLVING INTO SHADOWS-- CLEVER. BUT YOU OVERESTIMATE YOUR SKILLS, BOY.
LET'S SEE WHAT MASTER KUSHO TAUGHT YOU!
FOOL. I AM MORE THAN A KINKOU.

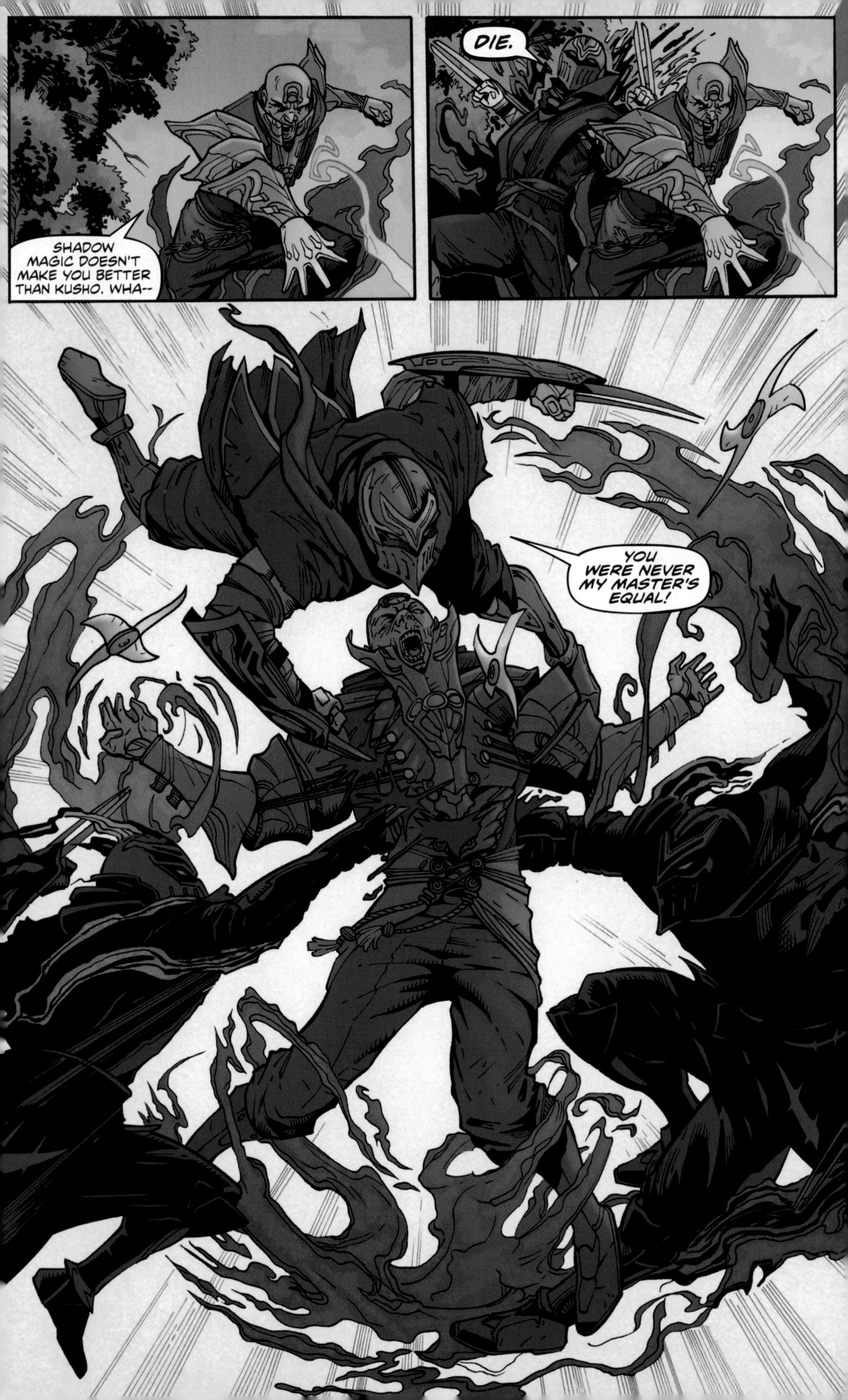
SHADOW MAGIC DOESN'T MAKE YOU BETTER THAN KUSHO. WHA--
DIE.
YOU WERE NEVER MY MASTER'S EQUAL!

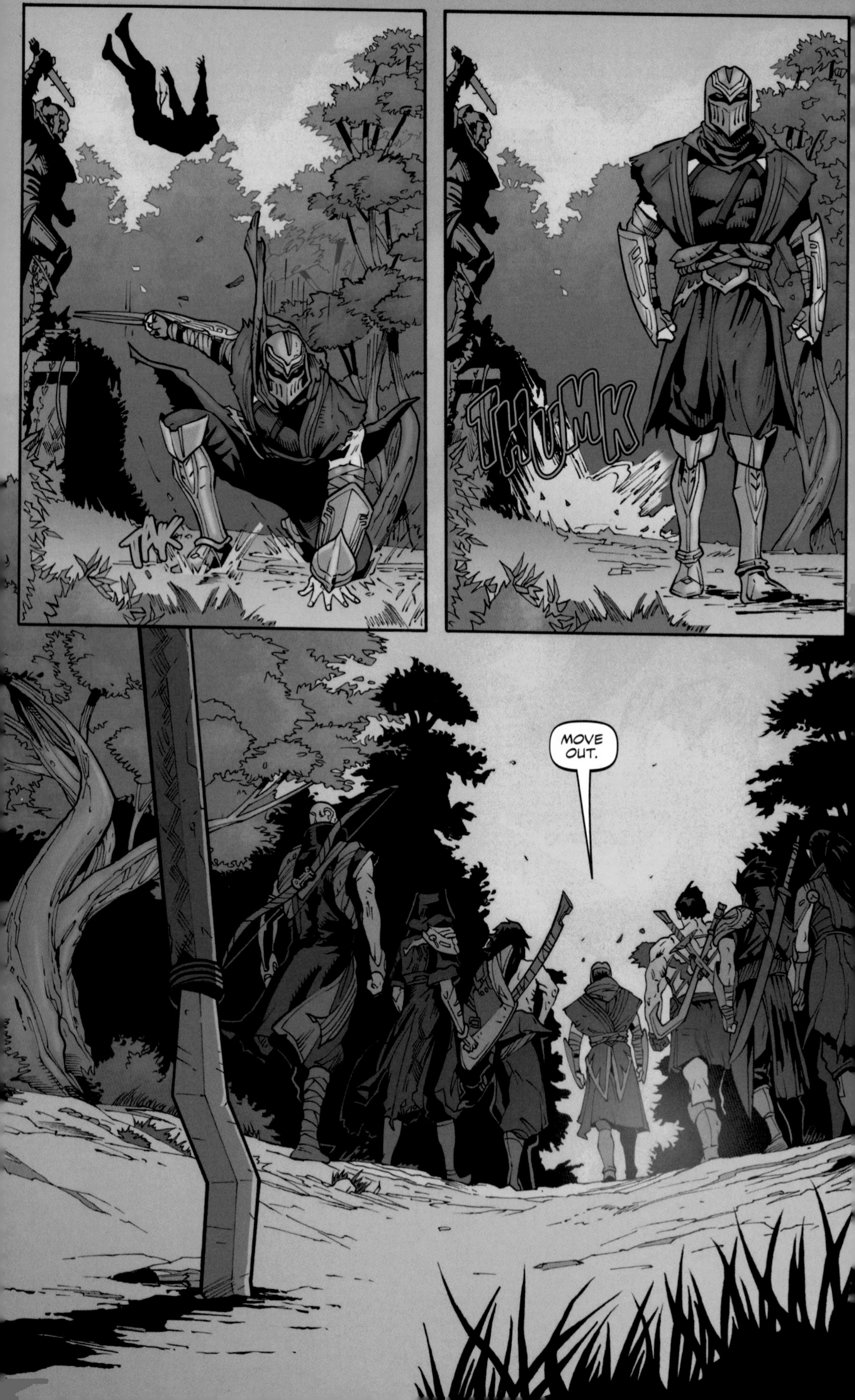
TAK
THUMK
MOVE OUT.

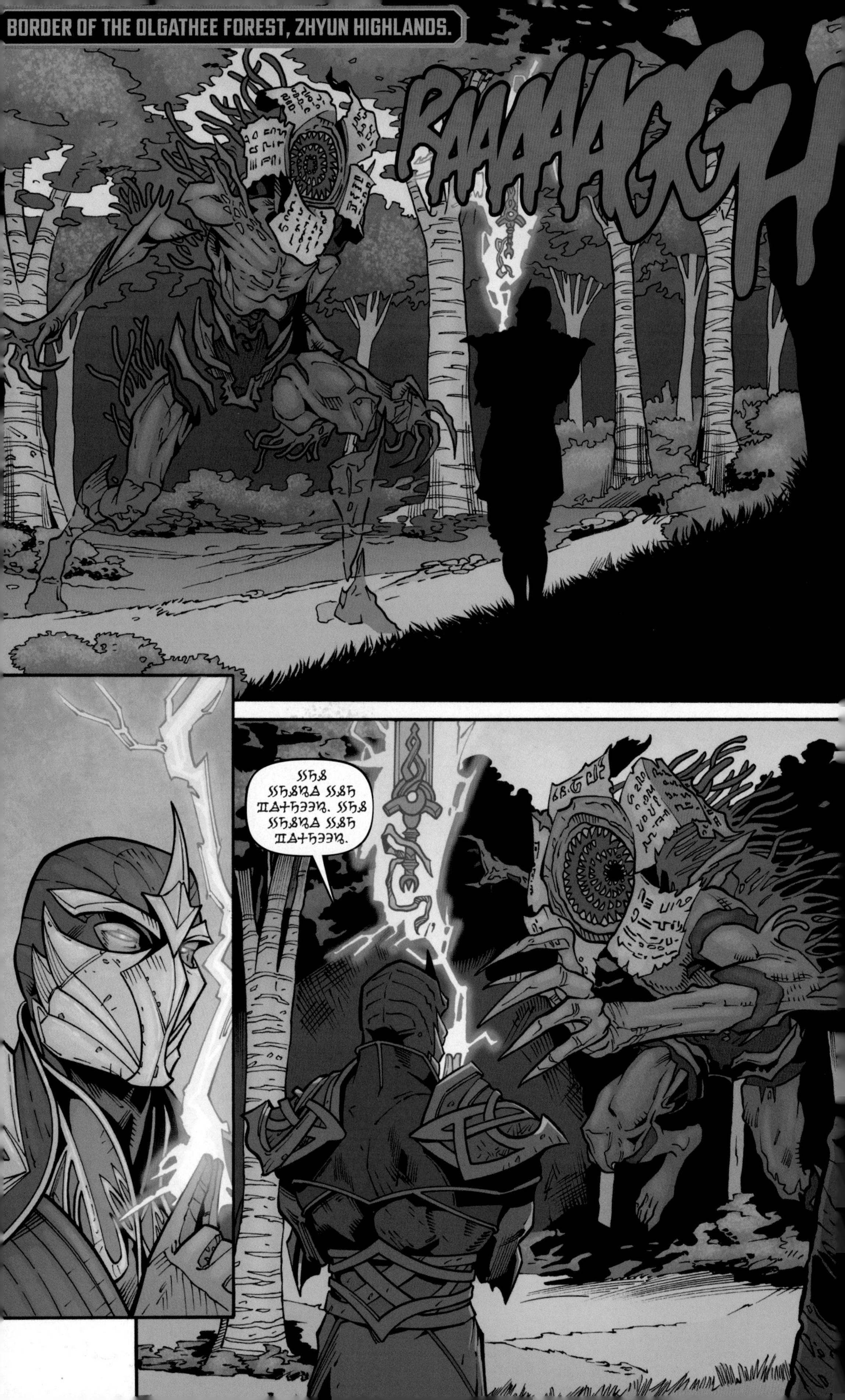
BORDER OF THE OLGATHEE FOREST, ZHYUN HIGHLANDS.

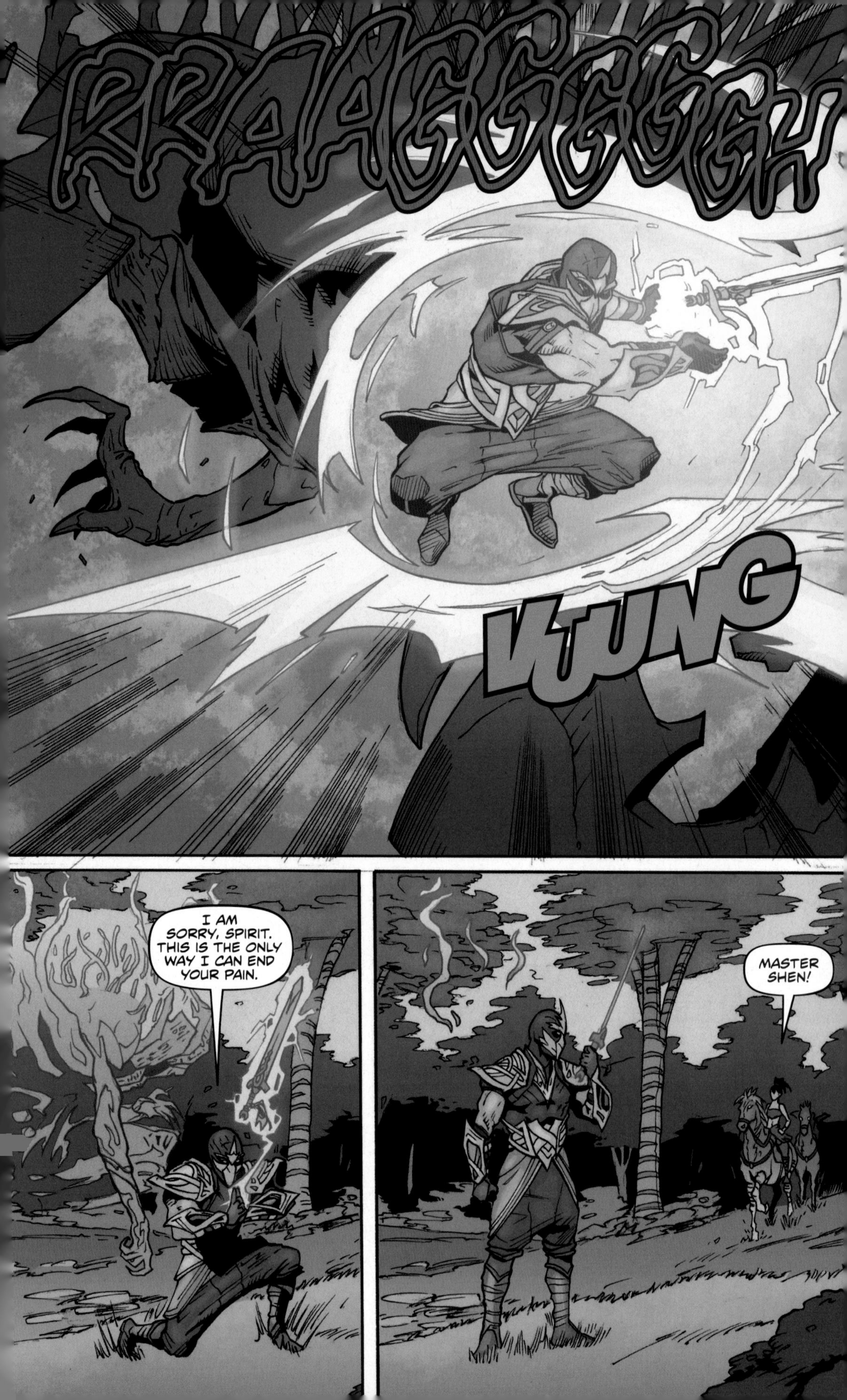
RRAAGGGGGH!
VUUNG
I AM SORRY, SPIRIT. THIS IS THE ONLY WAY I CAN END YOUR PAIN.
MASTER SHEN!

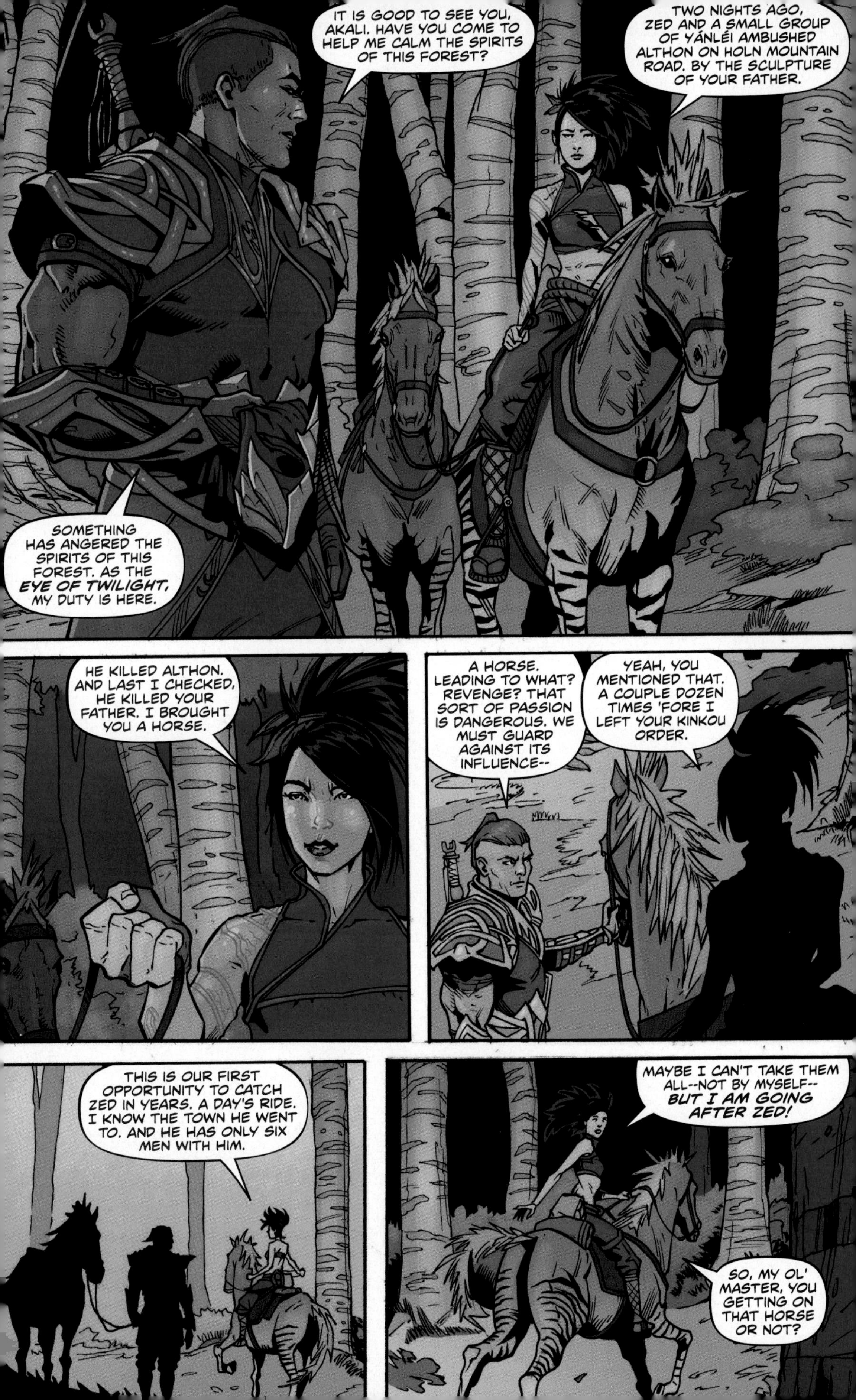
IT IS GOOD TO SEE YOU, AKALI. HAVE YOU COME TO HELP ME CALM THE SPIRITS OF THIS FOREST?
TWO NIGHTS AGO, ZED AND A SMALL GROUP OF YÁNLÉI AMBUSHED ALTHON ON HOLN MOUNTAIN ROAD. BY THE SCULPTURE OF YOUR FATHER.
SOMETHING HAS ANGERED THE SPIRITS OF THIS FOREST. AS THE *EYE OF TWILIGHT,* MY DUTY IS HERE.
HE KILLED ALTHON. AND LAST I CHECKED, HE KILLED YOUR FATHER. I BROUGHT YOU A HORSE.
A HORSE. LEADING TO WHAT? REVENGE? THAT SORT OF PASSION IS DANGEROUS. WE MUST GUARD AGAINST ITS INFLUENCE--
YEAH, YOU MENTIONED THAT. A COUPLE DOZEN TIMES 'FORE I LEFT YOUR KINKOU ORDER.
THIS IS OUR FIRST OPPORTUNITY TO CATCH ZED IN YEARS. A DAY'S RIDE. I KNOW THE TOWN HE WENT TO. AND HE HAS ONLY SIX MEN WITH HIM.
MAYBE I CAN'T TAKE THEM ALL--NOT BY MYSELF-- ***BUT I AM GOING AFTER ZED!***
SO, MY OL' MASTER, YOU GETTING ON THAT HORSE OR NOT?

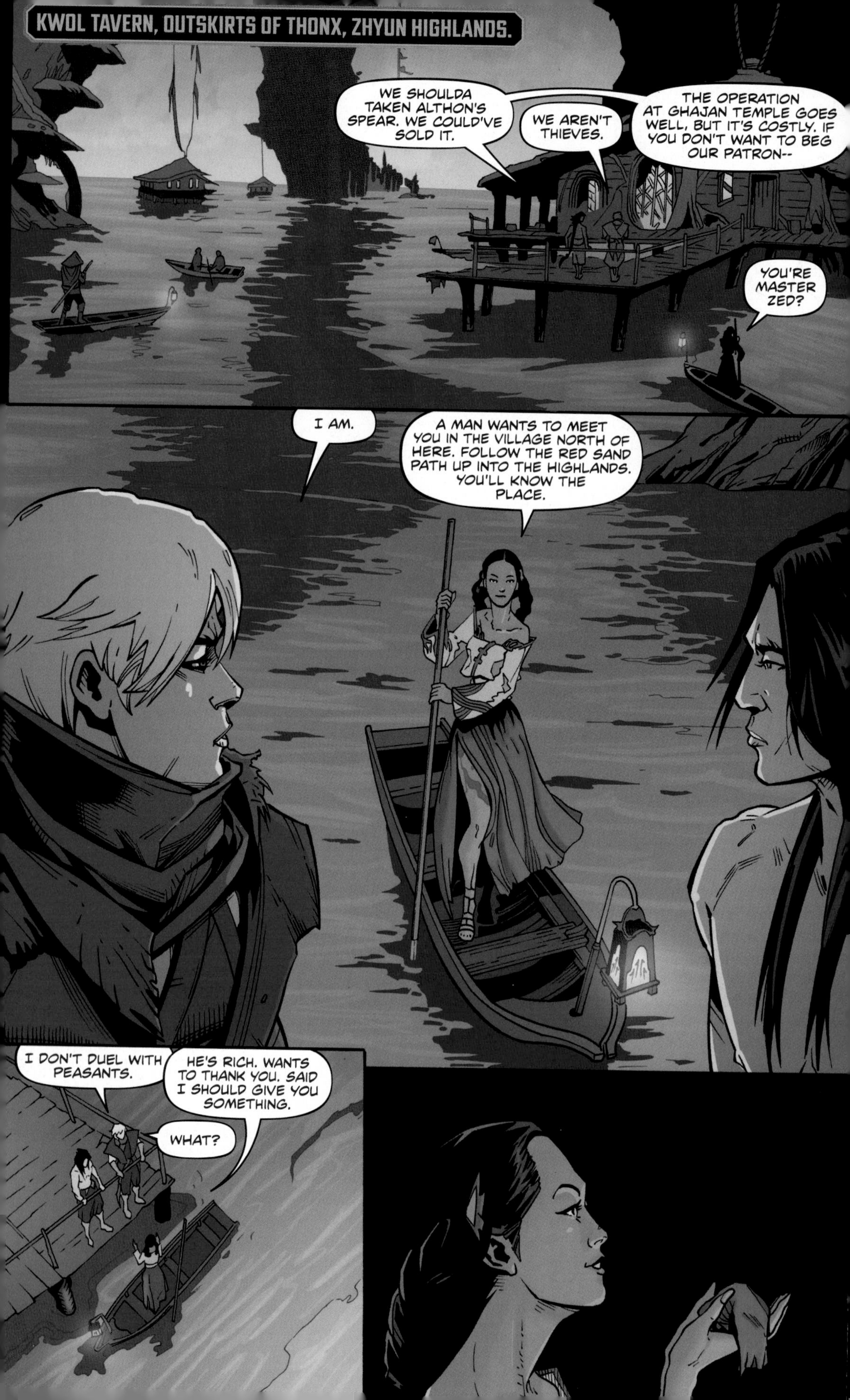

KWOL TAVERN, OUTSKIRTS OF THONX, ZHYUN HIGHLANDS.
WE SHOULDA TAKEN ALTHON'S SPEAR. WE COULD'VE SOLD IT.
WE AREN'T THIEVES.
THE OPERATION AT GHAJAN TEMPLE GOES WELL, BUT IT'S COSTLY. IF YOU DON'T WANT TO BEG OUR PATRON--
YOU'RE MASTER ZED?
I AM.
A MAN WANTS TO MEET YOU IN THE VILLAGE NORTH OF HERE. FOLLOW THE RED SAND PATH UP INTO THE HIGHLANDS. YOU'LL KNOW THE PLACE.
I DON'T DUEL WITH PEASANTS.
HE'S RICH. WANTS TO THANK YOU. SAID I SHOULD GIVE YOU SOMETHING.
WHAT?

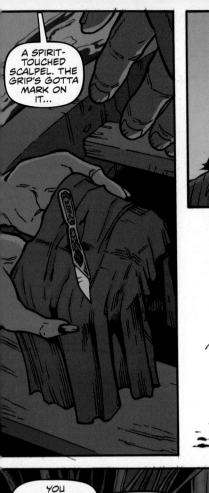

A SPIRIT-TOUCHED SCALPEL. THE GRIP'S GOTTA MARK ON IT...

THE MARK OF THE KINKOU. WHY DOES IT GLOW NOW?

LONG AGO, IT WAS ATTUNED TO MY SPIRIT.

YEAH. HE SAID IT WOULD MEAN SOMETHING TO YOU.

SOOO... OBVIOUSLY WE CAN'T TRUST HER--

WHAT DO YOU MEAN "NO MORE CREDIT"?!

SOUNDS LIKE JOVN'S DRUNK.

YOU WOULDN'T HAVE A TOWN WITHOUT GUYS LIKE ME!

WHEN THE FOREIGNERS INVADED! WHEN THE WAR CAME! WHERE IN THE HELLS WERE YOU?!

SET HIM DOWN, JOVN.

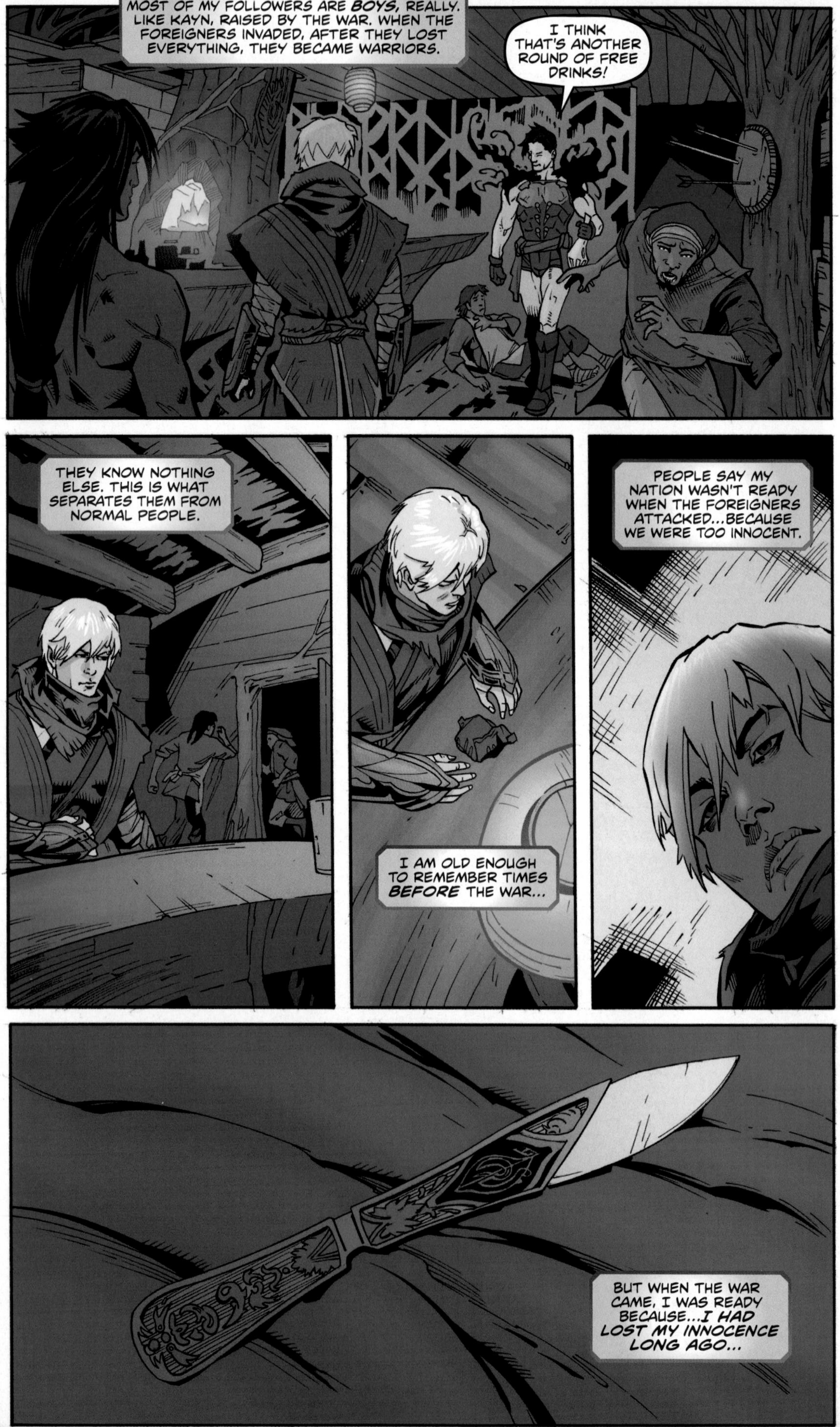

MOST OF MY FOLLOWERS ARE *BOYS*, REALLY. LIKE KAYN, RAISED BY THE WAR. WHEN THE FOREIGNERS INVADED, AFTER THEY LOST EVERYTHING, THEY BECAME WARRIORS.
I THINK THAT'S ANOTHER ROUND OF FREE DRINKS!
THEY KNOW NOTHING ELSE. THIS IS WHAT SEPARATES THEM FROM NORMAL PEOPLE.
I AM OLD ENOUGH TO REMEMBER TIMES *BEFORE* THE WAR...
PEOPLE SAY MY NATION WASN'T READY WHEN THE FOREIGNERS ATTACKED...BECAUSE WE WERE TOO INNOCENT.
BUT WHEN THE WAR CAME, I WAS READY BECAUSE...*I HAD LOST MY INNOCENCE LONG AGO...*

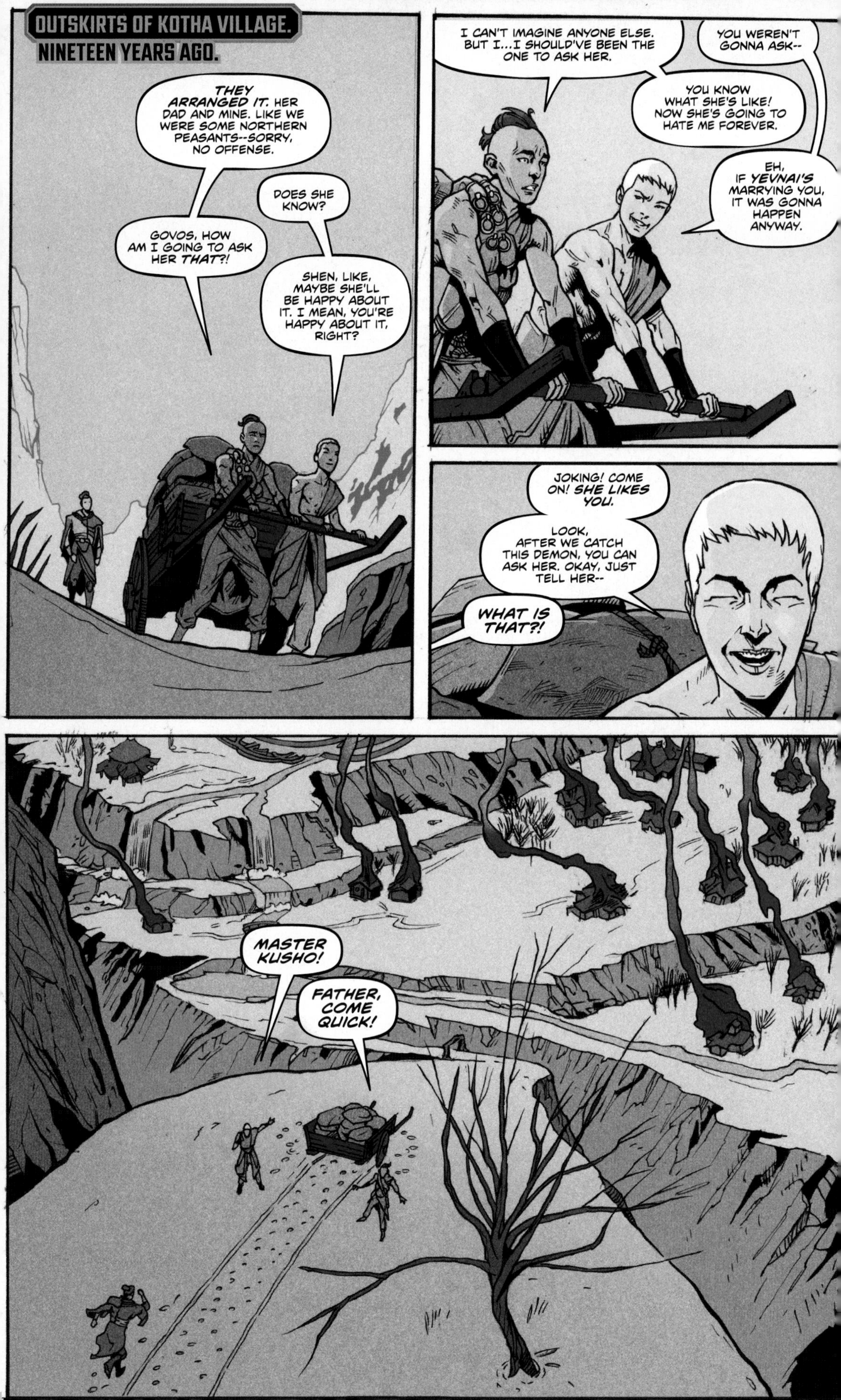
OUTSKIRTS OF KOTHA VILLAGE.
NINETEEN YEARS AGO.
THEY ARRANGED IT. HER DAD AND MINE. LIKE WE WERE SOME NORTHERN PEASANTS--SORRY, NO OFFENSE.
DOES SHE KNOW?
GOVOS, HOW AM I GOING TO ASK HER THAT?!
SHEN, LIKE, MAYBE SHE'LL BE HAPPY ABOUT IT. I MEAN, YOU'RE HAPPY ABOUT IT, RIGHT?
I CAN'T IMAGINE ANYONE ELSE. BUT I...I SHOULD'VE BEEN THE ONE TO ASK HER.
YOU WEREN'T GONNA ASK--
YOU KNOW WHAT SHE'S LIKE! NOW SHE'S GOING TO HATE ME FOREVER.
EH, IF YEVNAI'S MARRYING YOU, IT WAS GONNA HAPPEN ANYWAY.
JOKING! COME ON! SHE LIKES YOU.
LOOK, AFTER WE CATCH THIS DEMON, YOU CAN ASK HER. OKAY, JUST TELL HER--
WHAT IS THAT?!
MASTER KUSHO!
FATHER, COME QUICK!

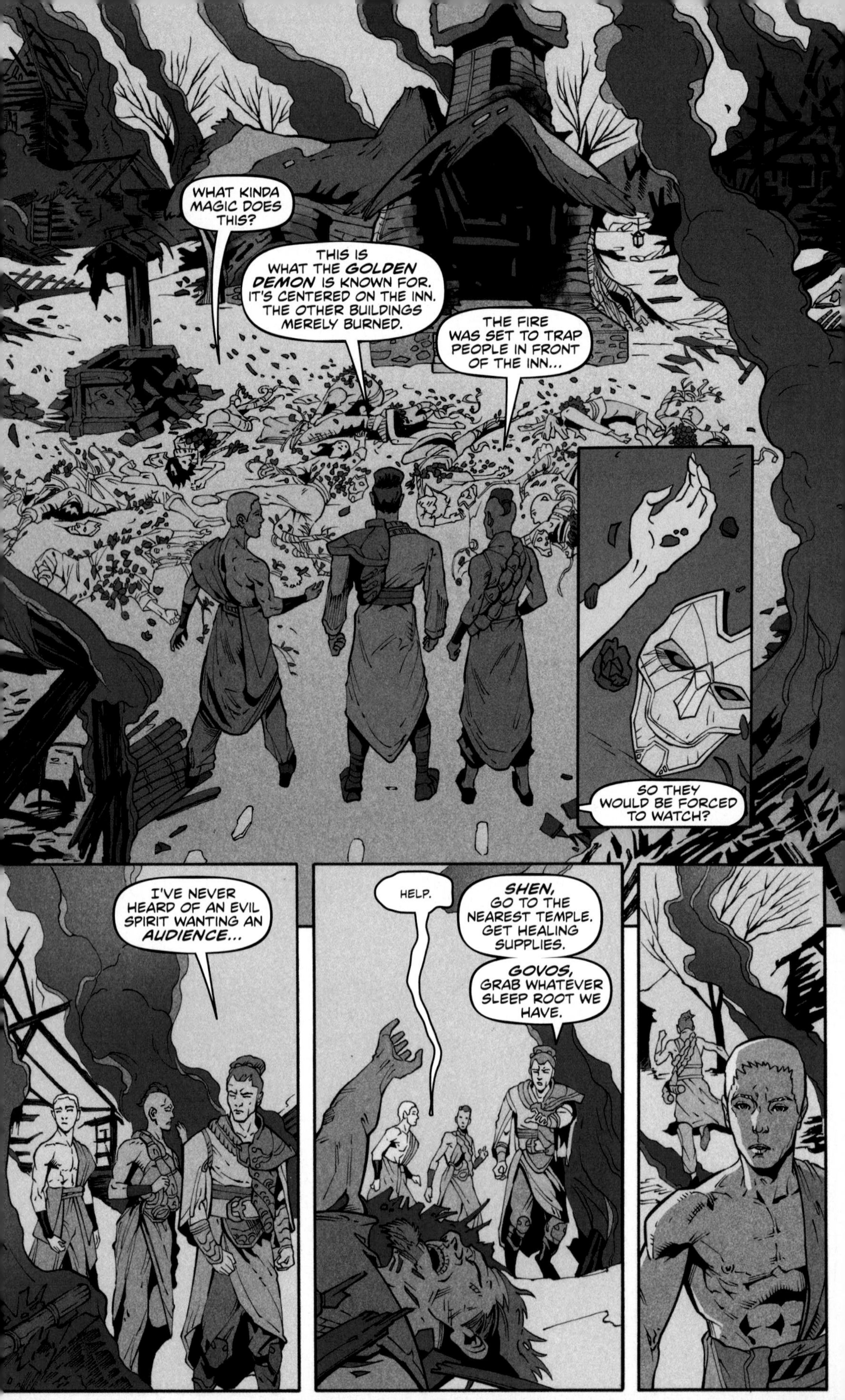
WHAT KINDA MAGIC DOES THIS?
THIS IS WHAT THE GOLDEN DEMON IS KNOWN FOR. IT'S CENTERED ON THE INN. THE OTHER BUILDINGS MERELY BURNED.
THE FIRE WAS SET TO TRAP PEOPLE IN FRONT OF THE INN...
SO THEY WOULD BE FORCED TO WATCH?
I'VE NEVER HEARD OF AN EVIL SPIRIT WANTING AN AUDIENCE...
HELP.
SHEN, GO TO THE NEAREST TEMPLE. GET HEALING SUPPLIES.
GOVOS, GRAB WHATEVER SLEEP ROOT WE HAVE.

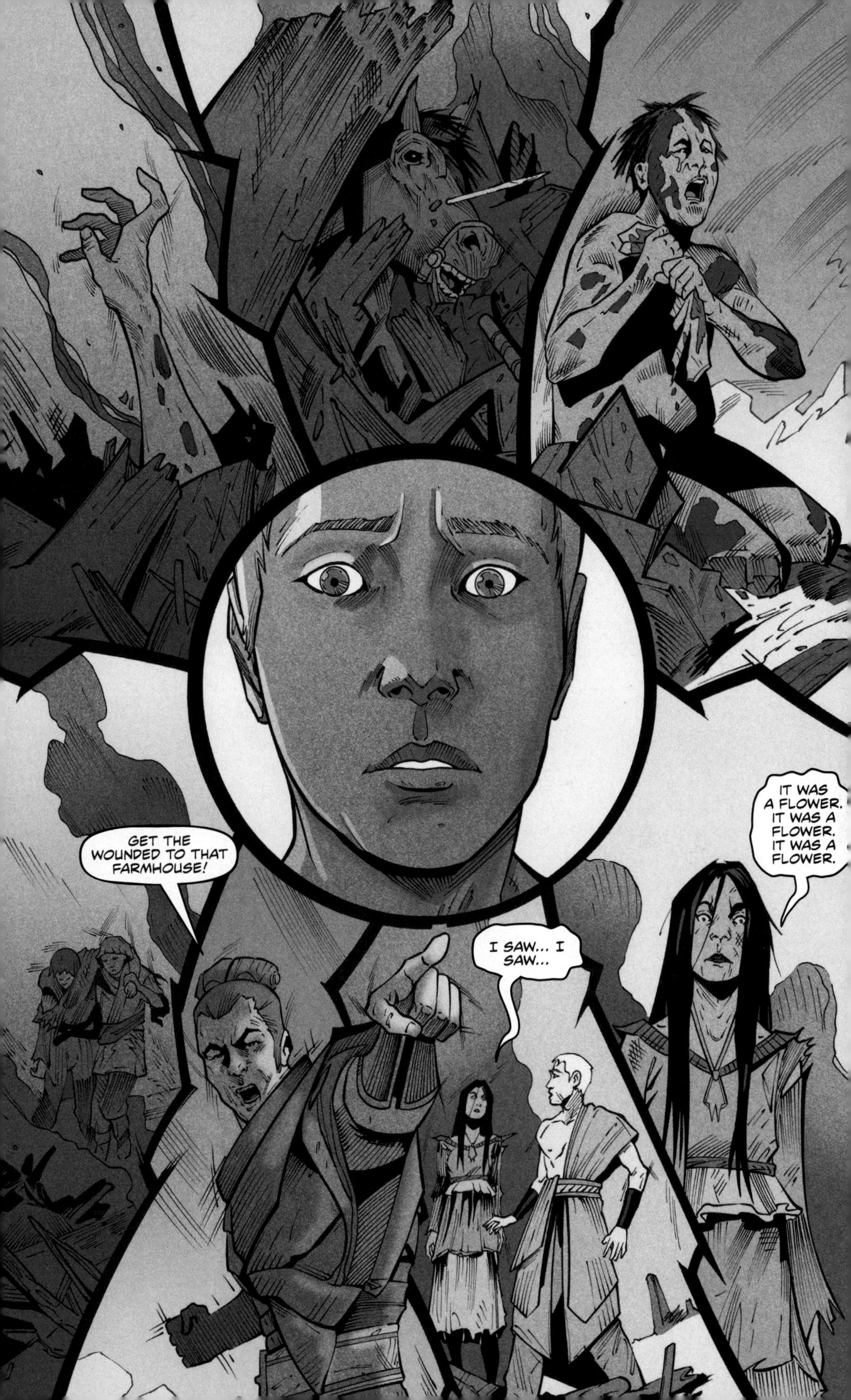
GET THE WOUNDED TO THAT FARMHOUSE!
I SAW... I SAW...
IT WAS A FLOWER. IT WAS A FLOWER. IT WAS A FLOWER.

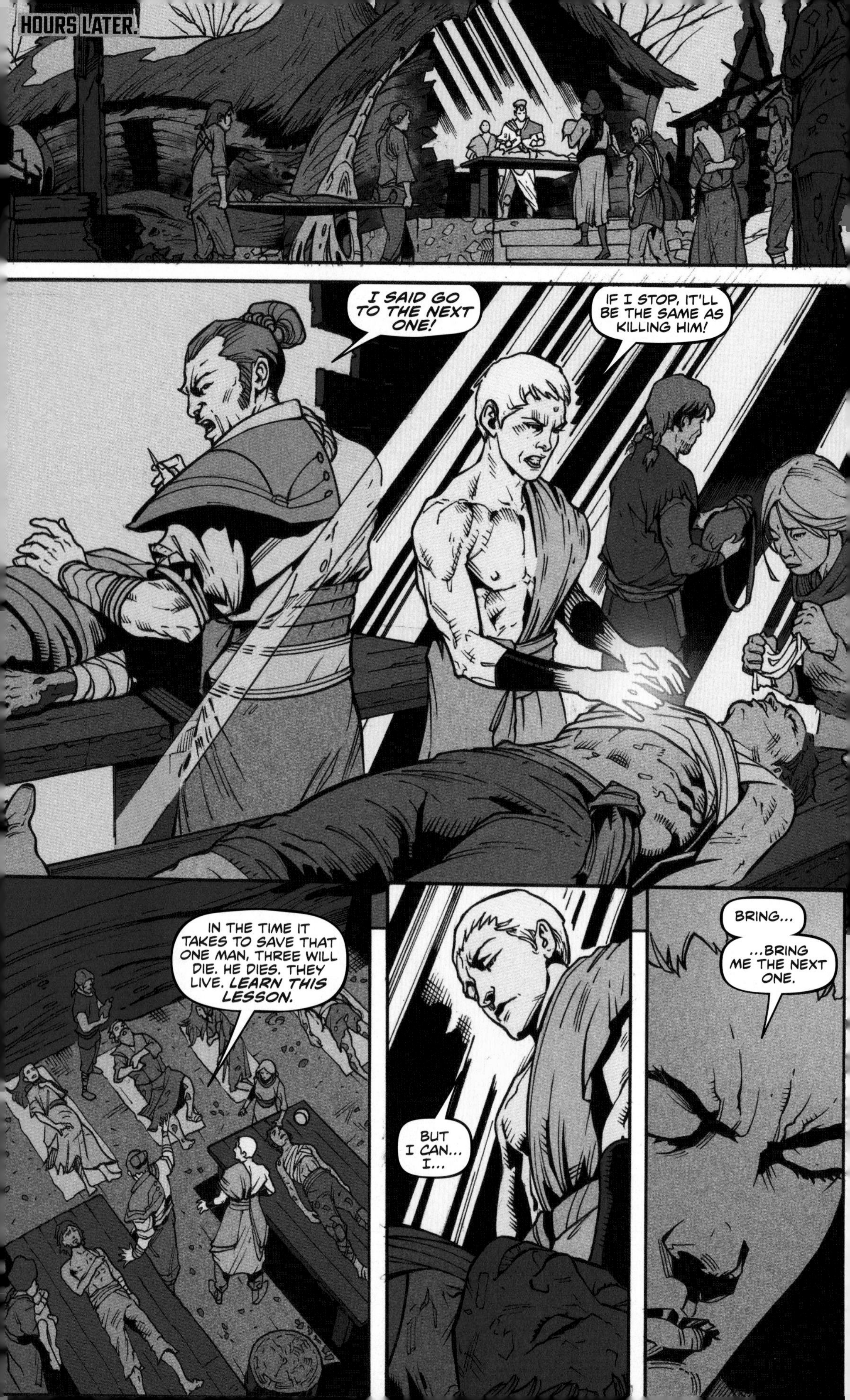
HOURS LATER.
I SAID GO TO THE NEXT ONE!
IF I STOP, IT'LL BE THE SAME AS KILLING HIM!
IN THE TIME IT TAKES TO SAVE THAT ONE MAN, THREE WILL DIE. HE DIES. THEY LIVE. LEARN THIS LESSON.
BUT I CAN... I...
BRING...
...BRING ME THE NEXT ONE.

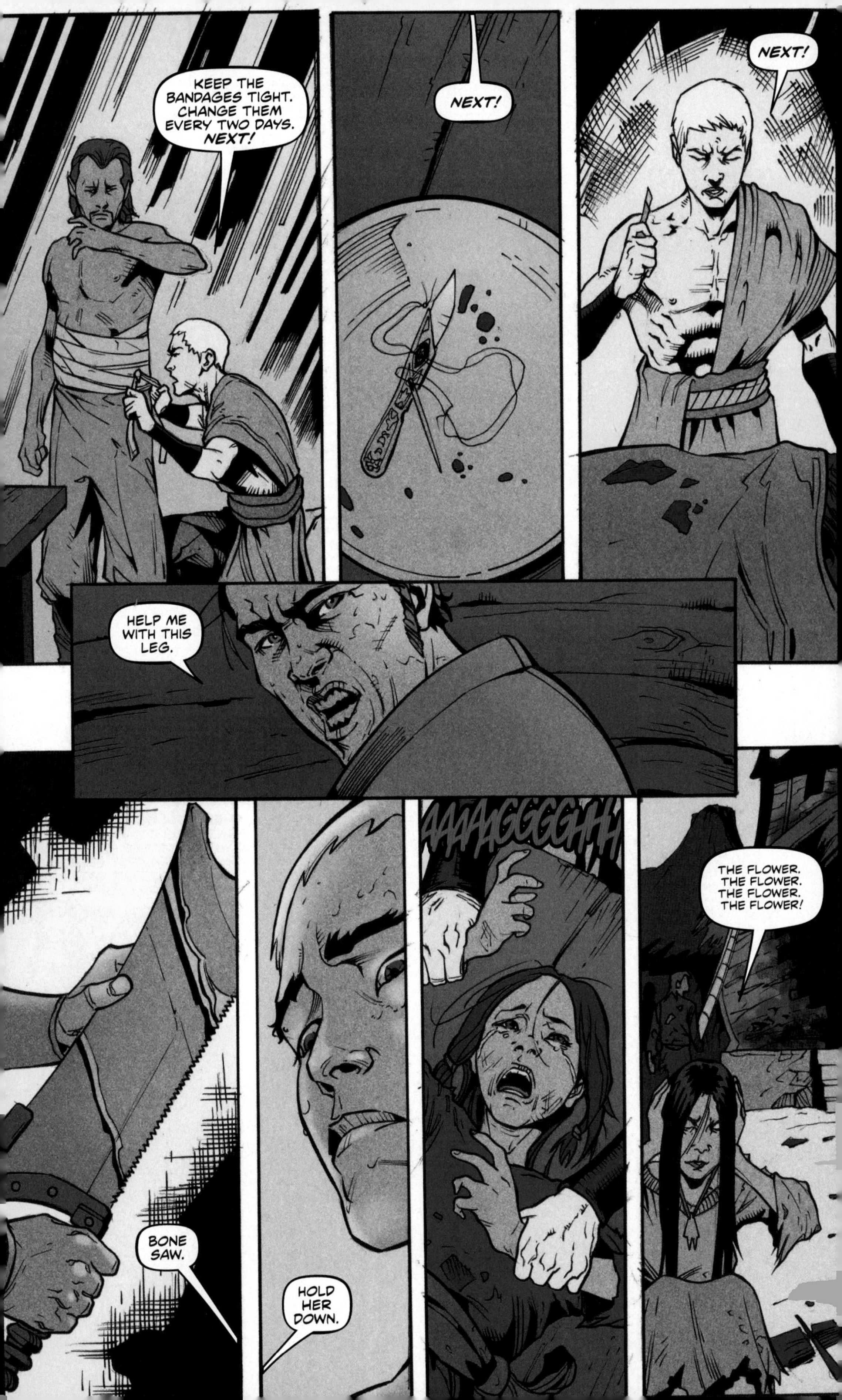
KEEP THE BANDAGES TIGHT. CHANGE THEM EVERY TWO DAYS. NEXT!
NEXT!
NEXT!
HELP ME WITH THIS LEG.
BONE SAW.
HOLD HER DOWN.
AAAAAGGGGHHH
THE FLOWER. THE FLOWER. THE FLOWER. THE FLOWER!

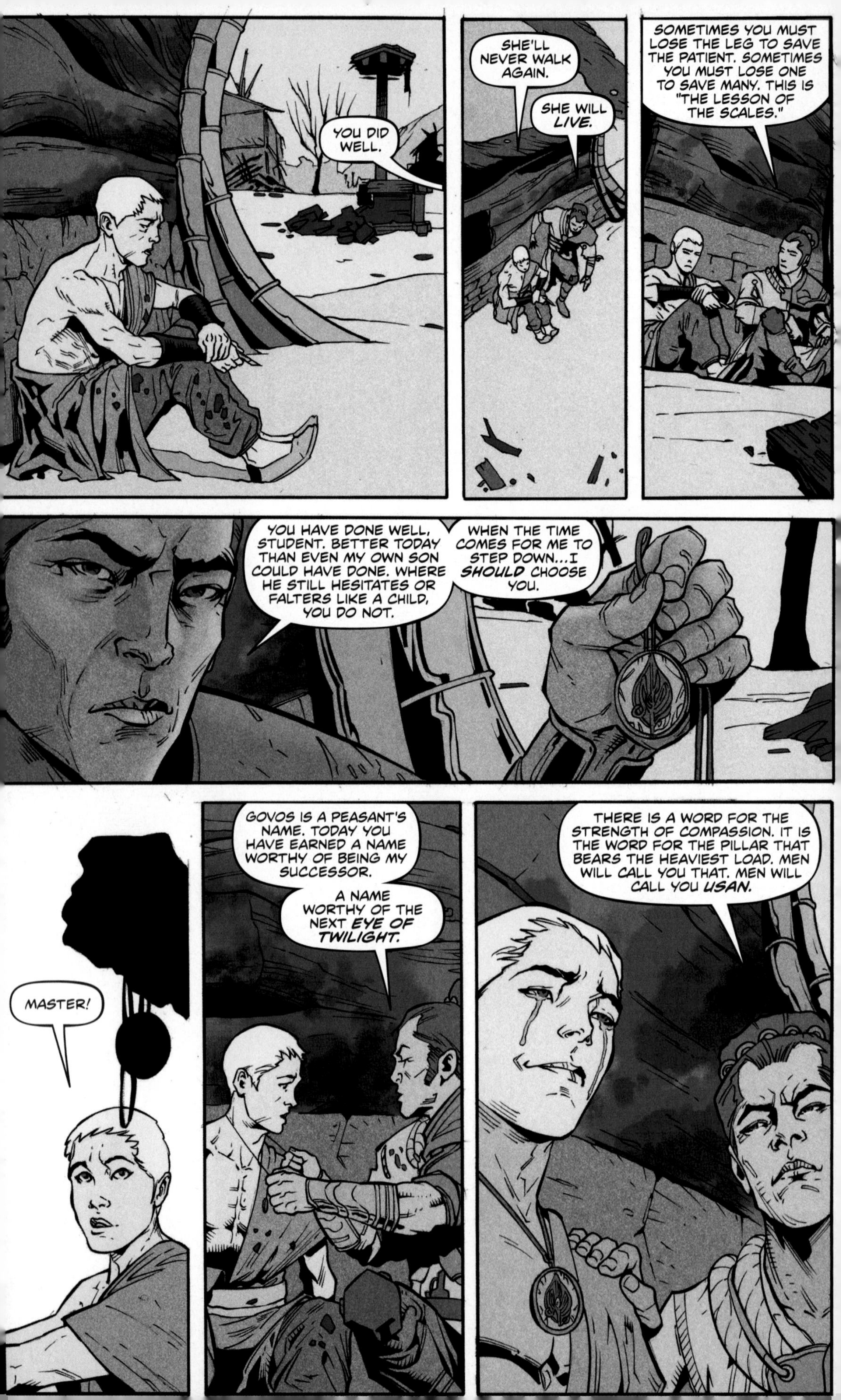
YOU DID WELL.
SHE'LL NEVER WALK AGAIN.
SHE WILL *LIVE.*
SOMETIMES YOU MUST LOSE THE LEG TO SAVE THE PATIENT. SOMETIMES YOU MUST LOSE ONE TO SAVE MANY. THIS IS "THE LESSON OF THE SCALES."
YOU HAVE DONE WELL, STUDENT. BETTER TODAY THAN EVEN MY OWN SON COULD HAVE DONE. WHERE HE STILL HESITATES OR FALTERS LIKE A CHILD, YOU DO NOT.
WHEN THE TIME COMES FOR ME TO STEP DOWN...I *SHOULD* CHOOSE YOU.
MASTER!
GOVOS IS A PEASANT'S NAME. TODAY YOU HAVE EARNED A NAME WORTHY OF BEING MY SUCCESSOR.
A NAME WORTHY OF THE NEXT *EYE OF TWILIGHT.*
THERE IS A WORD FOR THE STRENGTH OF COMPASSION. IT IS THE WORD FOR THE PILLAR THAT BEARS THE HEAVIEST LOAD. MEN WILL CALL YOU THAT. MEN WILL CALL YOU *USAN.*

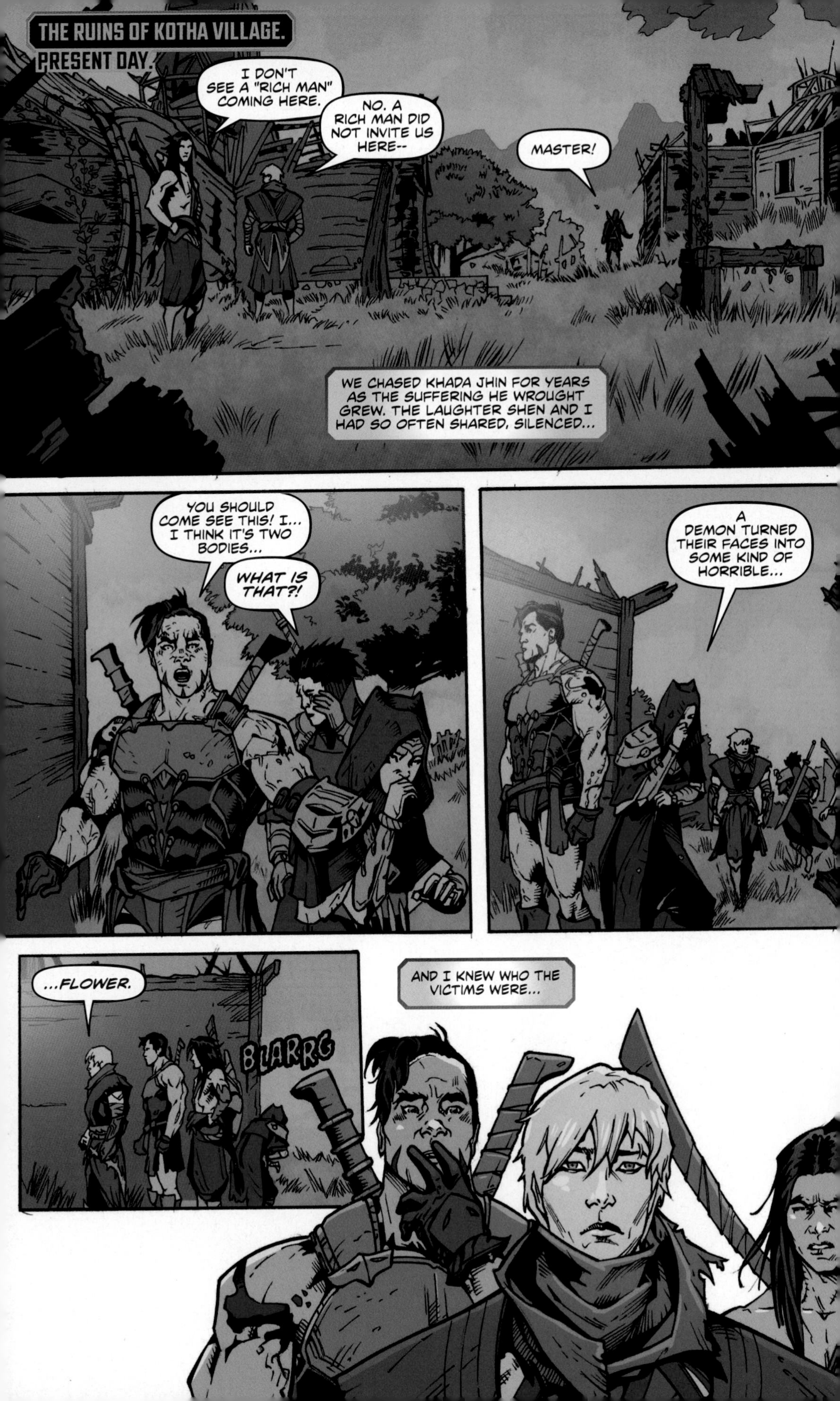
THE RUINS OF KOTHA VILLAGE.
PRESENT DAY.
I DON'T SEE A "RICH MAN" COMING HERE.
NO. A RICH MAN DID NOT INVITE US HERE--
MASTER!
WE CHASED KHADA JHIN FOR YEARS AS THE SUFFERING HE WROUGHT GREW. THE LAUGHTER SHEN AND I HAD SO OFTEN SHARED, SILENCED...
YOU SHOULD COME SEE THIS! I... I THINK IT'S TWO BODIES...
WHAT IS THAT?!
A DEMON TURNED THEIR FACES INTO SOME KIND OF HORRIBLE...
...FLOWER.
AND I KNEW WHO THE VICTIMS WERE...
BLARRG

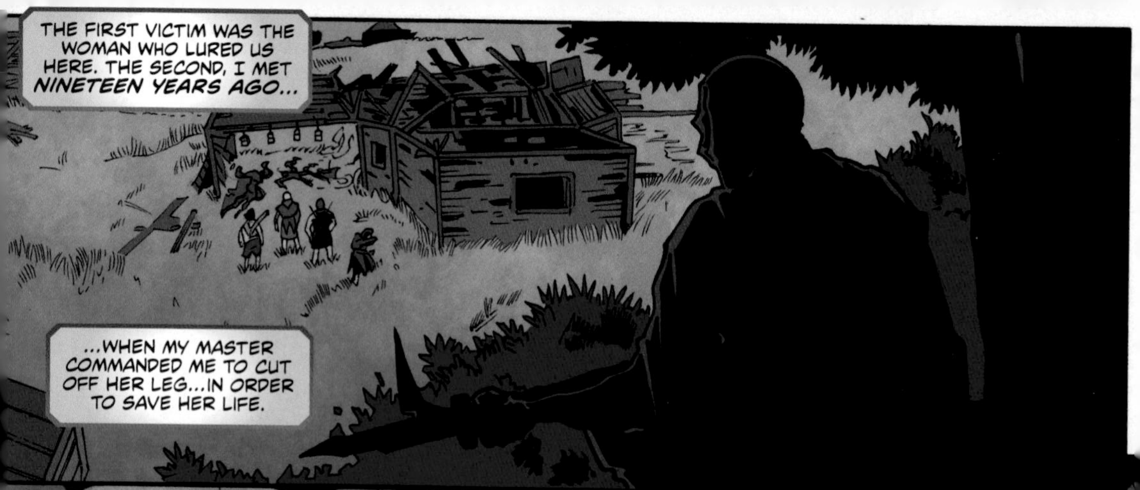
THE FIRST VICTIM WAS THE WOMAN WHO LURED US HERE. THE SECOND, I MET NINETEEN YEARS AGO...
...WHEN MY MASTER COMMANDED ME TO CUT OFF HER LEG...IN ORDER TO SAVE HER LIFE.

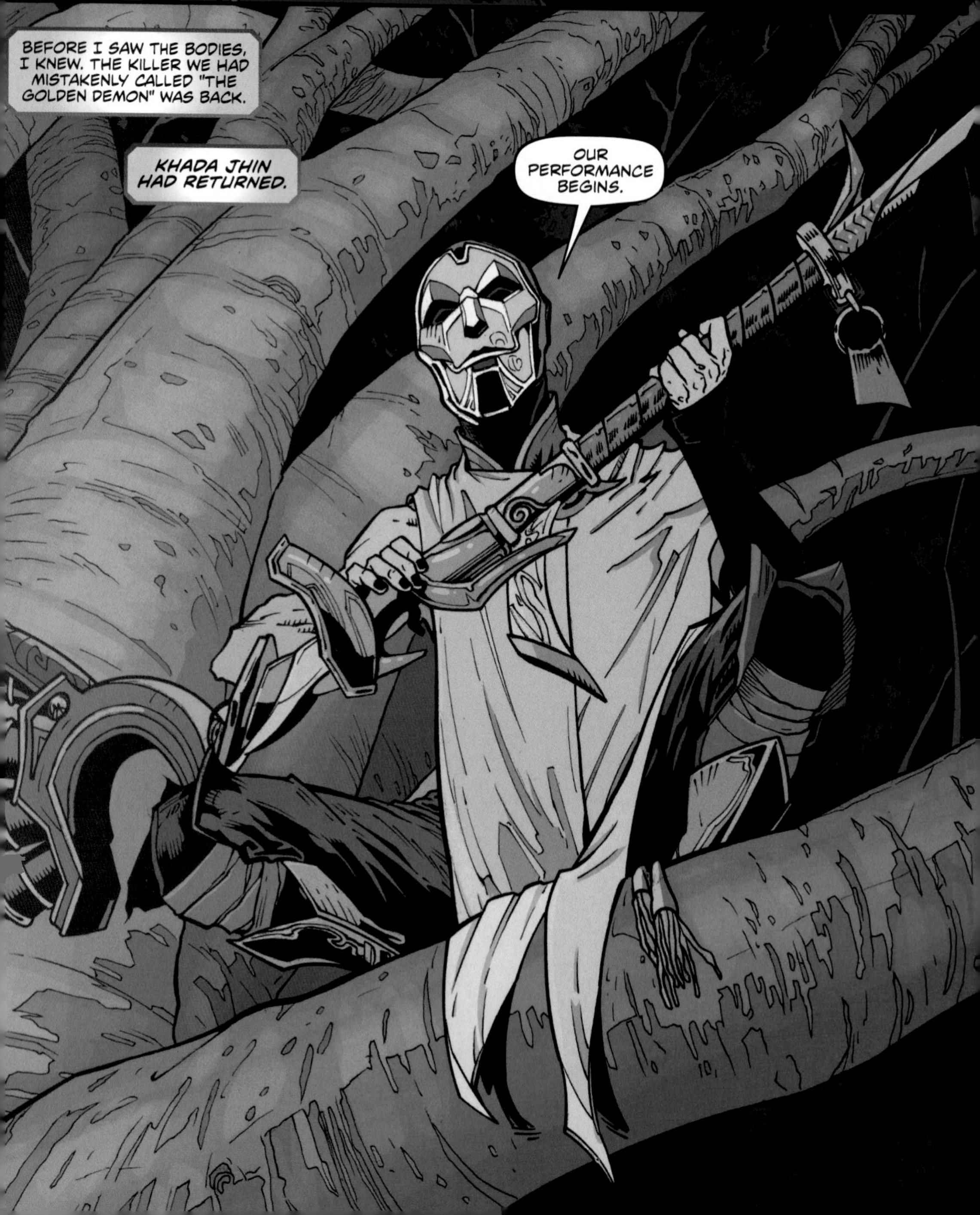
BEFORE I SAW THE BODIES, I KNEW. THE KILLER WE HAD MISTAKENLY CALLED "THE GOLDEN DEMON" WAS BACK.
KHADA JHIN HAD RETURNED.
OUR PERFORMANCE BEGINS.

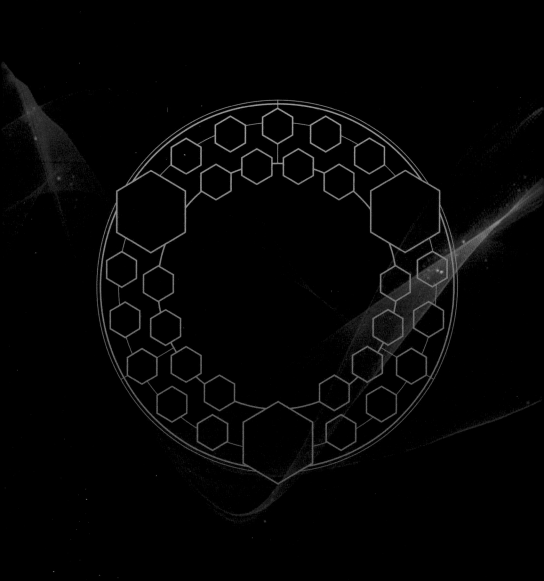

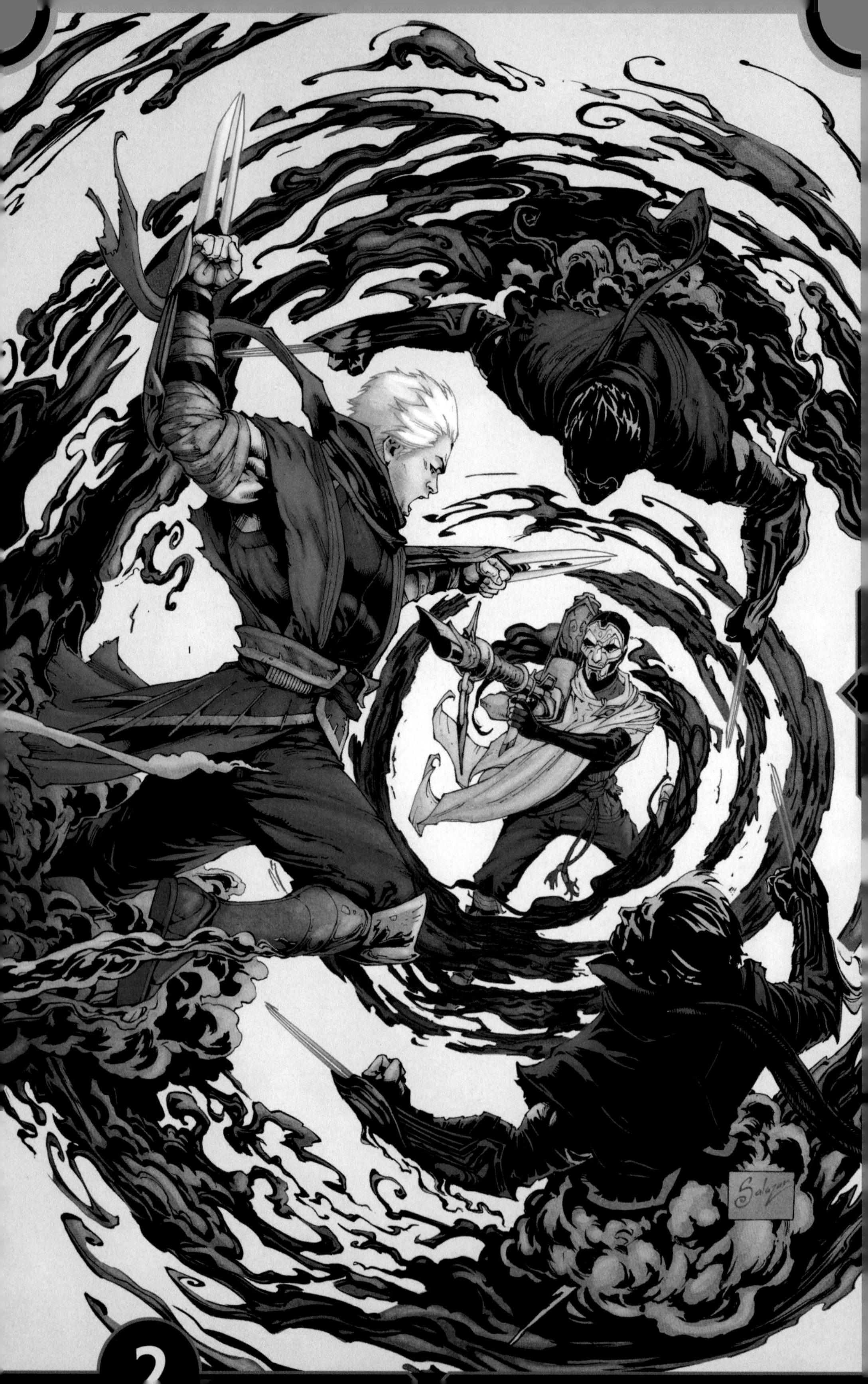
Salazar
2

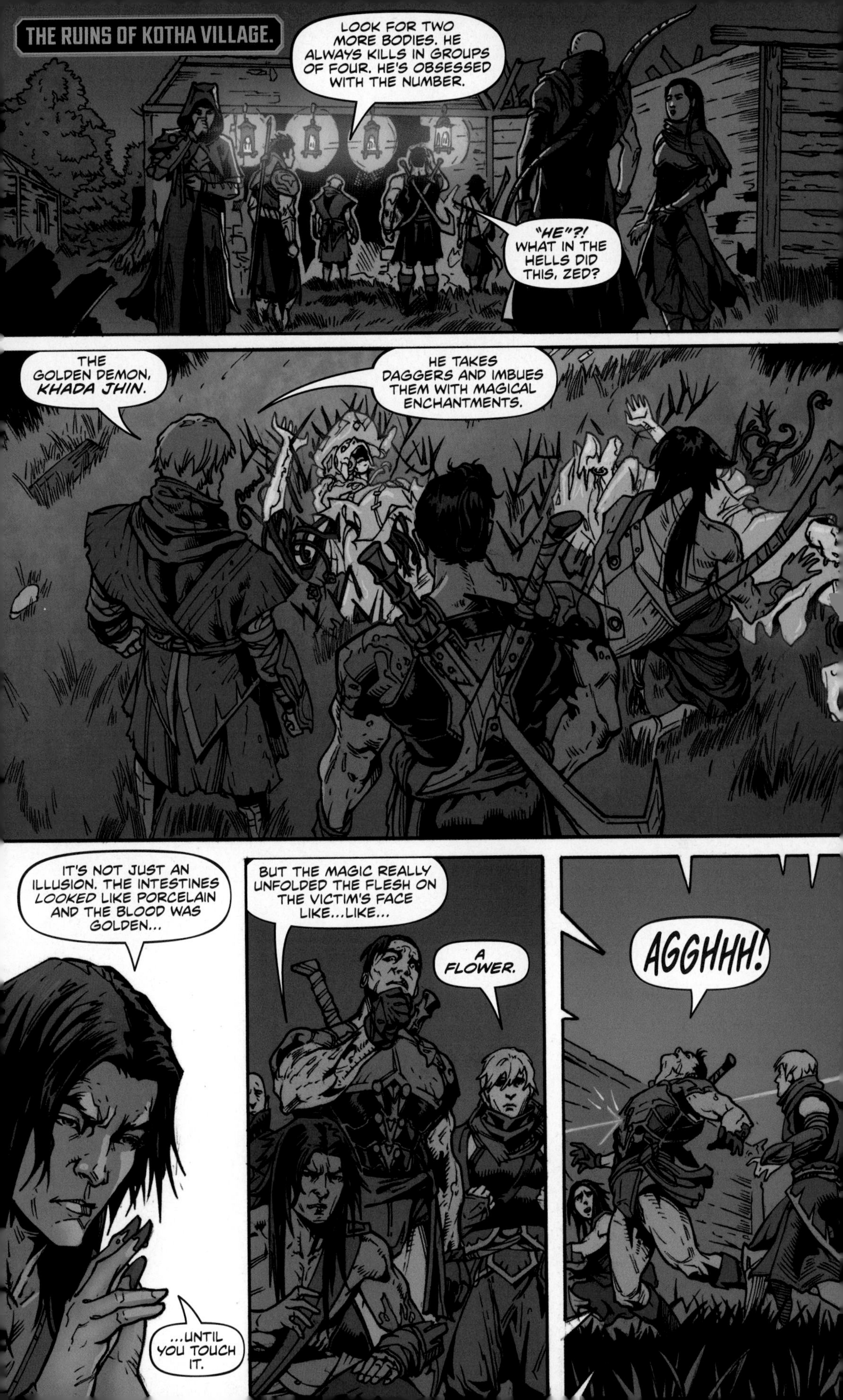
THE RUINS OF KOTHA VILLAGE.
LOOK FOR TWO MORE BODIES. HE ALWAYS KILLS IN GROUPS OF FOUR. HE'S OBSESSED WITH THE NUMBER.
"HE"?! WHAT IN THE HELLS DID THIS, ZED?
THE GOLDEN DEMON, KHADA JHIN.
HE TAKES DAGGERS AND IMBUES THEM WITH MAGICAL ENCHANTMENTS.
IT'S NOT JUST AN ILLUSION. THE INTESTINES LOOKED LIKE PORCELAIN AND THE BLOOD WAS GOLDEN...
...UNTIL YOU TOUCH IT.
BUT THE MAGIC REALLY UNFOLDED THE FLESH ON THE VICTIM'S FACE LIKE...LIKE...
A FLOWER.
AGGHHH!

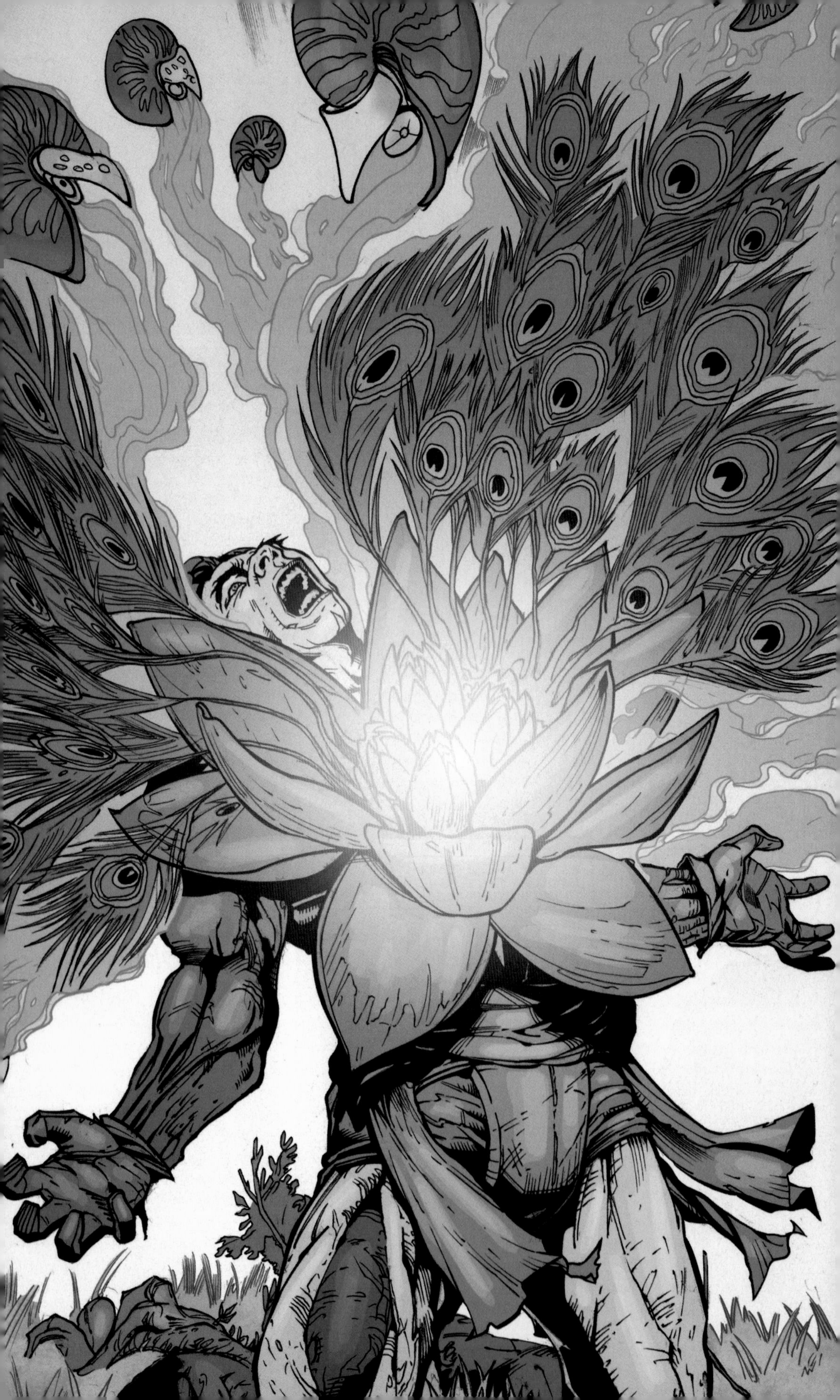

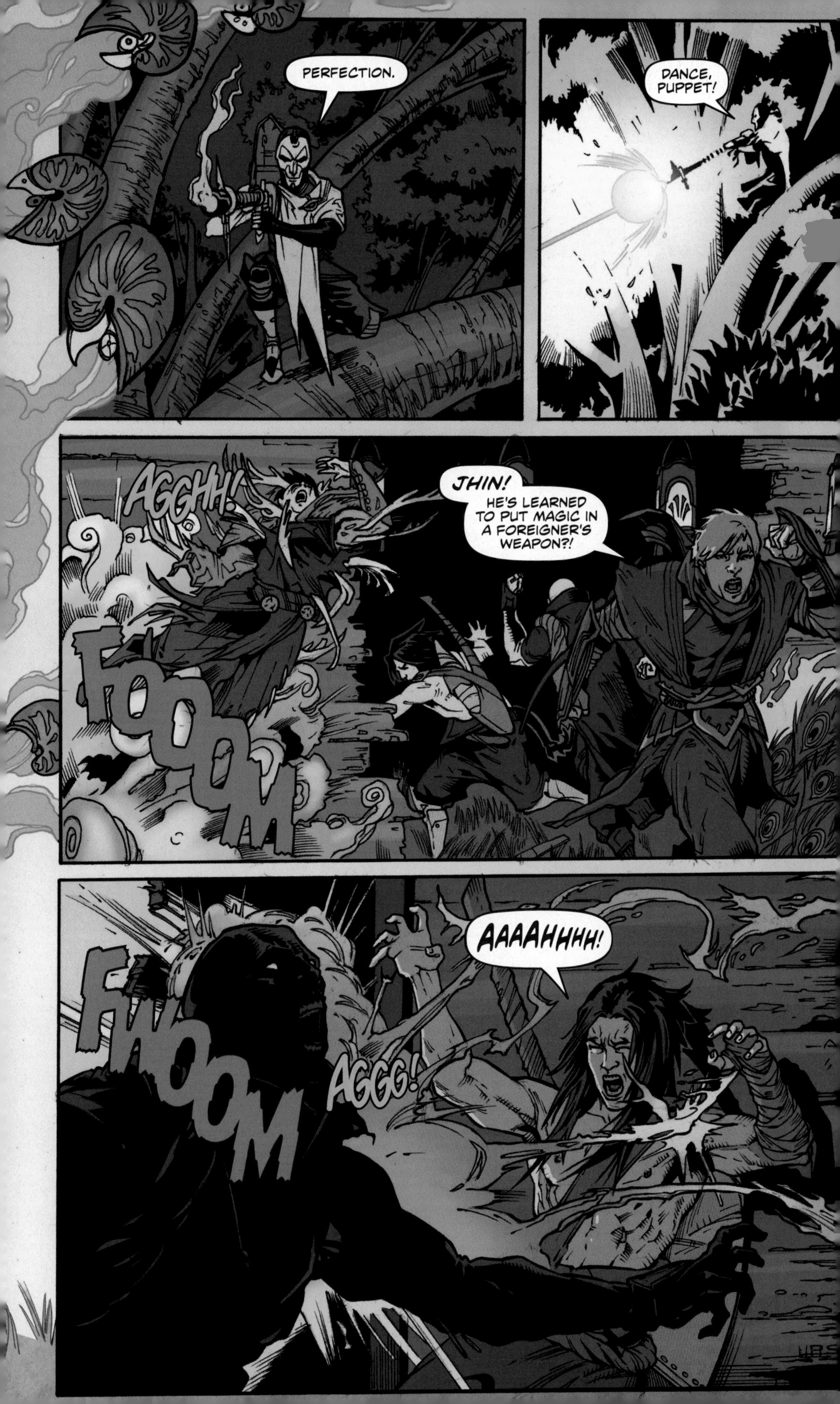
PERFECTION.
DANCE, PUPPET!
AGGHH!
FOOOM
JHIN!
HE'S LEARNED TO PUT MAGIC IN A FOREIGNER'S WEAPON?!
FWOOM
AAAAHHHH!
AGGG!

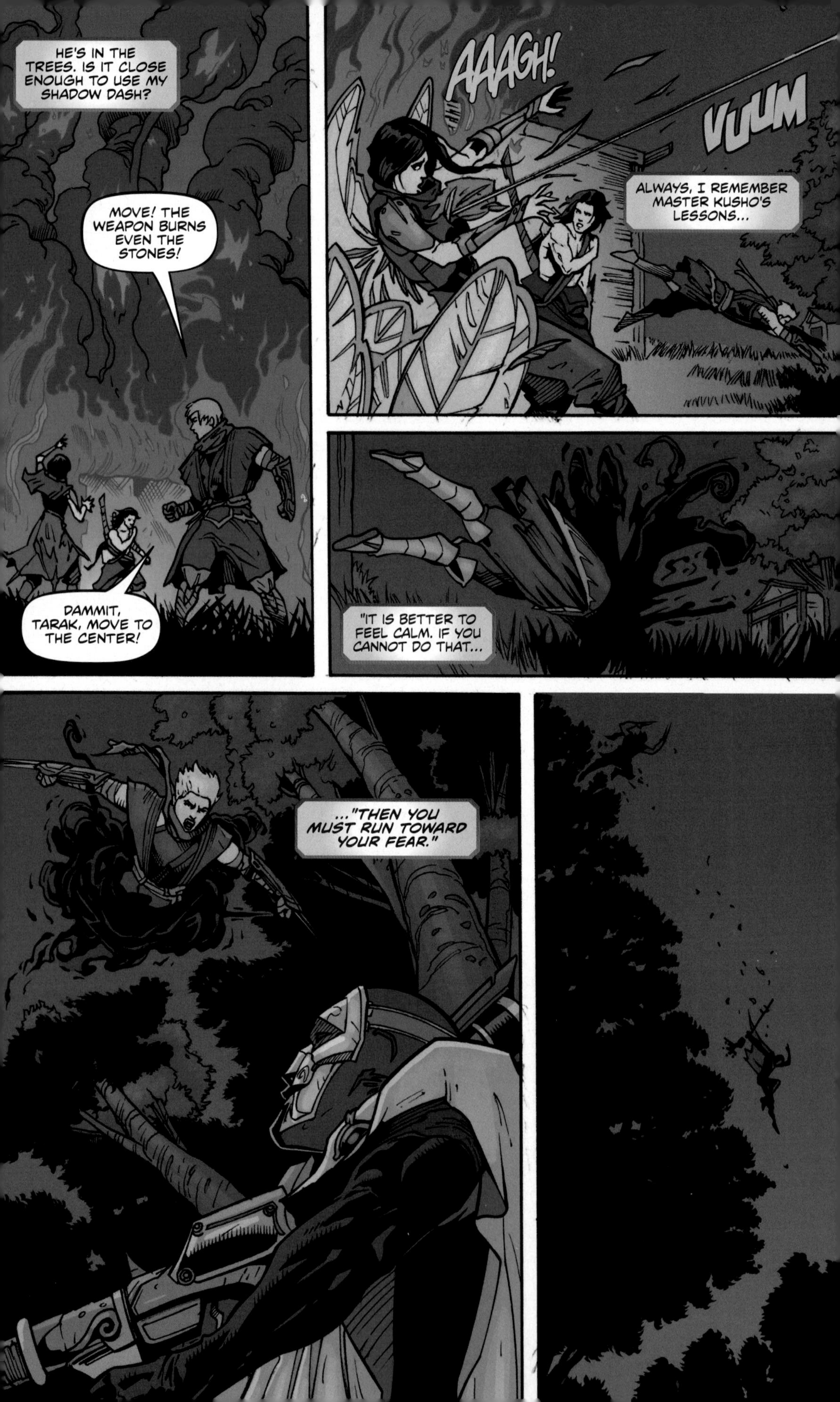
HE'S IN THE TREES. IS IT CLOSE ENOUGH TO USE MY SHADOW DASH?
MOVE! THE WEAPON BURNS EVEN THE STONES!
DAMMIT, TARAK, MOVE TO THE CENTER!
AAAGH!
VUUM
ALWAYS, I REMEMBER MASTER KUSHO'S LESSONS...
"IT IS BETTER TO FEEL CALM. IF YOU CANNOT DO THAT...
..."THEN YOU MUST RUN TOWARD YOUR FEAR."

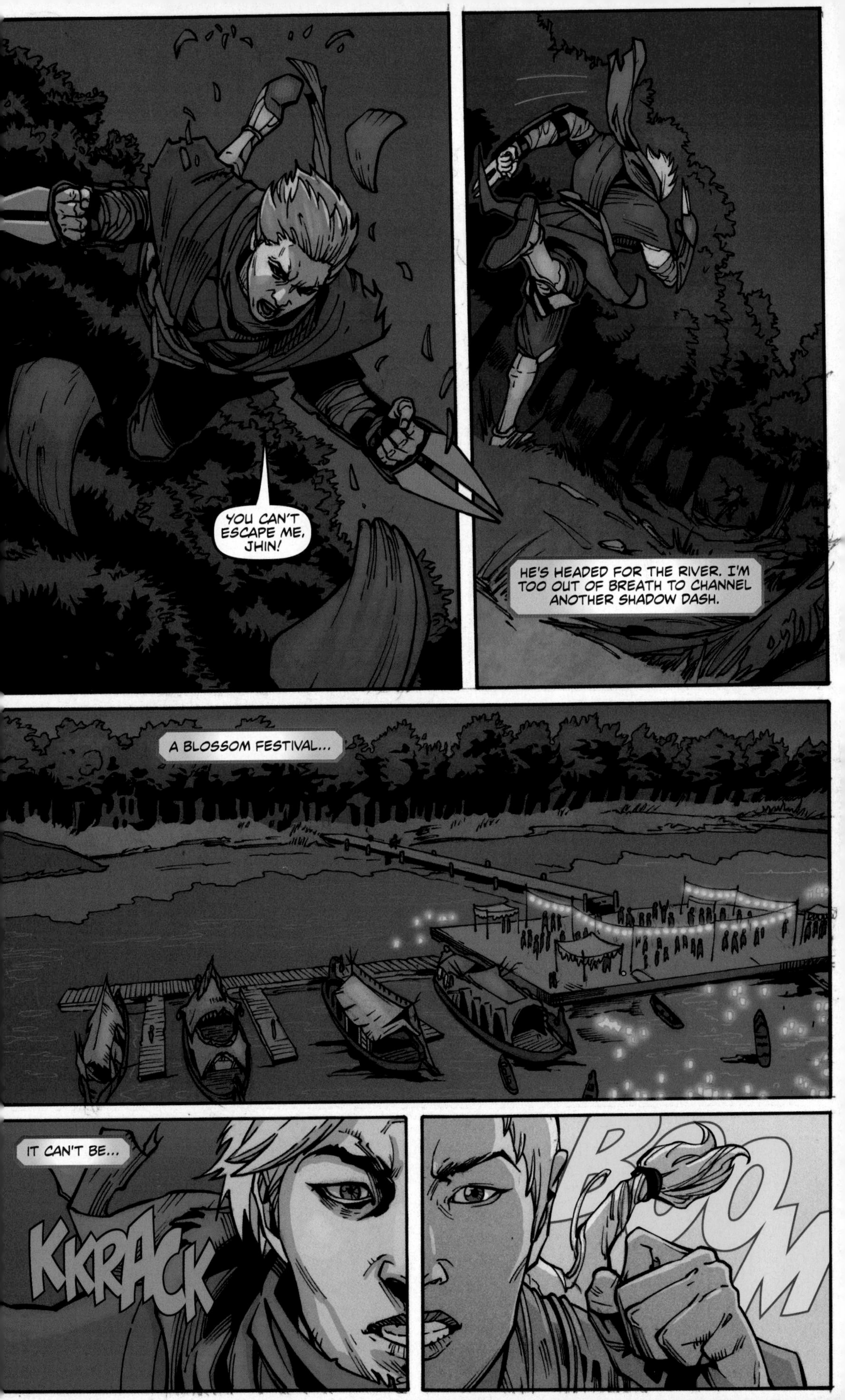
YOU CAN'T ESCAPE ME, JHIN!
HE'S HEADED FOR THE RIVER. I'M TOO OUT OF BREATH TO CHANNEL ANOTHER SHADOW DASH.
A BLOSSOM FESTIVAL...
IT CAN'T BE...
KKRACK
BOOM

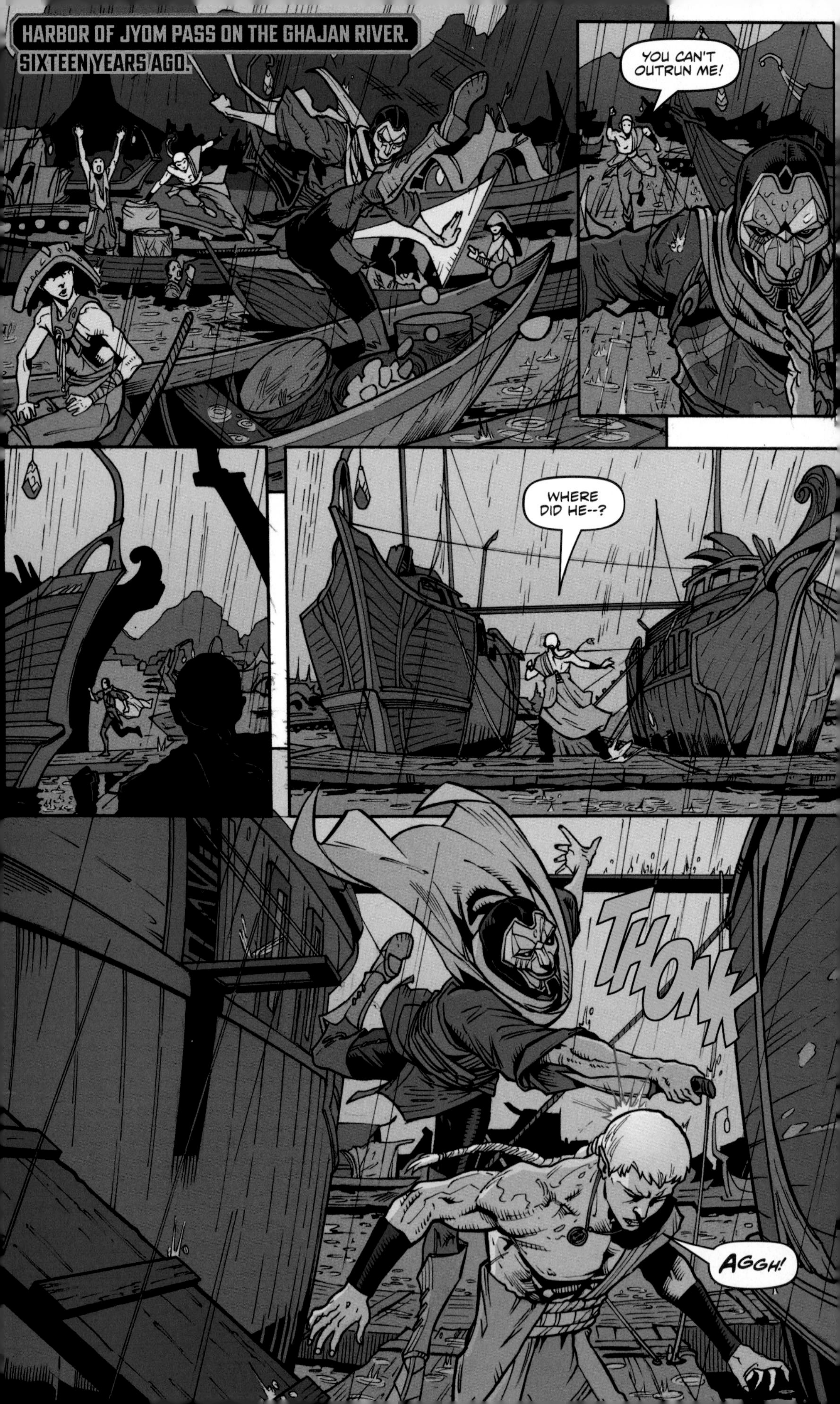
HARBOR OF JYOM PASS ON THE GHAJAN RIVER.
SIXTEEN YEARS AGO.
YOU CAN'T OUTRUN ME!
WHERE DID HE--?
THONK
AGGH!

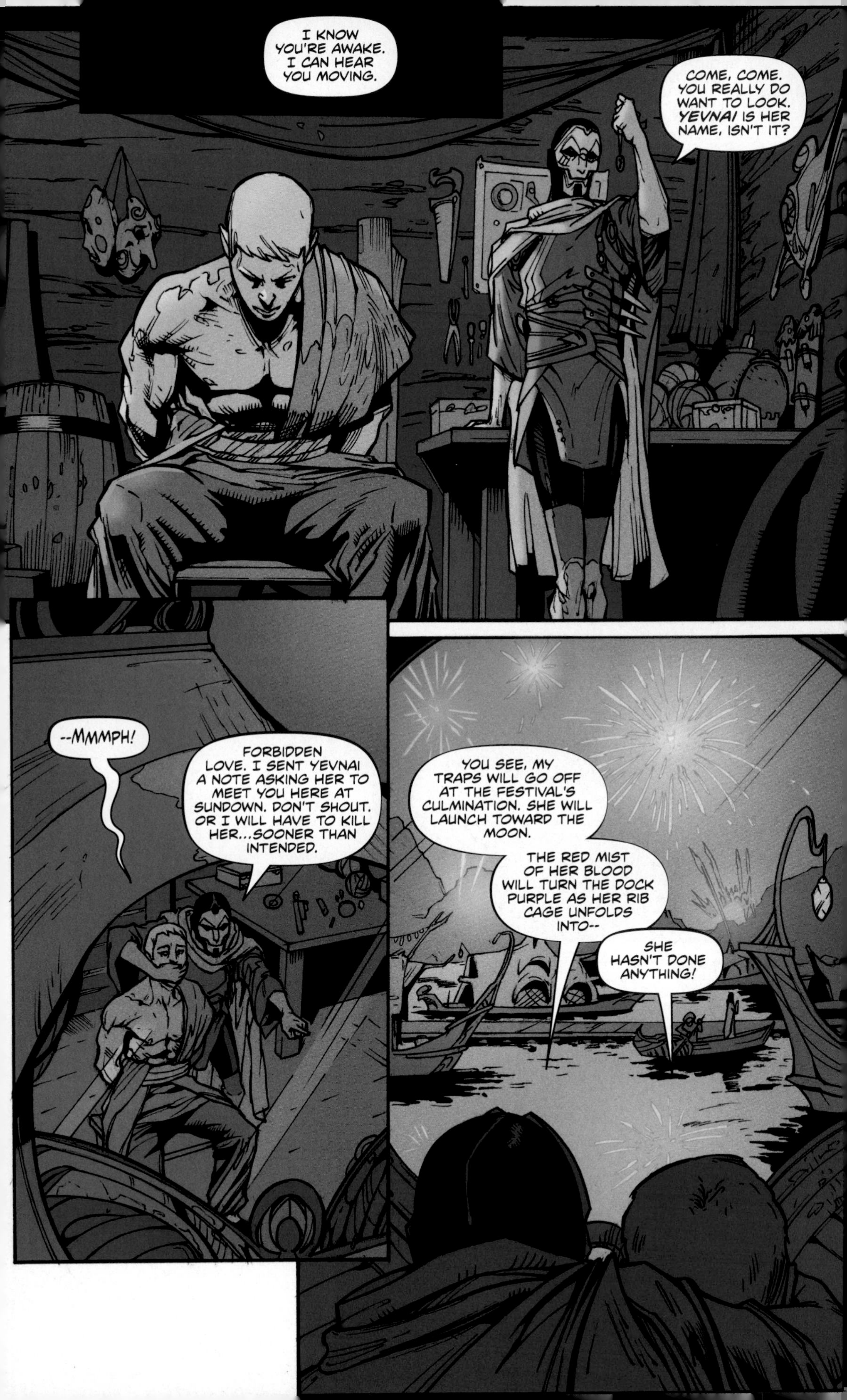
I KNOW YOU'RE AWAKE. I CAN HEAR YOU MOVING.
COME, COME. YOU REALLY DO WANT TO LOOK. *YEVNAI* IS HER NAME, ISN'T IT?
--MMMPH!
FORBIDDEN LOVE. I SENT YEVNAI A NOTE ASKING HER TO MEET YOU HERE AT SUNDOWN. DON'T SHOUT. OR I WILL HAVE TO KILL HER...SOONER THAN INTENDED.
YOU SEE, MY TRAPS WILL GO OFF AT THE FESTIVAL'S CULMINATION. SHE WILL LAUNCH TOWARD THE MOON.
THE RED MIST OF HER BLOOD WILL TURN THE DOCK PURPLE AS HER RIB CAGE UNFOLDS INTO--
SHE HASN'T DONE ANYTHING!

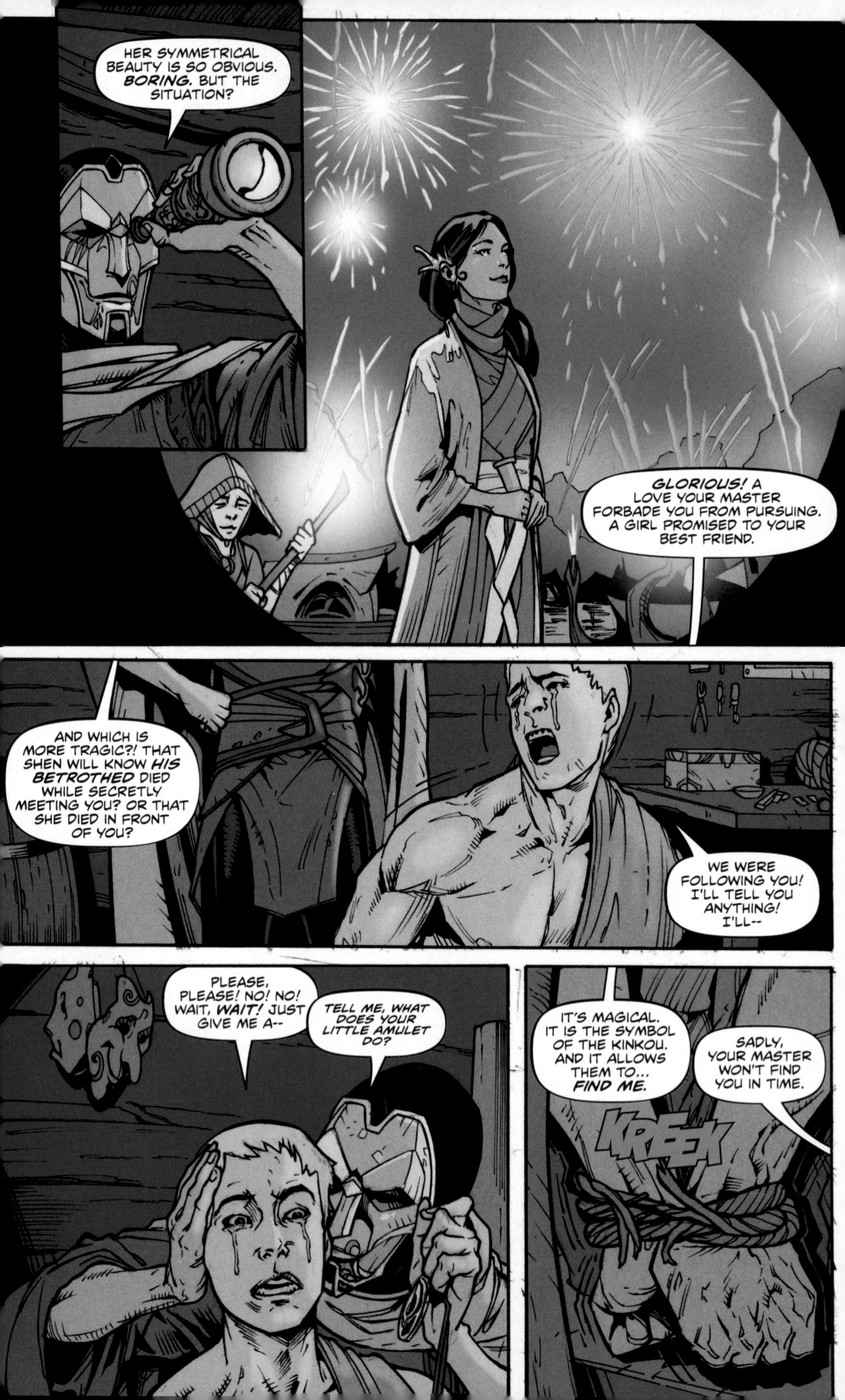

HER SYMMETRICAL BEAUTY IS SO OBVIOUS. BORING. BUT THE SITUATION?
GLORIOUS! A LOVE YOUR MASTER FORBADE YOU FROM PURSUING. A GIRL PROMISED TO YOUR BEST FRIEND.
AND WHICH IS MORE TRAGIC?! THAT SHEN WILL KNOW HIS BETROTHED DIED WHILE SECRETLY MEETING YOU? OR THAT SHE DIED IN FRONT OF YOU?
WE WERE FOLLOWING YOU! I'LL TELL YOU ANYTHING! I'LL--
PLEASE, PLEASE! NO! NO! WAIT, WAIT! JUST GIVE ME A--
TELL ME, WHAT DOES YOUR LITTLE AMULET DO?
IT'S MAGICAL. IT IS THE SYMBOL OF THE KINKOU. AND IT ALLOWS THEM TO... FIND ME.
SADLY, YOUR MASTER WON'T FIND YOU IN TIME.
KREEK

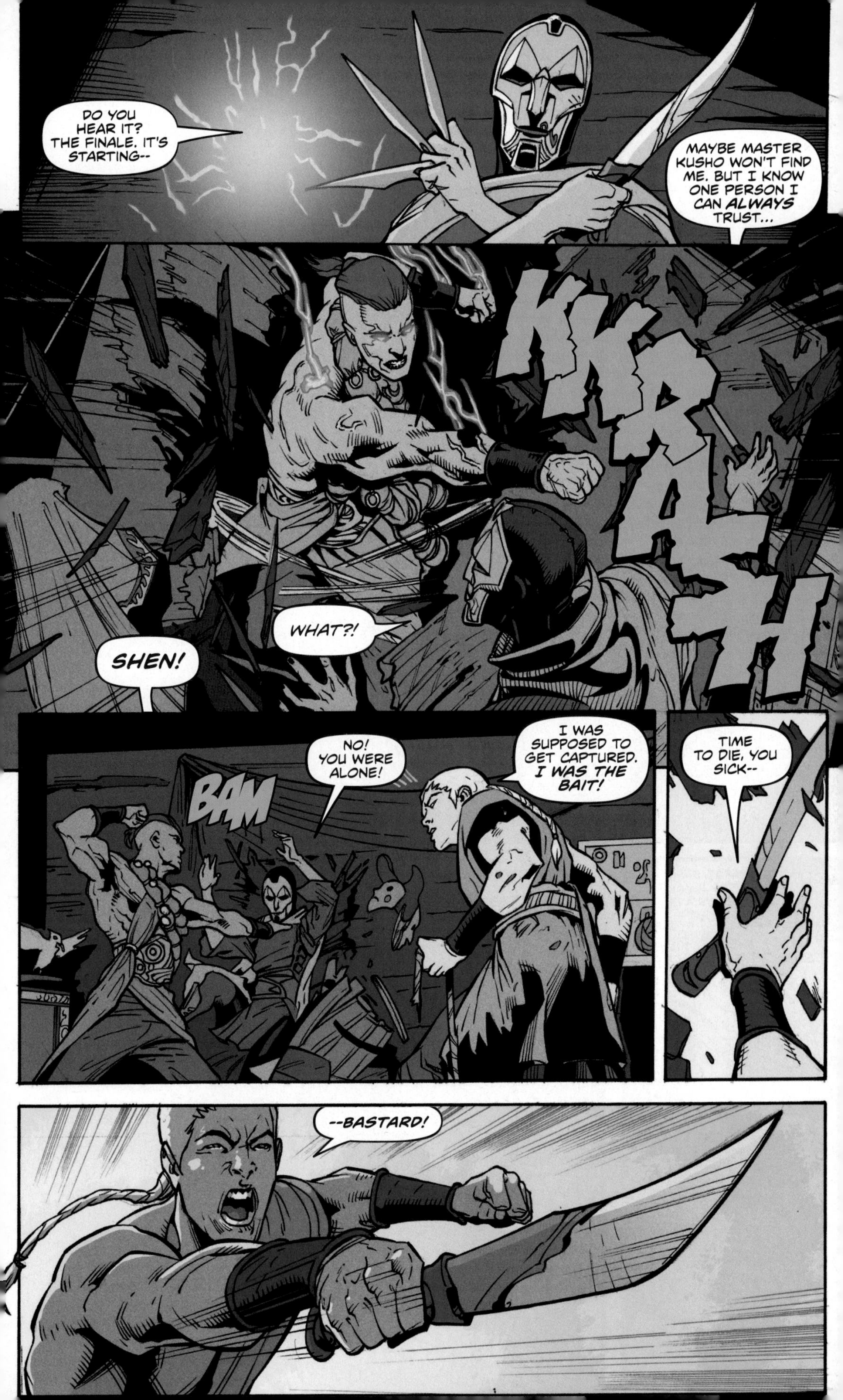
DO YOU HEAR IT? THE FINALE. IT'S STARTING--
MAYBE MASTER KUSHO WON'T FIND ME. BUT I KNOW ONE PERSON I CAN ALWAYS TRUST...
KKRASH
WHAT?!
SHEN!
BAM
NO! YOU WERE ALONE!
I WAS SUPPOSED TO GET CAPTURED. I WAS THE BAIT!
TIME TO DIE, YOU SICK--
--BASTARD!

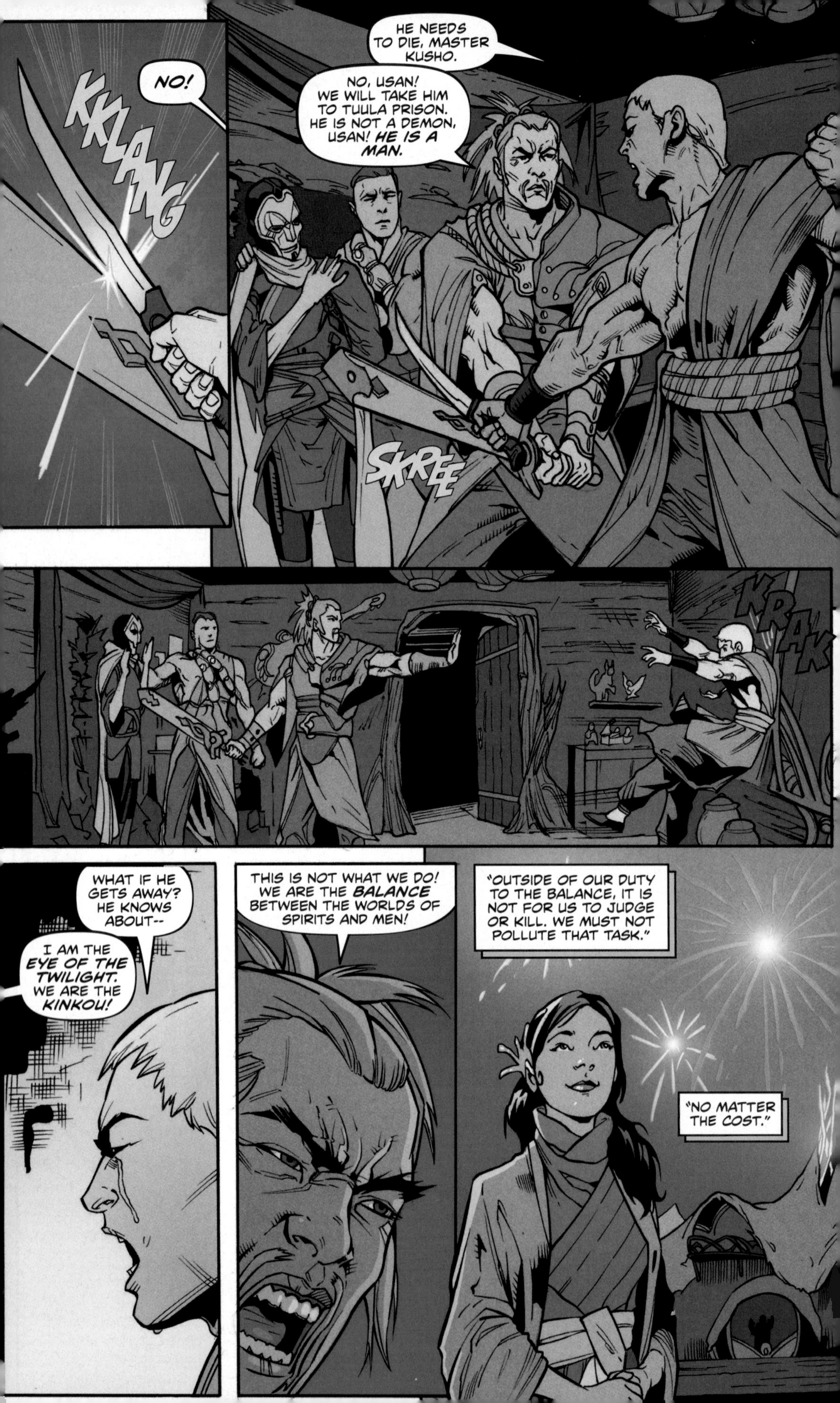

NO!
KKLANG
HE NEEDS TO DIE, MASTER KUSHO.
NO, USAN! WE WILL TAKE HIM TO TUULA PRISON. HE IS NOT A DEMON, USAN! *HE IS A MAN.*
SKREEE
KRAK
WHAT IF HE GETS AWAY? HE KNOWS ABOUT--
I AM THE *EYE OF THE TWILIGHT.* WE ARE THE *KINKOU!*
THIS IS NOT WHAT WE DO! WE ARE THE *BALANCE* BETWEEN THE WORLDS OF SPIRITS AND MEN!
"OUTSIDE OF OUR DUTY TO THE BALANCE, IT IS NOT FOR US TO JUDGE OR KILL. WE MUST NOT POLLUTE THAT TASK."
"NO MATTER THE COST."

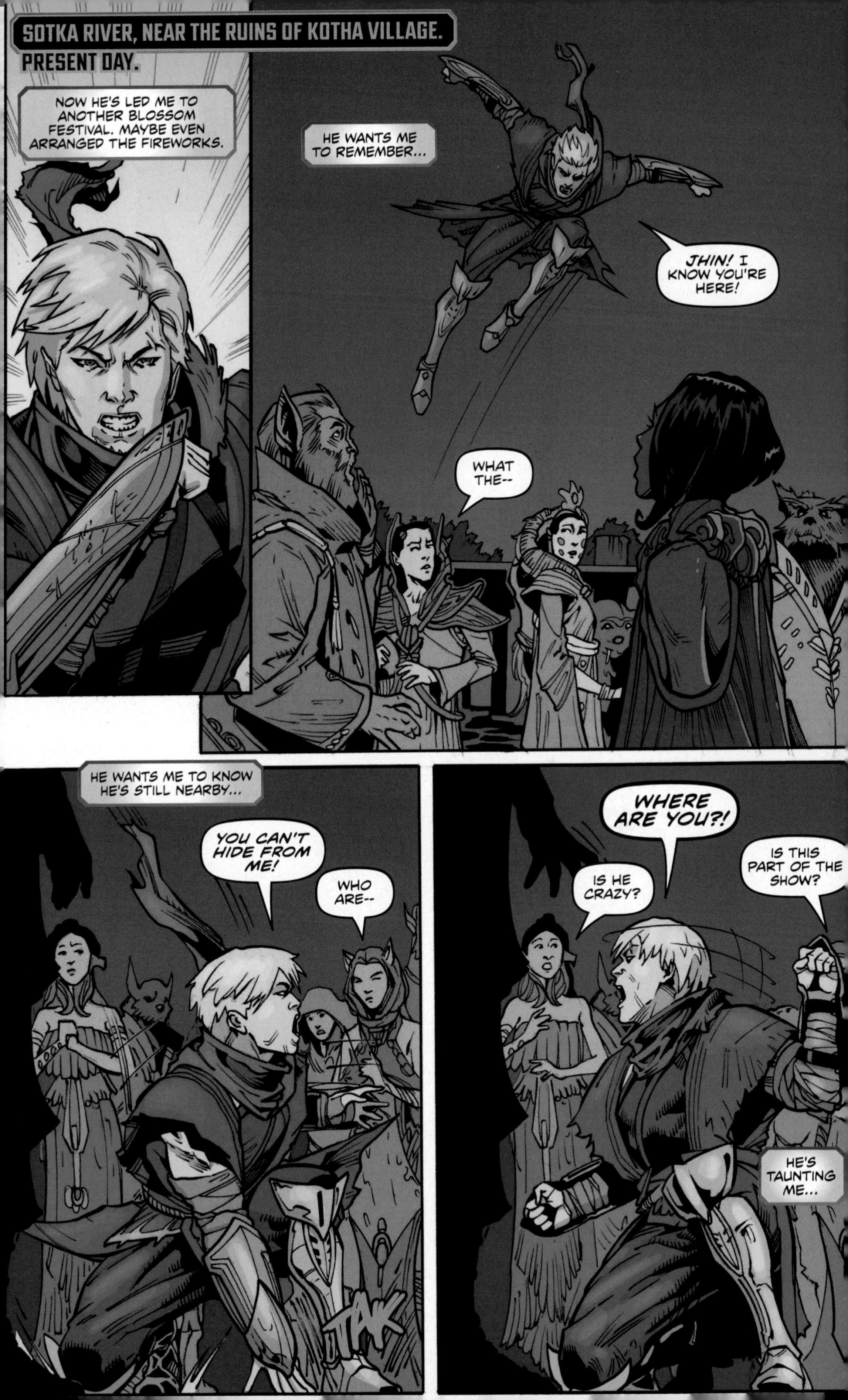
SOTKA RIVER, NEAR THE RUINS OF KOTHA VILLAGE.
PRESENT DAY.
NOW HE'S LED ME TO ANOTHER BLOSSOM FESTIVAL. MAYBE EVEN ARRANGED THE FIREWORKS.
HE WANTS ME TO REMEMBER...
JHIN! I KNOW YOU'RE HERE!
WHAT THE--
HE WANTS ME TO KNOW HE'S STILL NEARBY...
YOU CAN'T HIDE FROM ME!
WHO ARE--
TAK
WHERE ARE YOU?!
IS HE CRAZY?
IS THIS PART OF THE SHOW?
HE'S TAUNTING ME...

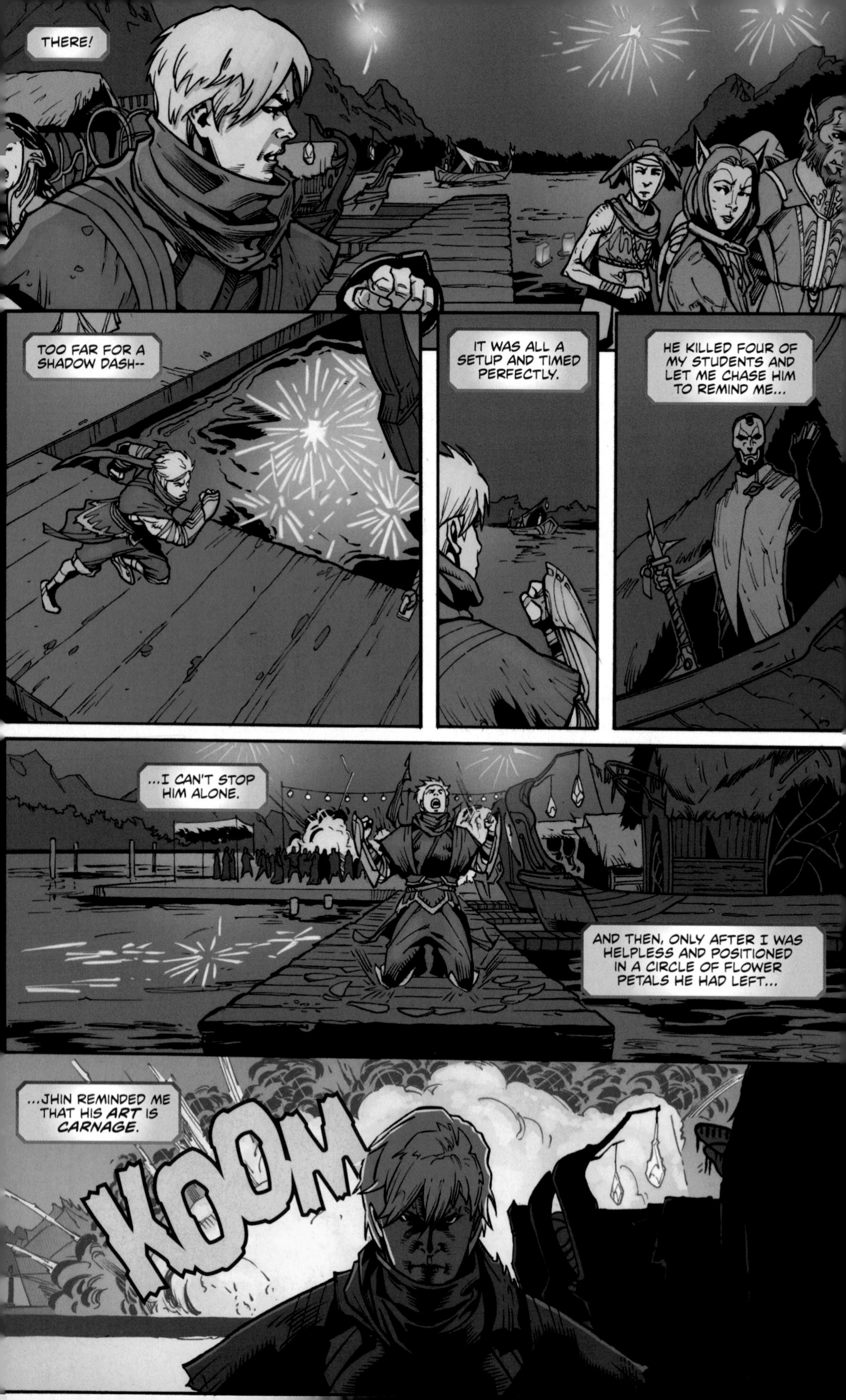
THERE!
TOO FAR FOR A SHADOW DASH--
IT WAS ALL A SETUP AND TIMED PERFECTLY.
HE KILLED FOUR OF MY STUDENTS AND LET ME CHASE HIM TO REMIND ME...
...I CAN'T STOP HIM ALONE.
AND THEN, ONLY AFTER I WAS HELPLESS AND POSITIONED IN A CIRCLE OF FLOWER PETALS HE HAD LEFT...
...JHIN REMINDED ME THAT HIS *ART* IS *CARNAGE*.
KOOM

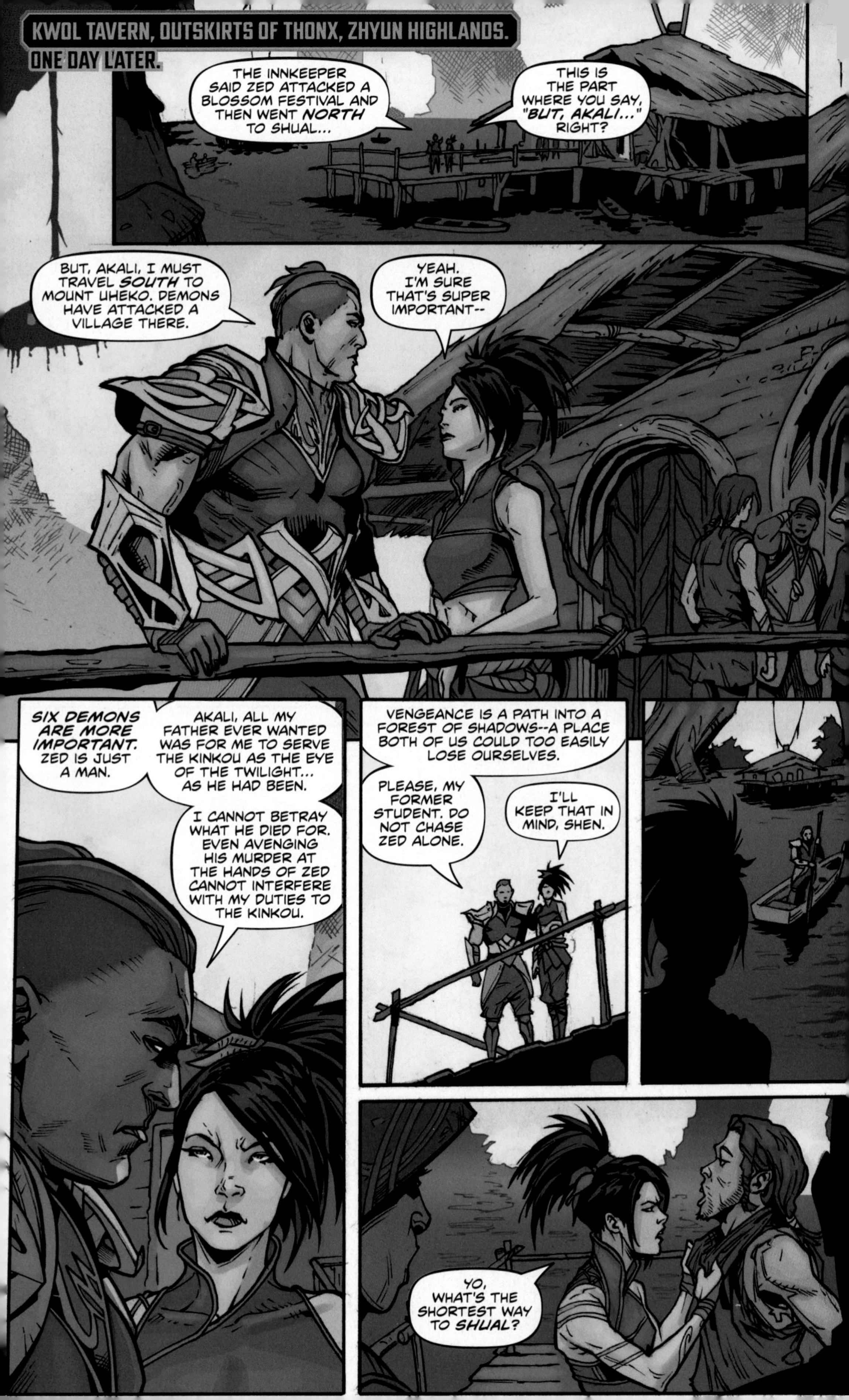
KWOL TAVERN, OUTSKIRTS OF THONX, ZHYUN HIGHLANDS.
ONE DAY LATER.
THE INNKEEPER SAID ZED ATTACKED A BLOSSOM FESTIVAL AND THEN WENT NORTH TO SHUAL...
THIS IS THE PART WHERE YOU SAY, "BUT, AKALI..." RIGHT?
BUT, AKALI, I MUST TRAVEL SOUTH TO MOUNT UHEKO. DEMONS HAVE ATTACKED A VILLAGE THERE.
YEAH. I'M SURE THAT'S SUPER IMPORTANT--
SIX DEMONS ARE MORE IMPORTANT. ZED IS JUST A MAN.
AKALI, ALL MY FATHER EVER WANTED WAS FOR ME TO SERVE THE KINKOU AS THE EYE OF THE TWILIGHT... AS HE HAD BEEN.
I CANNOT BETRAY WHAT HE DIED FOR. EVEN AVENGING HIS MURDER AT THE HANDS OF ZED CANNOT INTERFERE WITH MY DUTIES TO THE KINKOU.
VENGEANCE IS A PATH INTO A FOREST OF SHADOWS--A PLACE BOTH OF US COULD TOO EASILY LOSE OURSELVES.
PLEASE, MY FORMER STUDENT. DO NOT CHASE ZED ALONE.
I'LL KEEP THAT IN MIND, SHEN.
YO, WHAT'S THE SHORTEST WAY TO SHUAL?

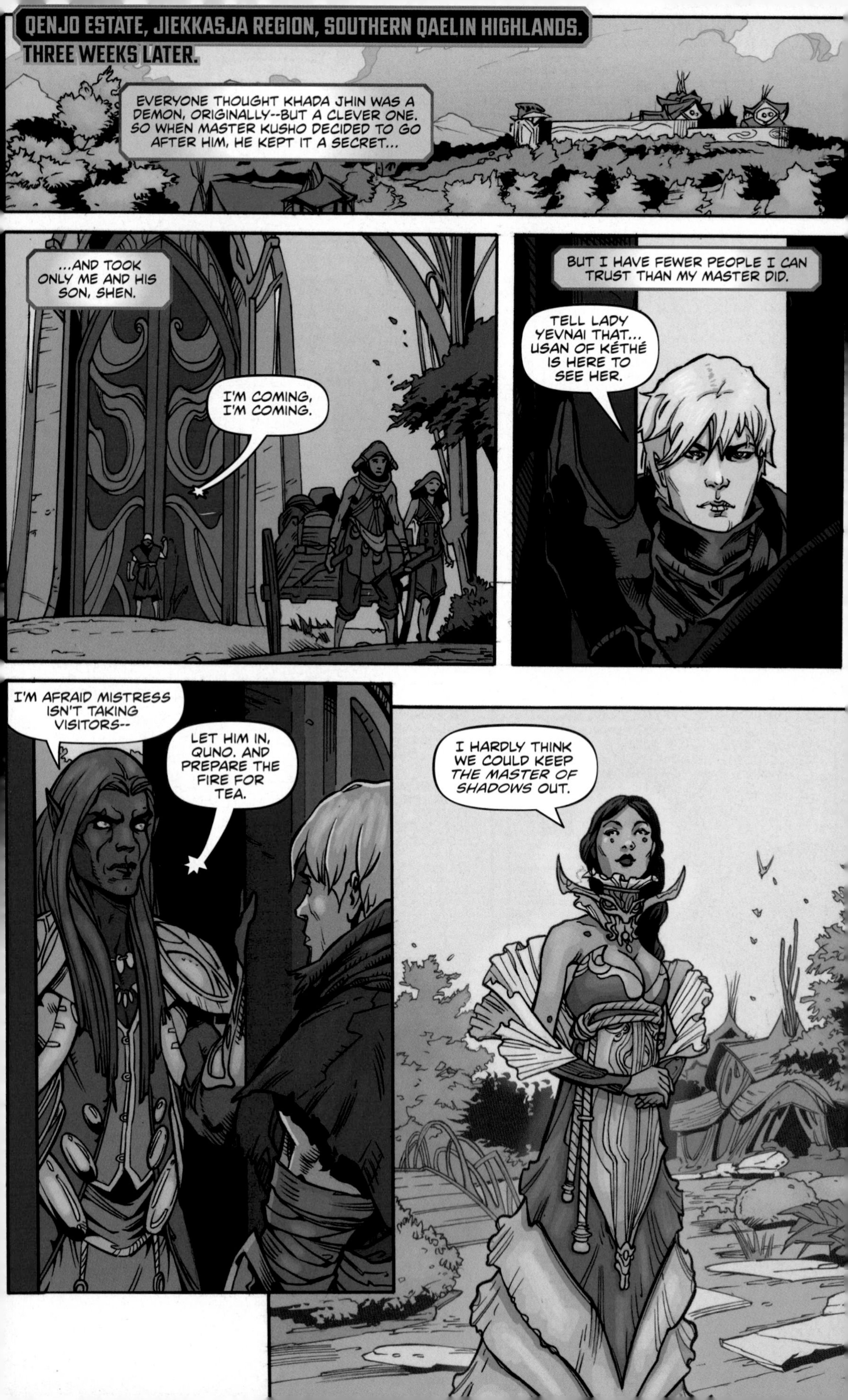

QENJO ESTATE, JIEKKASJA REGION, SOUTHERN QAELIN HIGHLANDS.
THREE WEEKS LATER.
EVERYONE THOUGHT KHADA JHIN WAS A DEMON, ORIGINALLY--BUT A CLEVER ONE. SO WHEN MASTER KUSHO DECIDED TO GO AFTER HIM, HE KEPT IT A SECRET...
...AND TOOK ONLY ME AND HIS SON, SHEN.
I'M COMING, I'M COMING.
BUT I HAVE FEWER PEOPLE I CAN TRUST THAN MY MASTER DID.
TELL LADY YEVNAI THAT... USAN OF KÉTHÉ IS HERE TO SEE HER.
I'M AFRAID MISTRESS ISN'T TAKING VISITORS--
LET HIM IN, QUNO. AND PREPARE THE FIRE FOR TEA.
I HARDLY THINK WE COULD KEEP *THE MASTER OF SHADOWS* OUT.

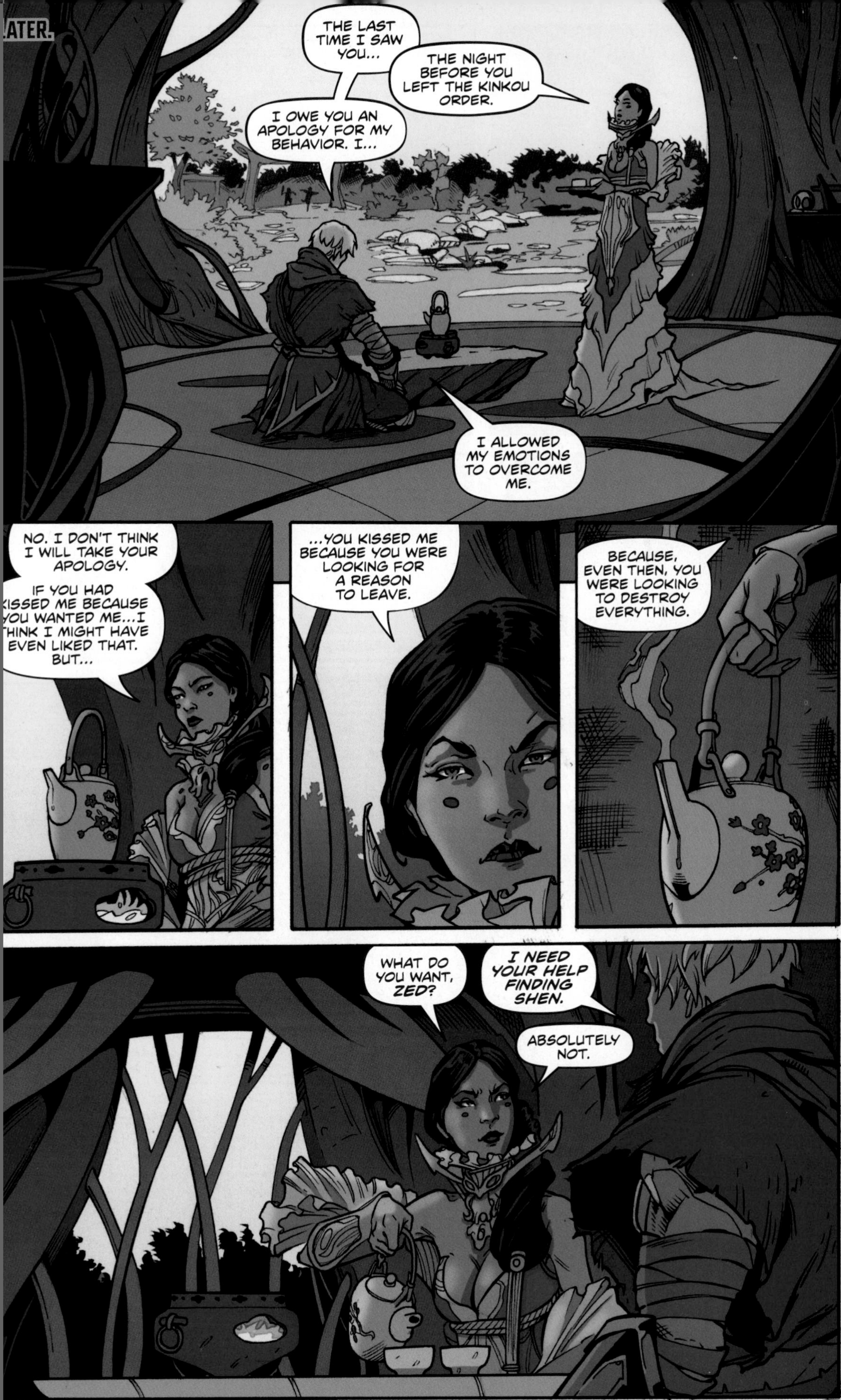
LATER.
THE LAST TIME I SAW YOU...
THE NIGHT BEFORE YOU LEFT THE KINKOU ORDER.
I OWE YOU AN APOLOGY FOR MY BEHAVIOR. I...
I ALLOWED MY EMOTIONS TO OVERCOME ME.
NO. I DON'T THINK I WILL TAKE YOUR APOLOGY.
IF YOU HAD KISSED ME BECAUSE YOU WANTED ME...I THINK I MIGHT HAVE EVEN LIKED THAT. BUT...
...YOU KISSED ME BECAUSE YOU WERE LOOKING FOR A REASON TO LEAVE.
BECAUSE, EVEN THEN, YOU WERE LOOKING TO DESTROY EVERYTHING.
WHAT DO YOU WANT, ZED?
I NEED YOUR HELP FINDING SHEN.
ABSOLUTELY NOT.

YOUR ENGAGEMENT WITH SHEN--

WAS CALLED OFF WHEN YOU KILLED MASTER KUSHO.

I GOT OVER THAT AND MARRIED LORD QENJO. HE WAS KIND AND RICH. AND I...I HAVE HAD A NICE LIFE...

BUT SHEN--HE WAS FORCED TO BECOME THE EYE OF THE TWILIGHT. A DUTY AND TITLE HE NEVER WANTED.

YOU KILLED HIS FATHER. NOW YOU SEEK TO DESTROY THE KINKOU?

HAVE YOU NO SHAME AT ALL?

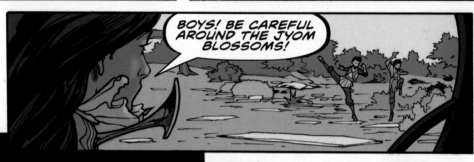

BOYS! BE CAREFUL AROUND THE JYOM BLOSSOMS!

SHINGK

YOU WILL TELL ME WHERE SHEN IS.

NO, USAN, I WILL NOT.

I WILL MAKE YOU ONE MORE CUP OF TEA. THEN YOU WILL GET OUT OF MY HOME AND NEVER RETURN.

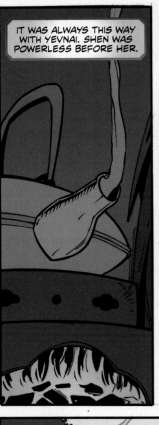

IT WAS ALWAYS THIS WAY WITH YEVNAI. SHEN WAS POWERLESS BEFORE HER.

I WAS TOO...AND FOR THE SAME REASON.

KHADA JHIN HAS RETURNED. I NEED SHEN'S HELP.

USAN, WHENEVER YOU SPEAK, NEW LIES ARE BORN.

MY RAIN STRIKE WILL DECIMATE YOUR ASH BLAST.

NO WAY!

HA HA HA

HA HA

HA

THEY HAVE YOUR GIFTS. YOUR YOUNGER SON'S MAGIC IS MUCH, MUCH STRONGER THAN HIS BROTHER'S.

BUT THE ELEMENTS AREN'T PURE.

THE YOUNGER SON HAS TRACES OF ANIMAL SPIRITS IN HIS MAGIC.

DOES YOUR HUSBAND KNOW?

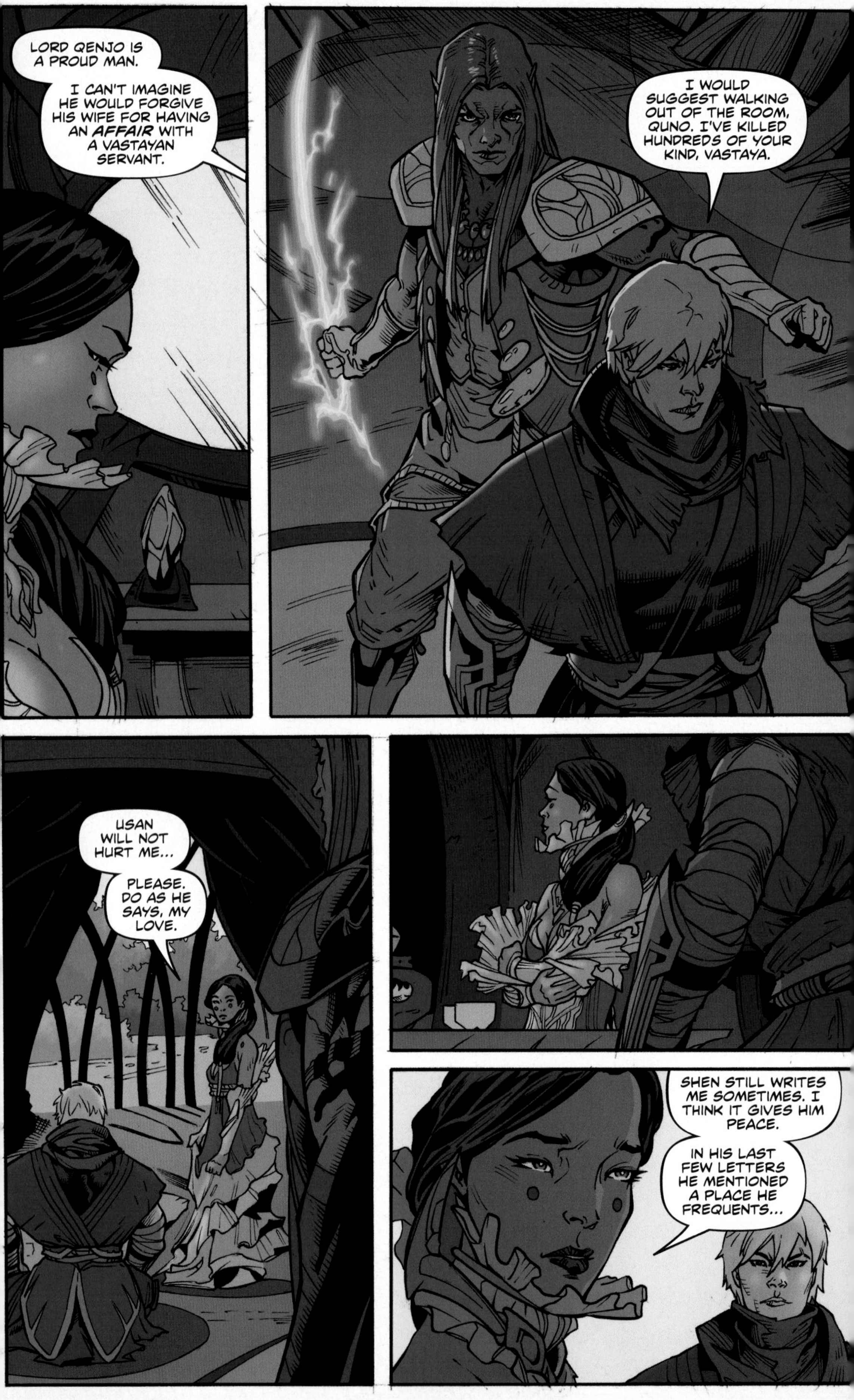
LORD QENJO IS A PROUD MAN.
I CAN'T IMAGINE HE WOULD FORGIVE HIS WIFE FOR HAVING AN *AFFAIR* WITH A VASTAYAN SERVANT.
I WOULD SUGGEST WALKING OUT OF THE ROOM, QUNO. I'VE KILLED HUNDREDS OF YOUR KIND, VASTAYA.
USAN WILL NOT HURT ME...
PLEASE. DO AS HE SAYS, MY LOVE.
SHEN STILL WRITES ME SOMETIMES. I THINK IT GIVES HIM PEACE.
IN HIS LAST FEW LETTERS HE MENTIONED A PLACE HE FREQUENTS...

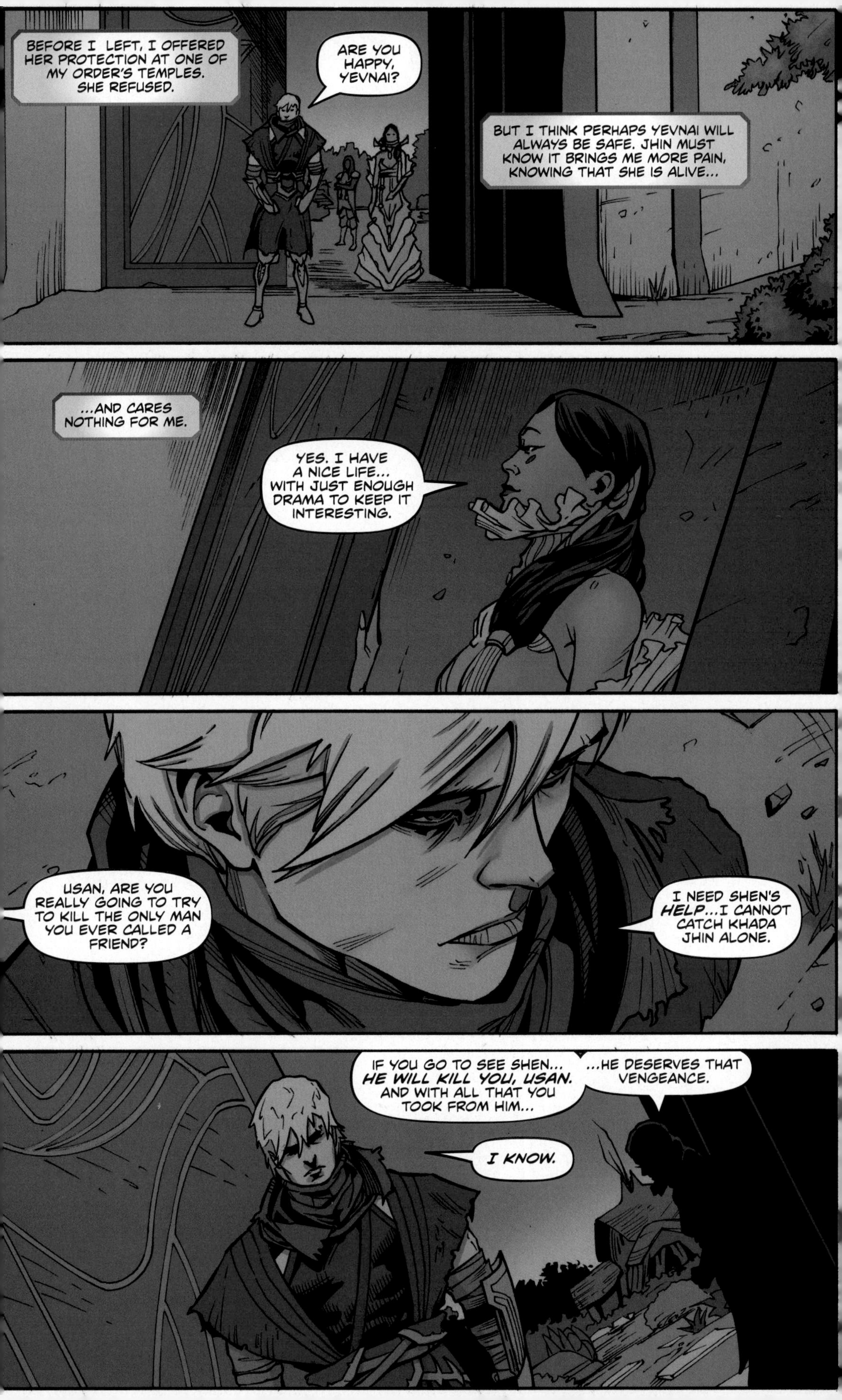
BEFORE I LEFT, I OFFERED HER PROTECTION AT ONE OF MY ORDER'S TEMPLES. SHE REFUSED.
ARE YOU HAPPY, YEVNAI?
BUT I THINK PERHAPS YEVNAI WILL ALWAYS BE SAFE. JHIN MUST KNOW IT BRINGS ME MORE PAIN, KNOWING THAT SHE IS ALIVE...
...AND CARES NOTHING FOR ME.
YES. I HAVE A NICE LIFE... WITH JUST ENOUGH DRAMA TO KEEP IT INTERESTING.
USAN, ARE YOU REALLY GOING TO TRY TO KILL THE ONLY MAN YOU EVER CALLED A FRIEND?
I NEED SHEN'S *HELP*...I CANNOT CATCH KHADA JHIN ALONE.
IF YOU GO TO SEE SHEN... *HE WILL KILL YOU, USAN.* AND WITH ALL THAT YOU TOOK FROM HIM...
...HE DESERVES THAT VENGEANCE.
I KNOW.

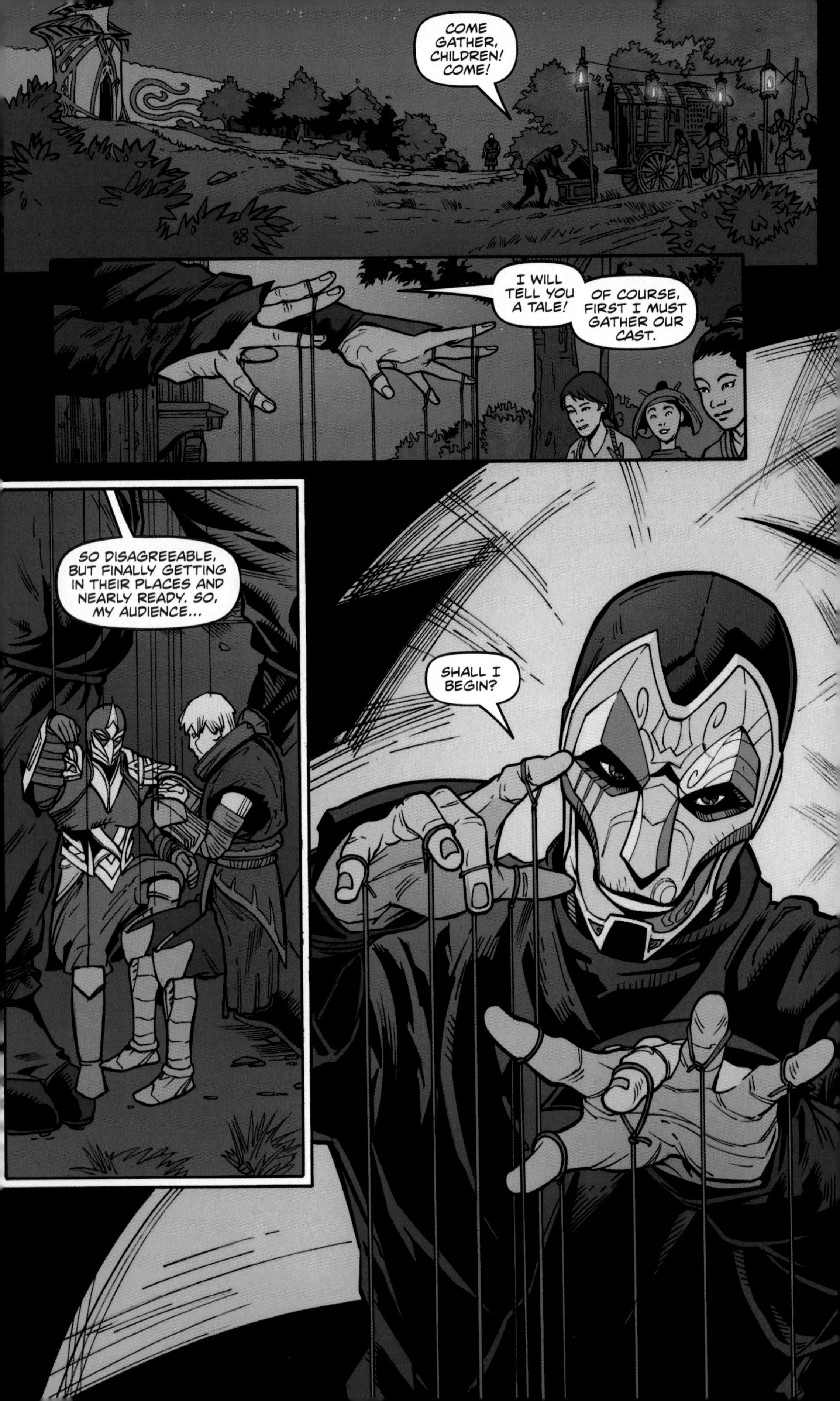

COME GATHER, CHILDREN! COME!
I WILL TELL YOU A TALE!
OF COURSE, FIRST I MUST GATHER OUR CAST.
SO DISAGREEABLE, BUT FINALLY GETTING IN THEIR PLACES AND NEARLY READY. SO, MY AUDIENCE...
SHALL I BEGIN?

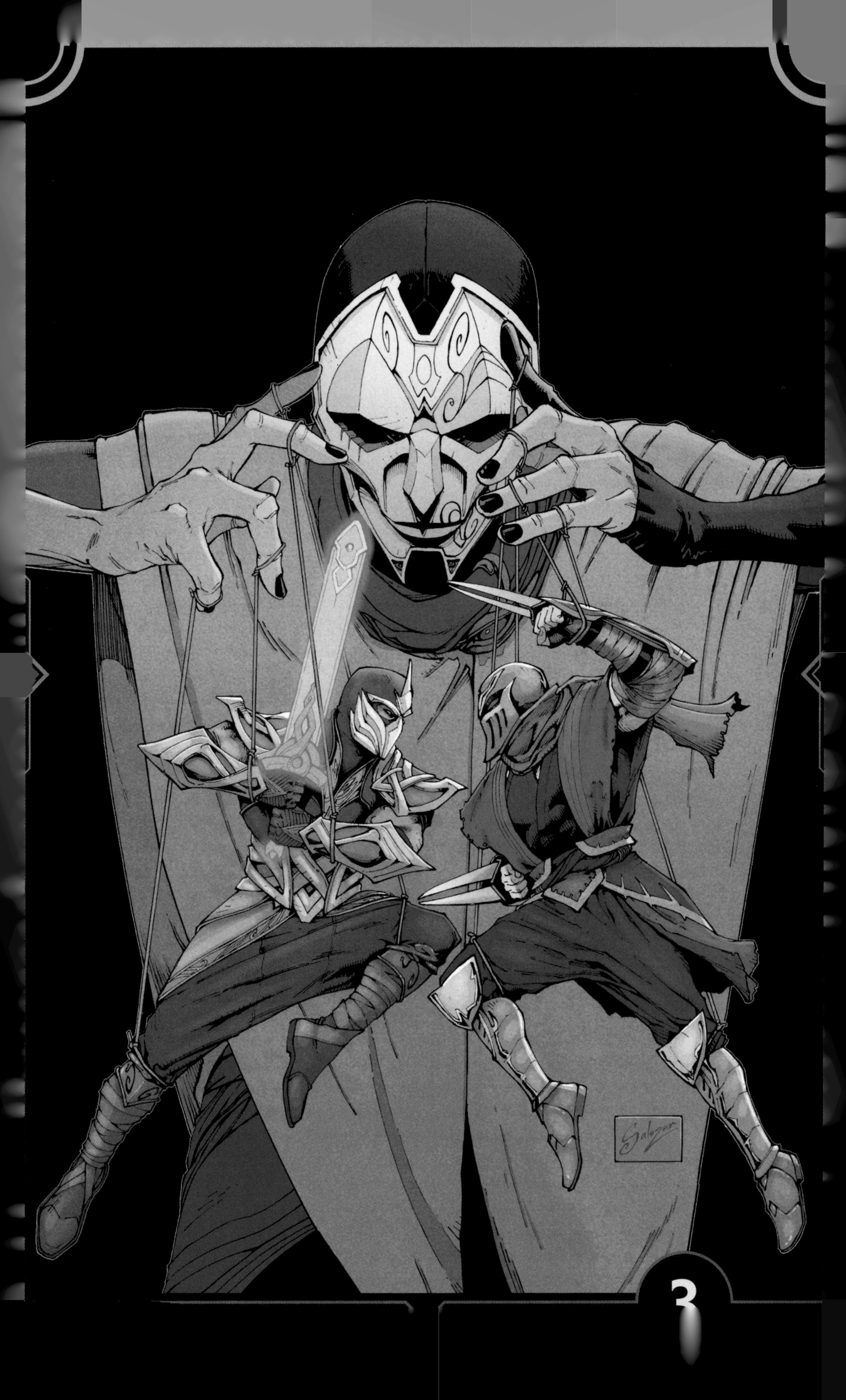
3

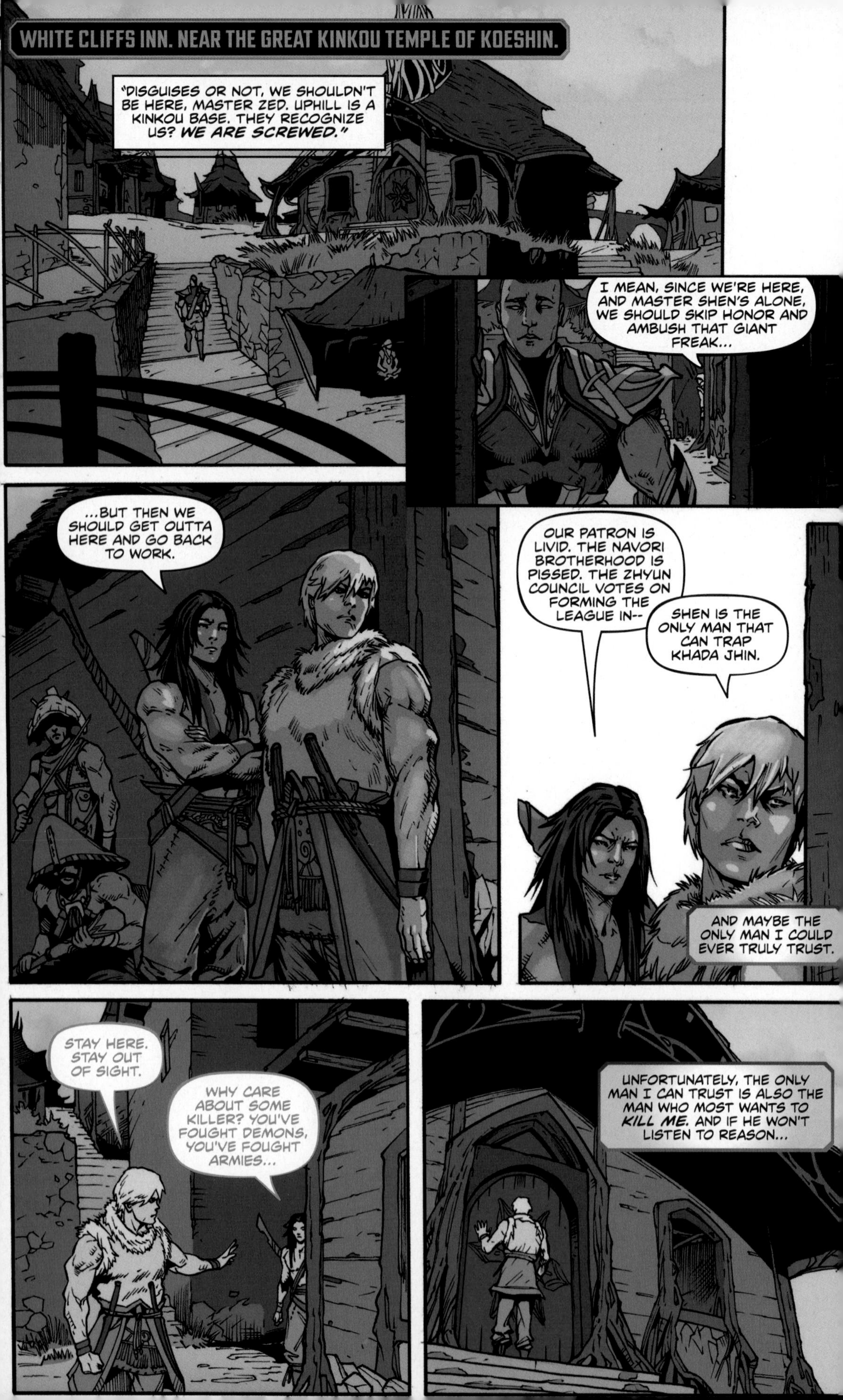
WHITE CLIFFS INN. NEAR THE GREAT KINKOU TEMPLE OF KOESHIN.
"DISGUISES OR NOT, WE SHOULDN'T BE HERE, MASTER ZED. UPHILL IS A KINKOU BASE. THEY RECOGNIZE US? WE ARE SCREWED."
I MEAN, SINCE WE'RE HERE, AND MASTER SHEN'S ALONE, WE SHOULD SKIP HONOR AND AMBUSH THAT GIANT FREAK...
...BUT THEN WE SHOULD GET OUTTA HERE AND GO BACK TO WORK.
OUR PATRON IS LIVID. THE NAVORI BROTHERHOOD IS PISSED. THE ZHYUN COUNCIL VOTES ON FORMING THE LEAGUE IN--
SHEN IS THE ONLY MAN THAT CAN TRAP KHADA JHIN.
AND MAYBE THE ONLY MAN I COULD EVER TRULY TRUST.
STAY HERE. STAY OUT OF SIGHT.
WHY CARE ABOUT SOME KILLER? YOU'VE FOUGHT DEMONS, YOU'VE FOUGHT ARMIES...
UNFORTUNATELY, THE ONLY MAN I CAN TRUST IS ALSO THE MAN WHO MOST WANTS TO KILL ME. AND IF HE WON'T LISTEN TO REASON...

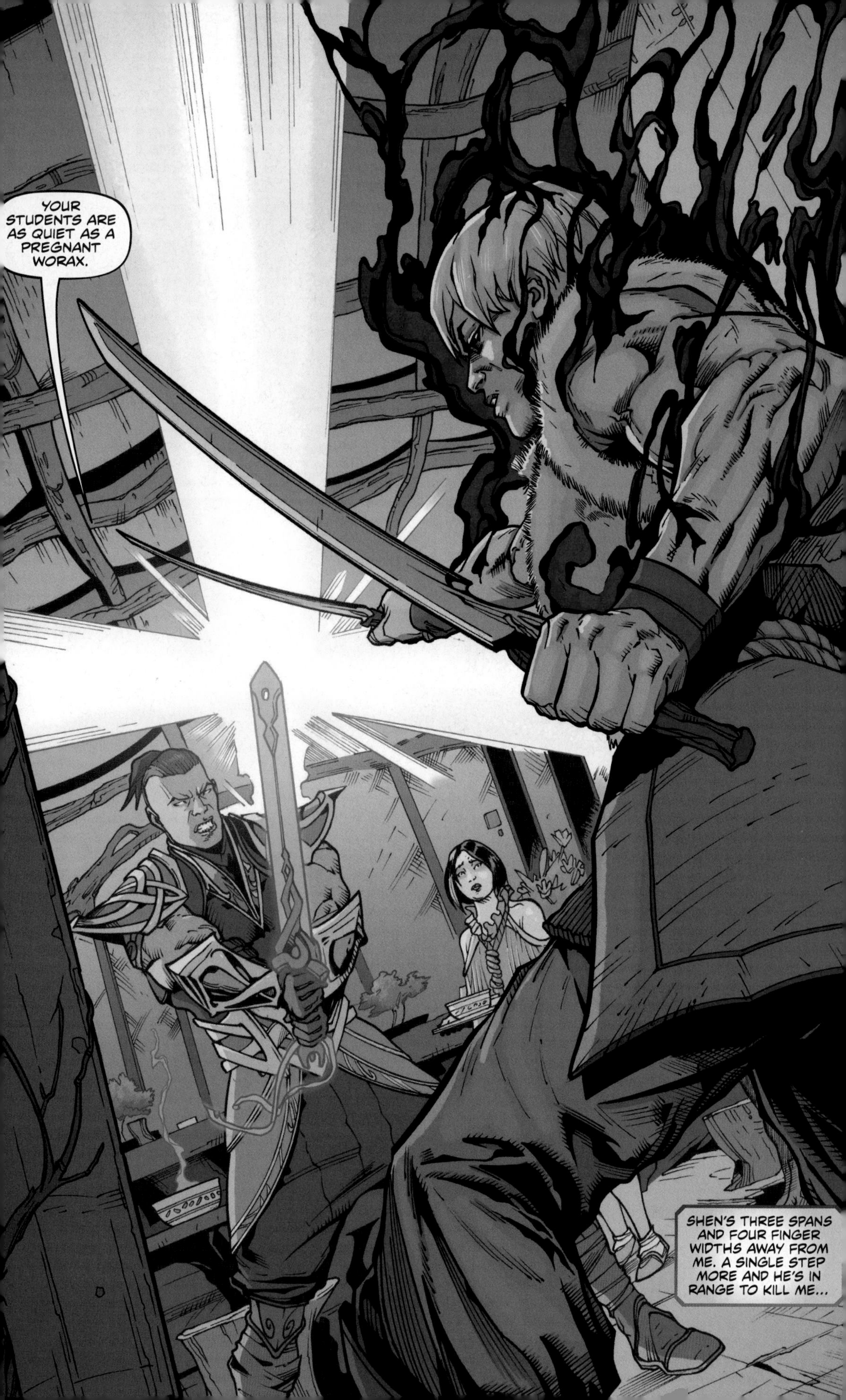
YOUR STUDENTS ARE AS QUIET AS A PREGNANT WORAX.
SHEN'S THREE SPANS AND FOUR FINGER WIDTHS AWAY FROM ME. A SINGLE STEP MORE AND HE'S IN RANGE TO KILL ME...

HE'LL TAKE CLOUD CUTS THE MOON STANCE NEXT.

STRIKING DISTANCE-- THREE SPANS, THREE FINGER WIDTHS FROM THE LEFT.

I AM KINKOU. I SHOULD NOT ACT OUT OF VENGEANCE FOR MY FATHER. BUT THIS IS NOT AN OPPORTUNITY I WILL PASS UP--

THE DISTANCE IS TWO SPANS AND ONE PALM-- HE'S GOING RIGHT!

ZRANG

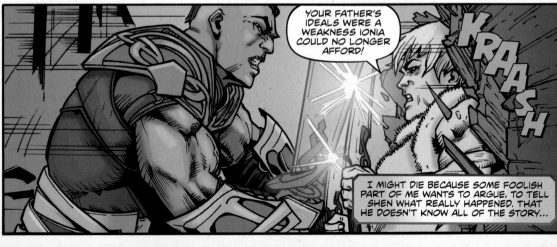

YOUR FATHER'S IDEALS WERE A WEAKNESS IONIA COULD NO LONGER AFFORD!

KRAASH

I MIGHT DIE BECAUSE SOME FOOLISH PART OF ME WANTS TO ARGUE, TO TELL SHEN WHAT REALLY HAPPENED. THAT HE DOESN'T KNOW ALL OF THE STORY...

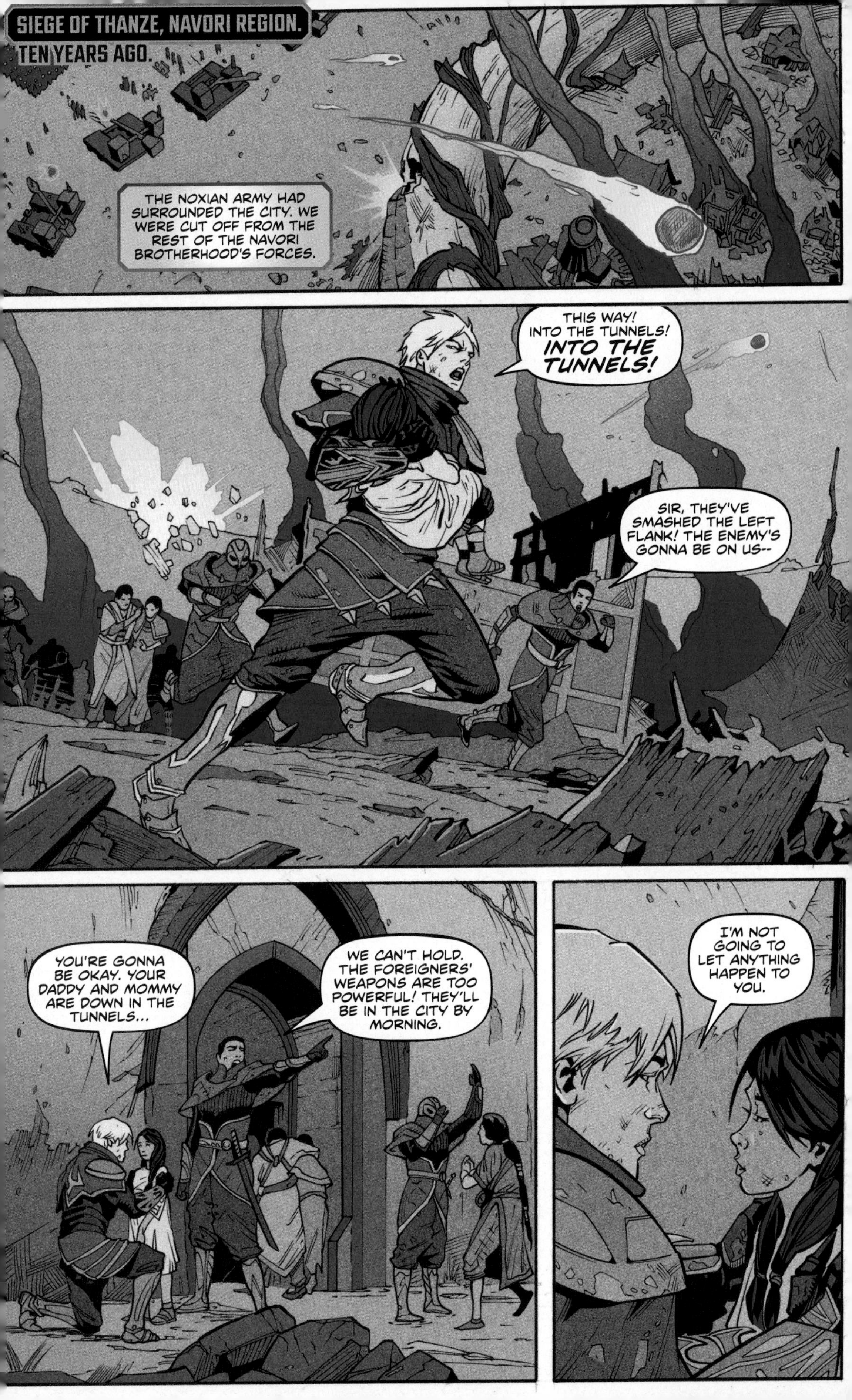
SIEGE OF THANZE, NAVORI REGION.
TEN YEARS AGO.
THE NOXIAN ARMY HAD SURROUNDED THE CITY. WE WERE CUT OFF FROM THE REST OF THE NAVORI BROTHERHOOD'S FORCES.
THIS WAY! INTO THE TUNNELS! INTO THE TUNNELS!
SIR, THEY'VE SMASHED THE LEFT FLANK! THE ENEMY'S GONNA BE ON US--
YOU'RE GONNA BE OKAY. YOUR DADDY AND MOMMY ARE DOWN IN THE TUNNELS...
WE CAN'T HOLD. THE FOREIGNERS' WEAPONS ARE TOO POWERFUL! THEY'LL BE IN THE CITY BY MORNING.
I'M NOT GOING TO LET ANYTHING HAPPEN TO YOU.

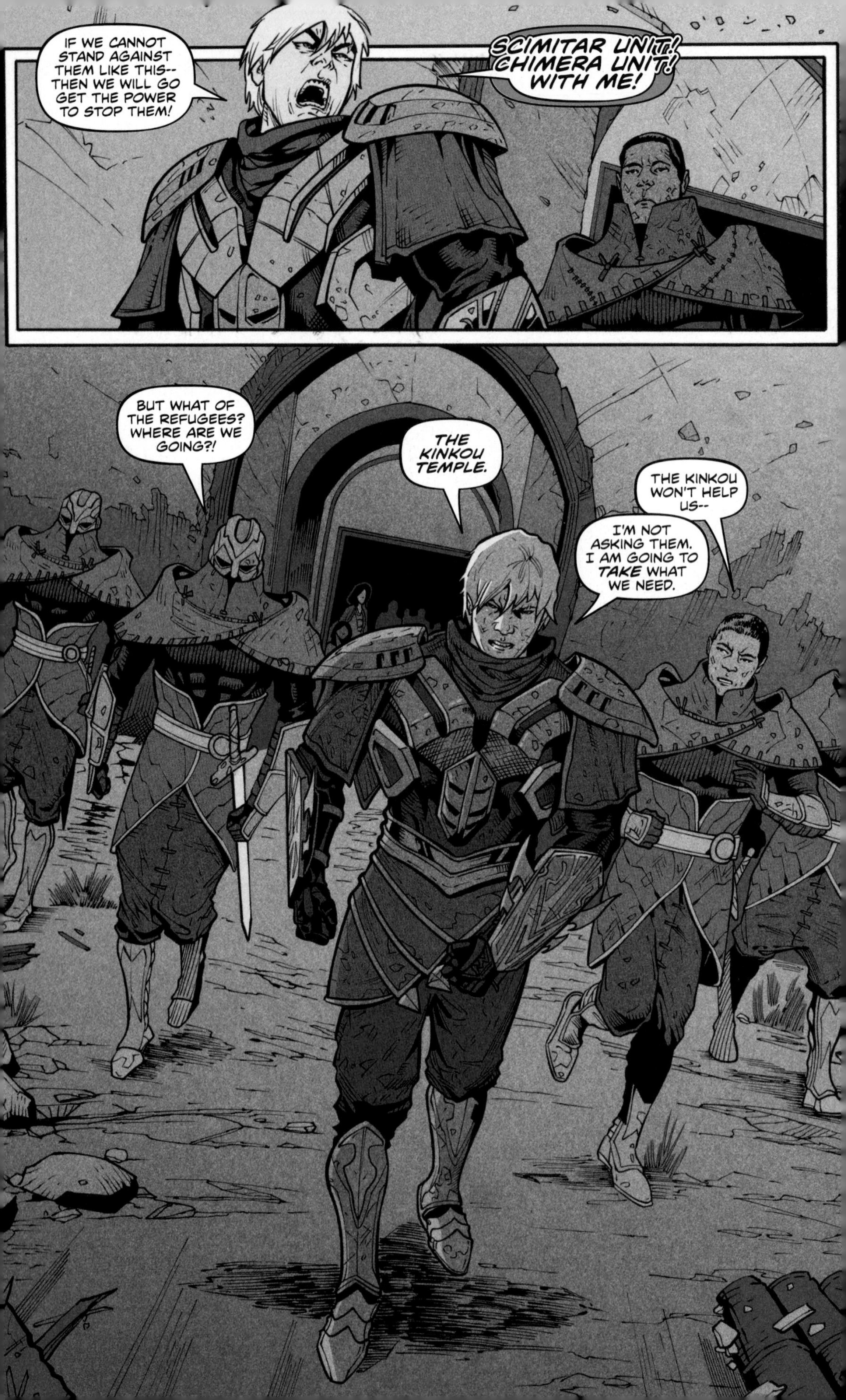
IF WE CANNOT STAND AGAINST THEM LIKE THIS-- THEN WE WILL GO GET THE POWER TO STOP THEM!
SCIMITAR UNIT! CHIMERA UNIT! WITH ME!
BUT WHAT OF THE REFUGEES? WHERE ARE WE GOING?!
THE KINKOU TEMPLE.
THE KINKOU WON'T HELP US--
I'M NOT ASKING THEM. I AM GOING TO TAKE WHAT WE NEED.

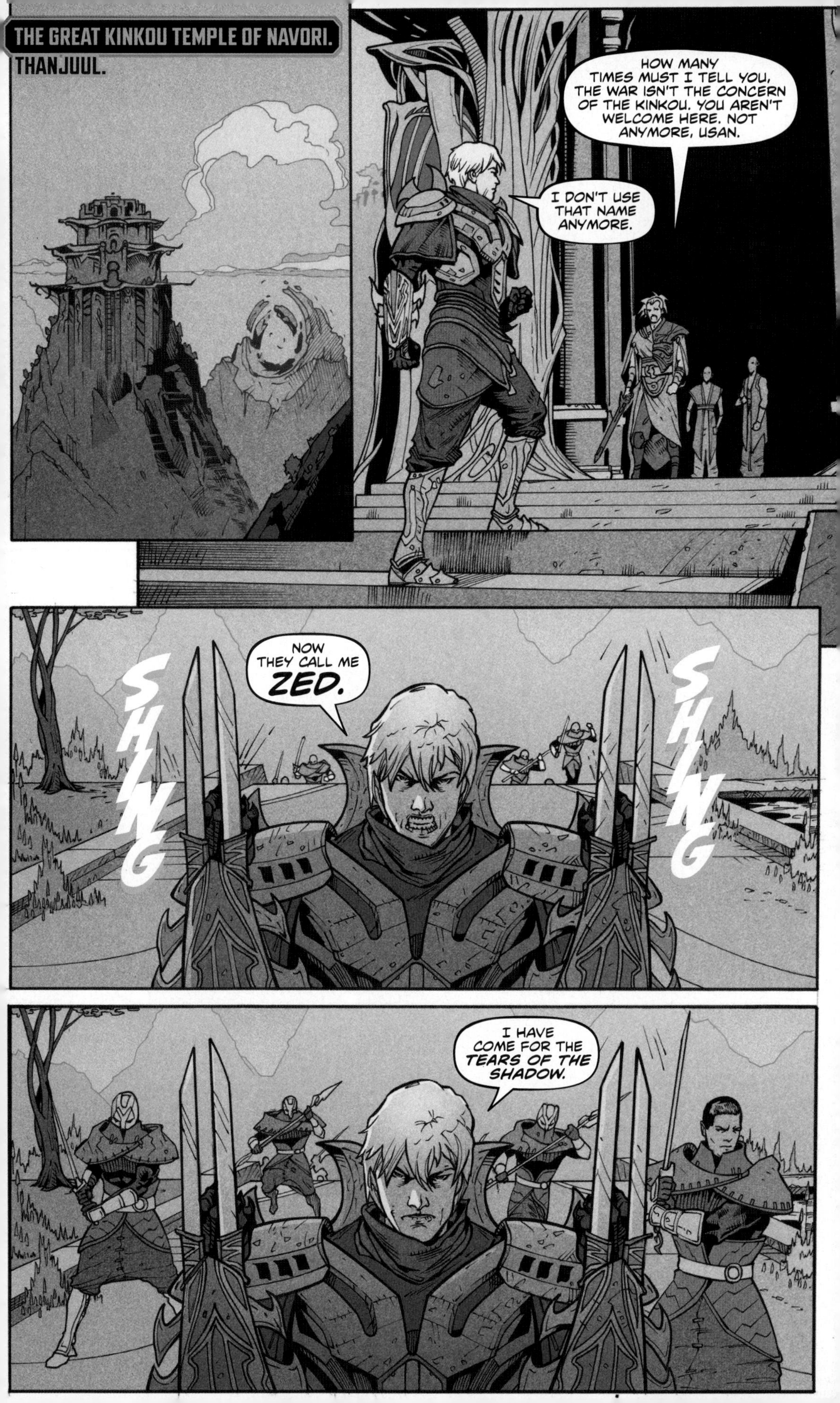
THE GREAT KINKOU TEMPLE OF NAVORI.
THANJUUL.
HOW MANY TIMES MUST I TELL YOU, THE WAR ISN'T THE CONCERN OF THE KINKOU. YOU AREN'T WELCOME HERE. NOT ANYMORE, USAN.
I DON'T USE THAT NAME ANYMORE.
NOW THEY CALL ME ZED.
SHING
SHING
I HAVE COME FOR THE TEARS OF THE SHADOW.

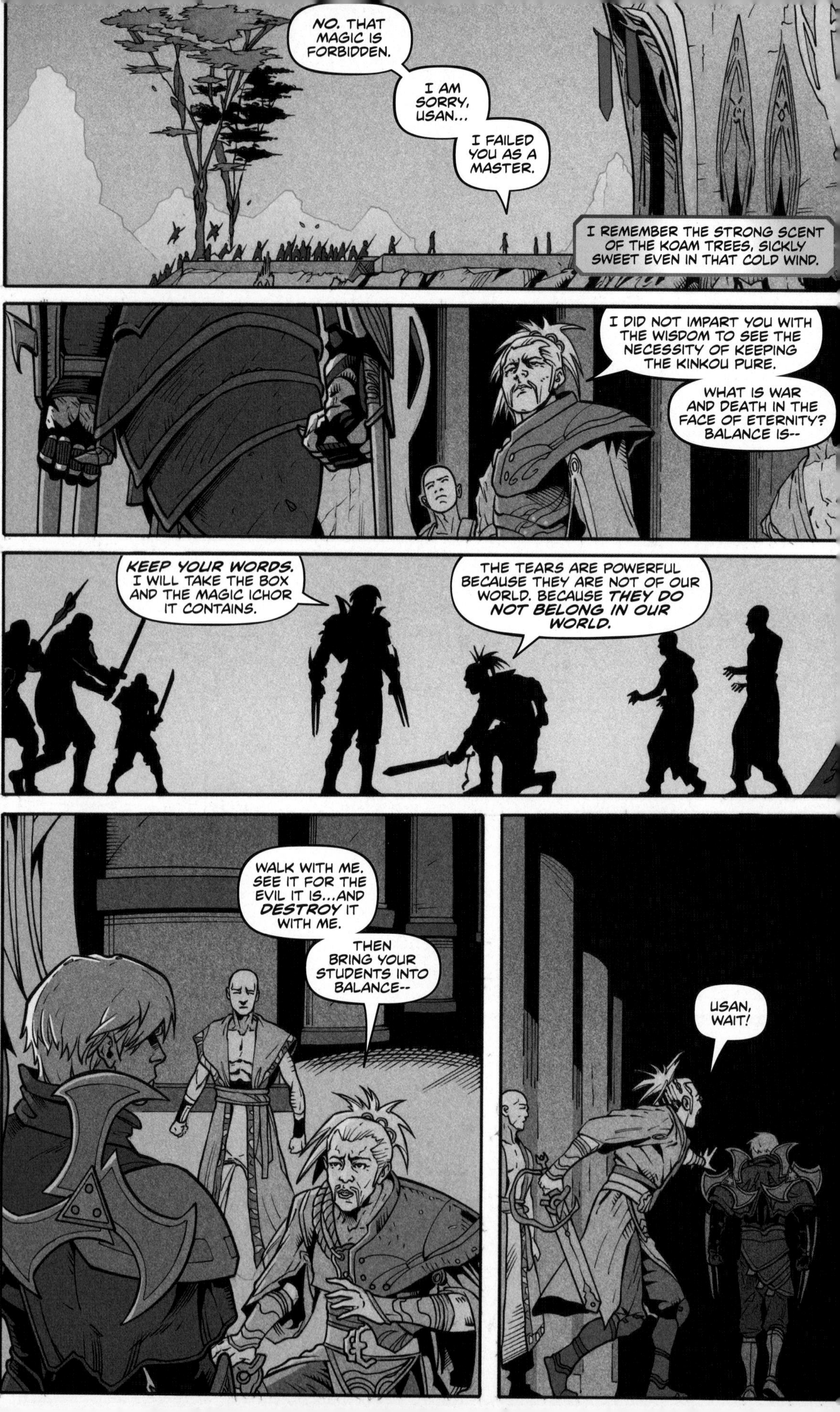

NO. THAT MAGIC IS FORBIDDEN.
I AM SORRY, USAN...
I FAILED YOU AS A MASTER.
I REMEMBER THE STRONG SCENT OF THE KOAM TREES, SICKLY SWEET EVEN IN THAT COLD WIND.
I DID NOT IMPART YOU WITH THE WISDOM TO SEE THE NECESSITY OF KEEPING THE KINKOU PURE.
WHAT IS WAR AND DEATH IN THE FACE OF ETERNITY? BALANCE IS--
KEEP YOUR WORDS. I WILL TAKE THE BOX AND THE MAGIC ICHOR IT CONTAINS.
THE TEARS ARE POWERFUL BECAUSE THEY ARE NOT OF OUR WORLD. BECAUSE THEY DO NOT BELONG IN OUR WORLD.
WALK WITH ME. SEE IT FOR THE EVIL IT IS...AND DESTROY IT WITH ME.
THEN BRING YOUR STUDENTS INTO BALANCE--
USAN, WAIT!

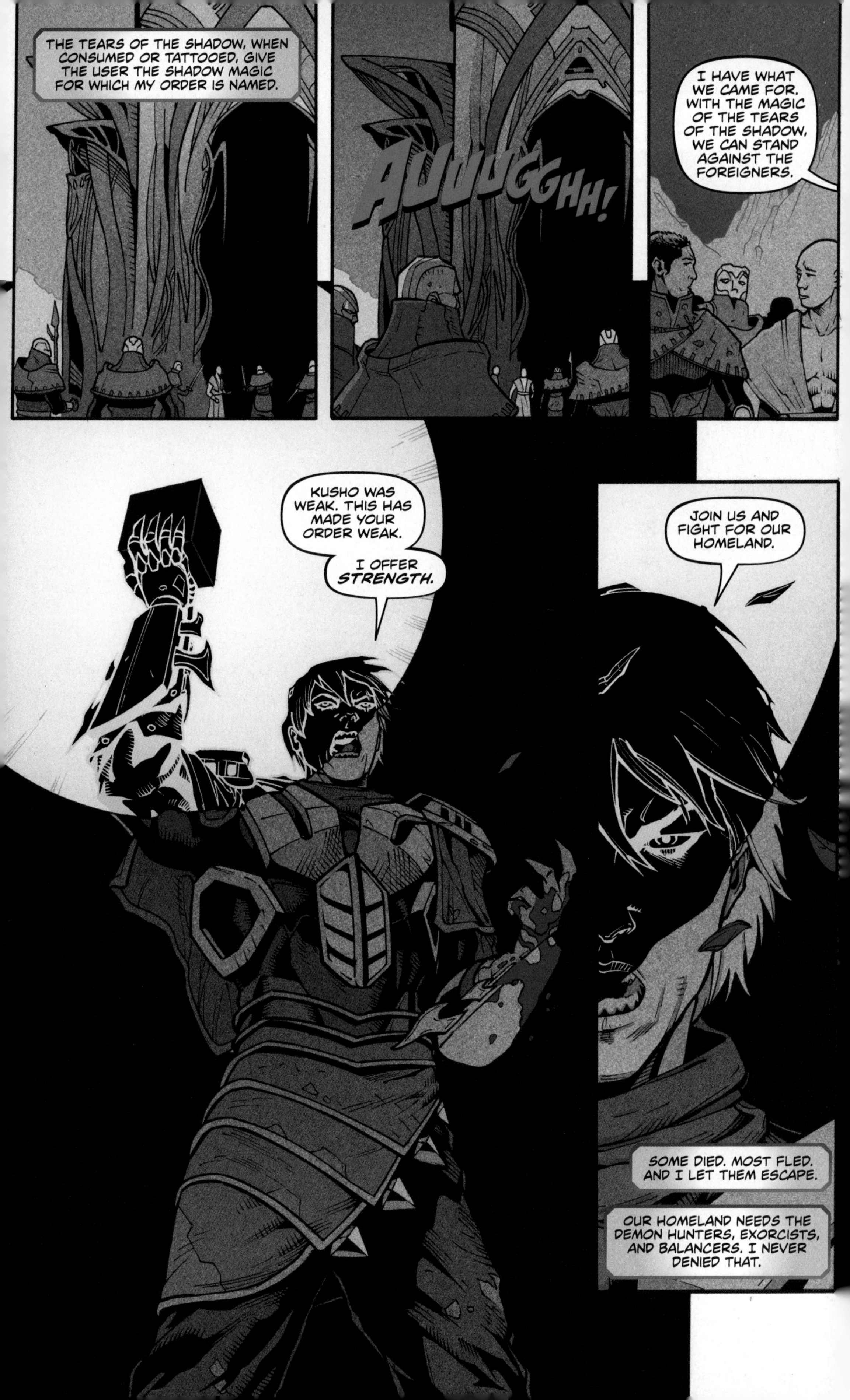
THE TEARS OF THE SHADOW, WHEN CONSUMED OR TATTOOED, GIVE THE USER THE SHADOW MAGIC FOR WHICH MY ORDER IS NAMED.
AUUUGGHH!
I HAVE WHAT WE CAME FOR. WITH THE MAGIC OF THE TEARS OF THE SHADOW, WE CAN STAND AGAINST THE FOREIGNERS.
KUSHO WAS WEAK. THIS HAS MADE YOUR ORDER WEAK.
I OFFER *STRENGTH.*
JOIN US AND FIGHT FOR OUR HOMELAND.
SOME DIED. MOST FLED. AND I LET THEM ESCAPE.
OUR HOMELAND NEEDS THE DEMON HUNTERS, EXORCISTS, AND BALANCERS. I NEVER DENIED THAT.

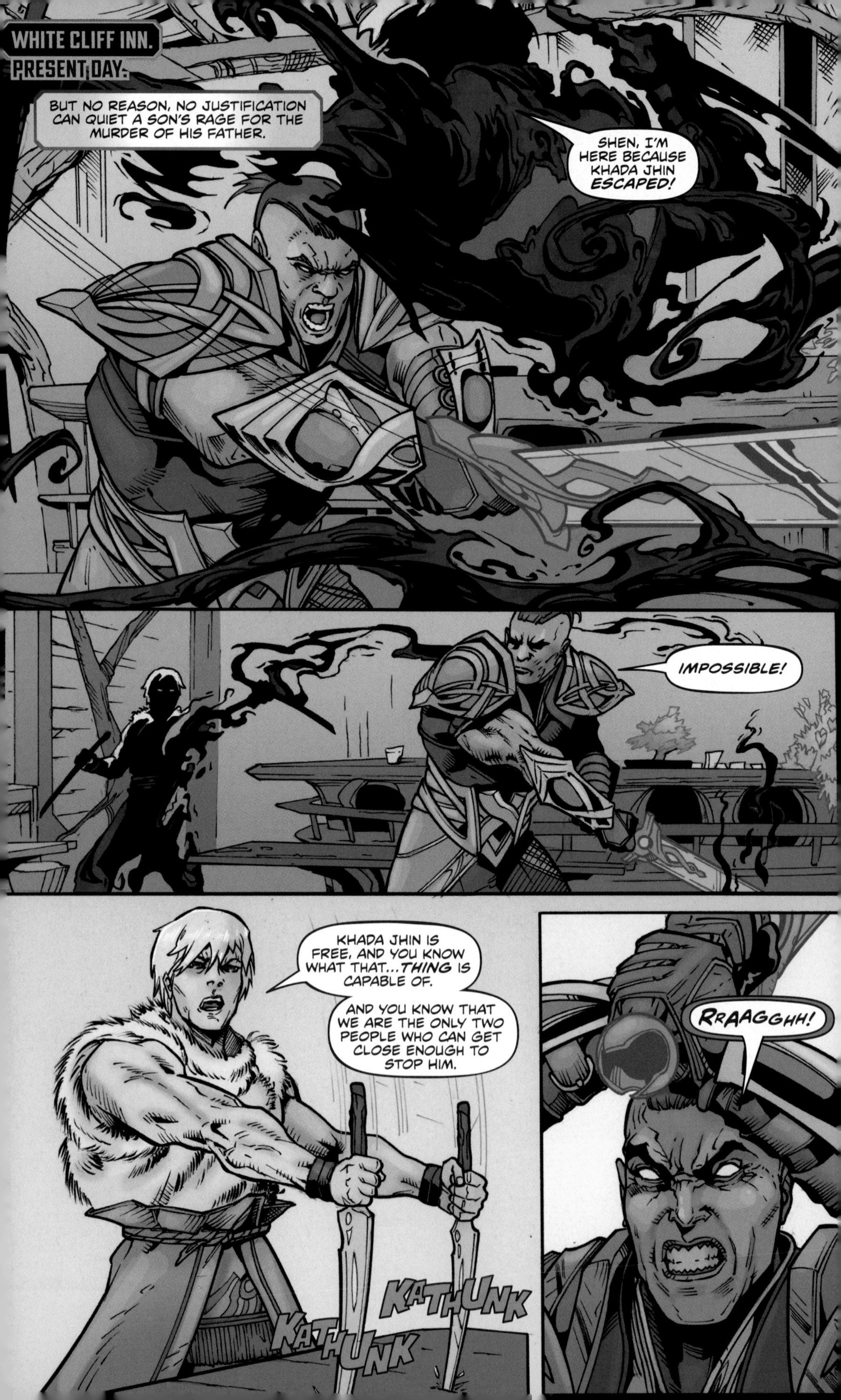
WHITE CLIFF INN. PRESENT DAY.
BUT NO REASON, NO JUSTIFICATION CAN QUIET A SON'S RAGE FOR THE MURDER OF HIS FATHER.
SHEN, I'M HERE BECAUSE KHADA JHIN ESCAPED!
IMPOSSIBLE!
KHADA JHIN IS FREE, AND YOU KNOW WHAT THAT...THING IS CAPABLE OF.
AND YOU KNOW THAT WE ARE THE ONLY TWO PEOPLE WHO CAN GET CLOSE ENOUGH TO STOP HIM.
KATHUNK
KATHUNK
RRAAGGHH!

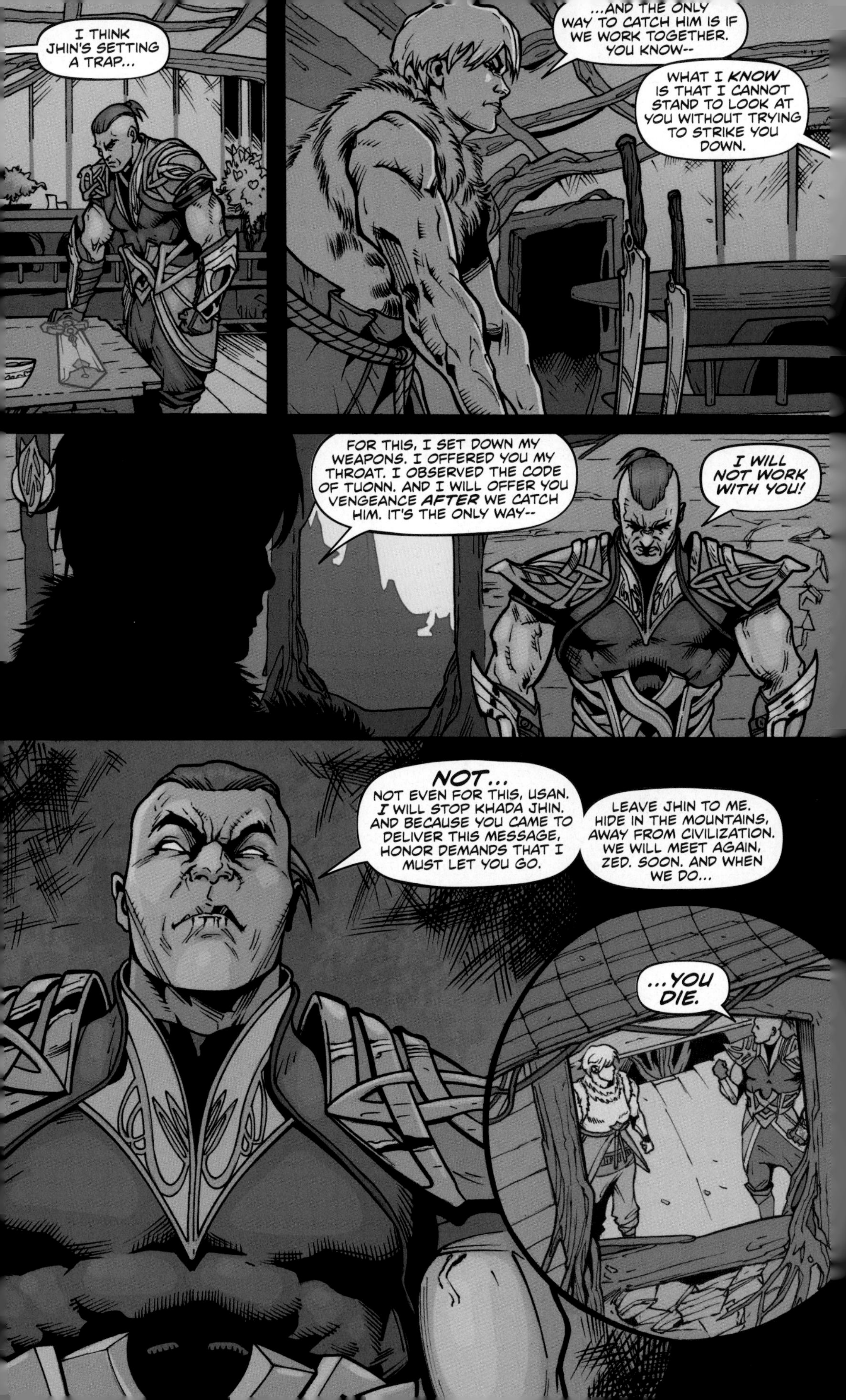
I THINK JHIN'S SETTING A TRAP...
...AND THE ONLY WAY TO CATCH HIM IS IF WE WORK TOGETHER. YOU KNOW--
WHAT I *KNOW* IS THAT I CANNOT STAND TO LOOK AT YOU WITHOUT TRYING TO STRIKE YOU DOWN.
FOR THIS, I SET DOWN MY WEAPONS. I OFFERED YOU MY THROAT. I OBSERVED THE CODE OF TUONN. AND I WILL OFFER YOU VENGEANCE *AFTER* WE CATCH HIM. IT'S THE ONLY WAY--
I WILL NOT WORK WITH YOU!
NOT...
NOT EVEN FOR THIS, USAN. *I* WILL STOP KHADA JHIN. AND BECAUSE YOU CAME TO DELIVER THIS MESSAGE, HONOR DEMANDS THAT I MUST LET YOU GO.
LEAVE JHIN TO ME. HIDE IN THE MOUNTAINS, AWAY FROM CIVILIZATION. WE WILL MEET AGAIN, ZED. SOON. AND WHEN WE DO...
...YOU DIE.

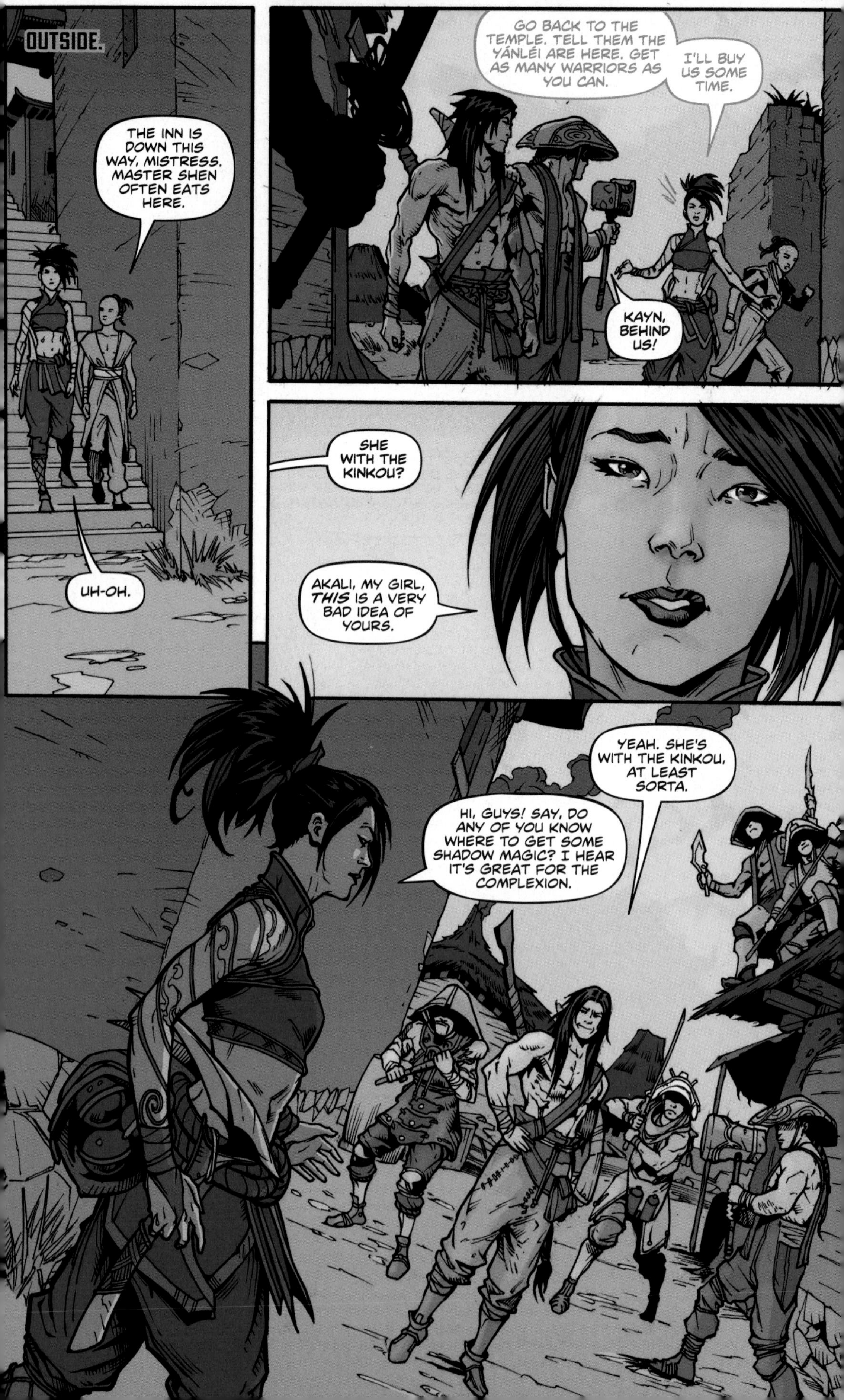
OUTSIDE.
THE INN IS DOWN THIS WAY, MISTRESS. MASTER SHEN OFTEN EATS HERE.
UH-OH.
GO BACK TO THE TEMPLE. TELL THEM THE YÁNLÉI ARE HERE. GET AS MANY WARRIORS AS YOU CAN.
I'LL BUY US SOME TIME.
KAYN, BEHIND US!
SHE WITH THE KINKOU?
AKALI, MY GIRL, THIS IS A VERY BAD IDEA OF YOURS.
YEAH. SHE'S WITH THE KINKOU, AT LEAST SORTA.
HI, GUYS! SAY, DO ANY OF YOU KNOW WHERE TO GET SOME SHADOW MAGIC? I HEAR IT'S GREAT FOR THE COMPLEXION.

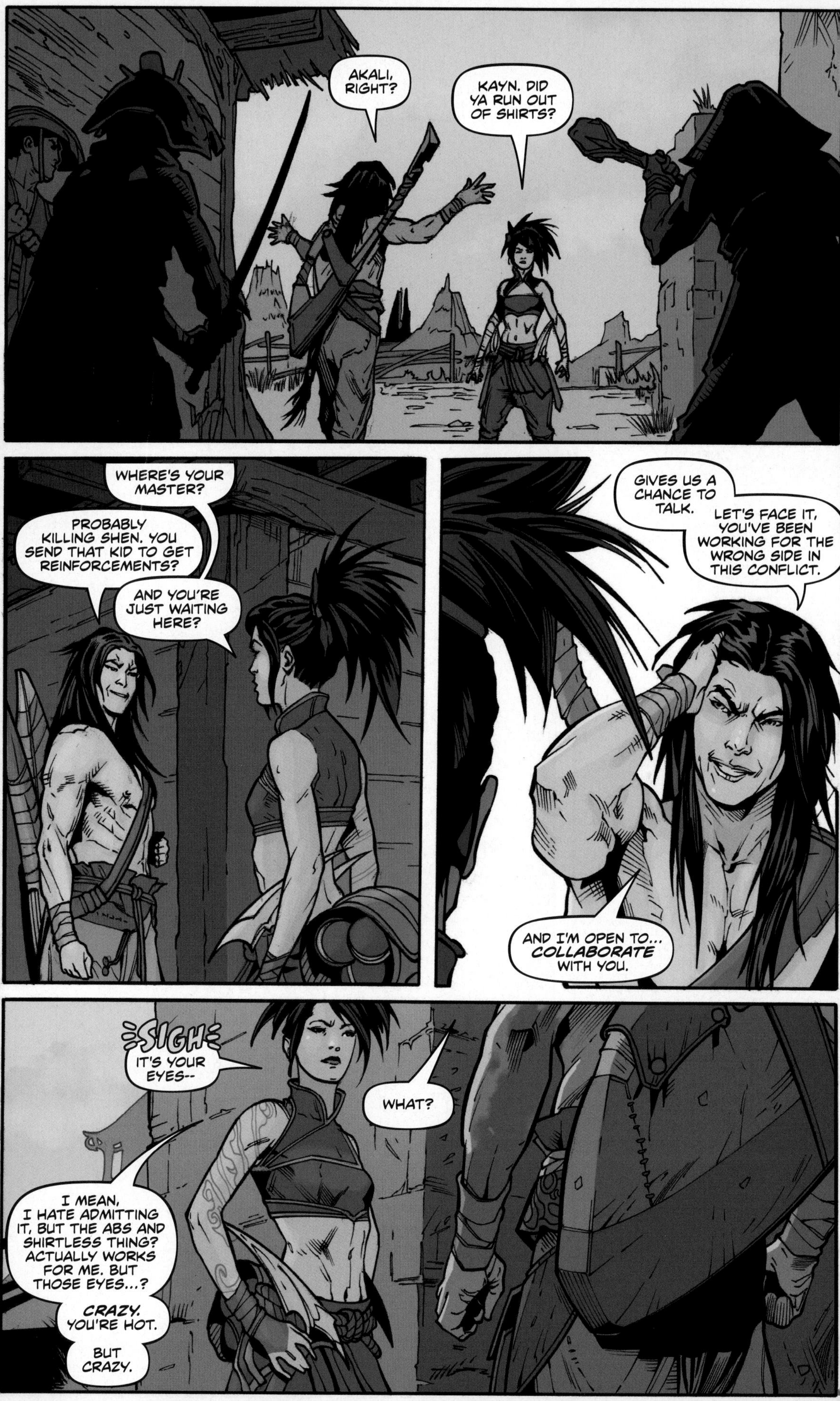
AKALI, RIGHT?
KAYN. DID YA RUN OUT OF SHIRTS?
WHERE'S YOUR MASTER?
PROBABLY KILLING SHEN. YOU SEND THAT KID TO GET REINFORCEMENTS?
AND YOU'RE JUST WAITING HERE?
GIVES US A CHANCE TO TALK.
LET'S FACE IT, YOU'VE BEEN WORKING FOR THE WRONG SIDE IN THIS CONFLICT.
AND I'M OPEN TO... *COLLABORATE* WITH YOU.
SIGH
IT'S YOUR EYES--
WHAT?
I MEAN, I HATE ADMITTING IT, BUT THE ABS AND SHIRTLESS THING? ACTUALLY WORKS FOR ME. BUT THOSE EYES...?
CRAZY. YOU'RE HOT.
BUT CRAZY.

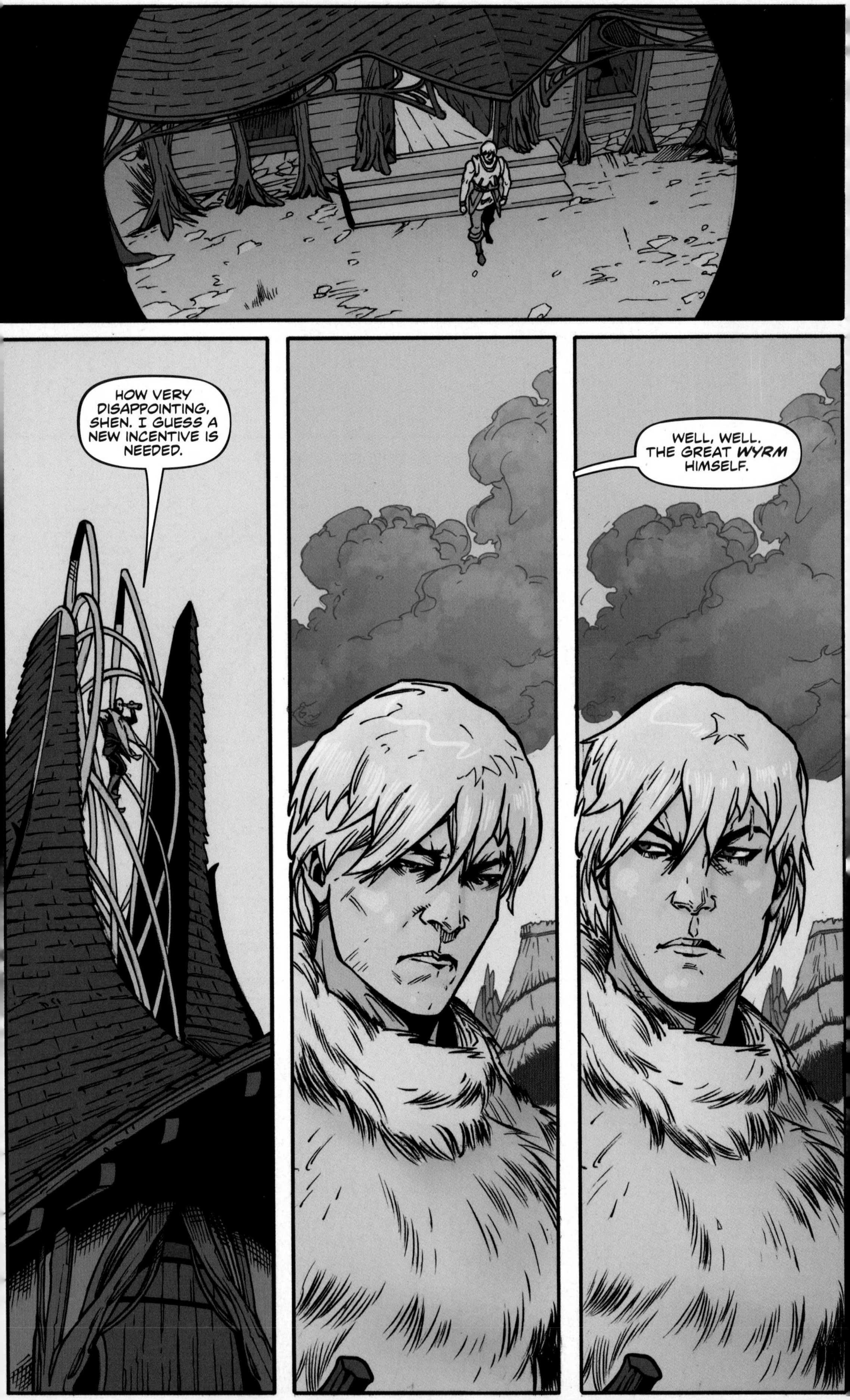
HOW VERY DISAPPOINTING, SHEN. I GUESS A NEW INCENTIVE IS NEEDED.
WELL, WELL. THE GREAT **WYRM** HIMSELF.

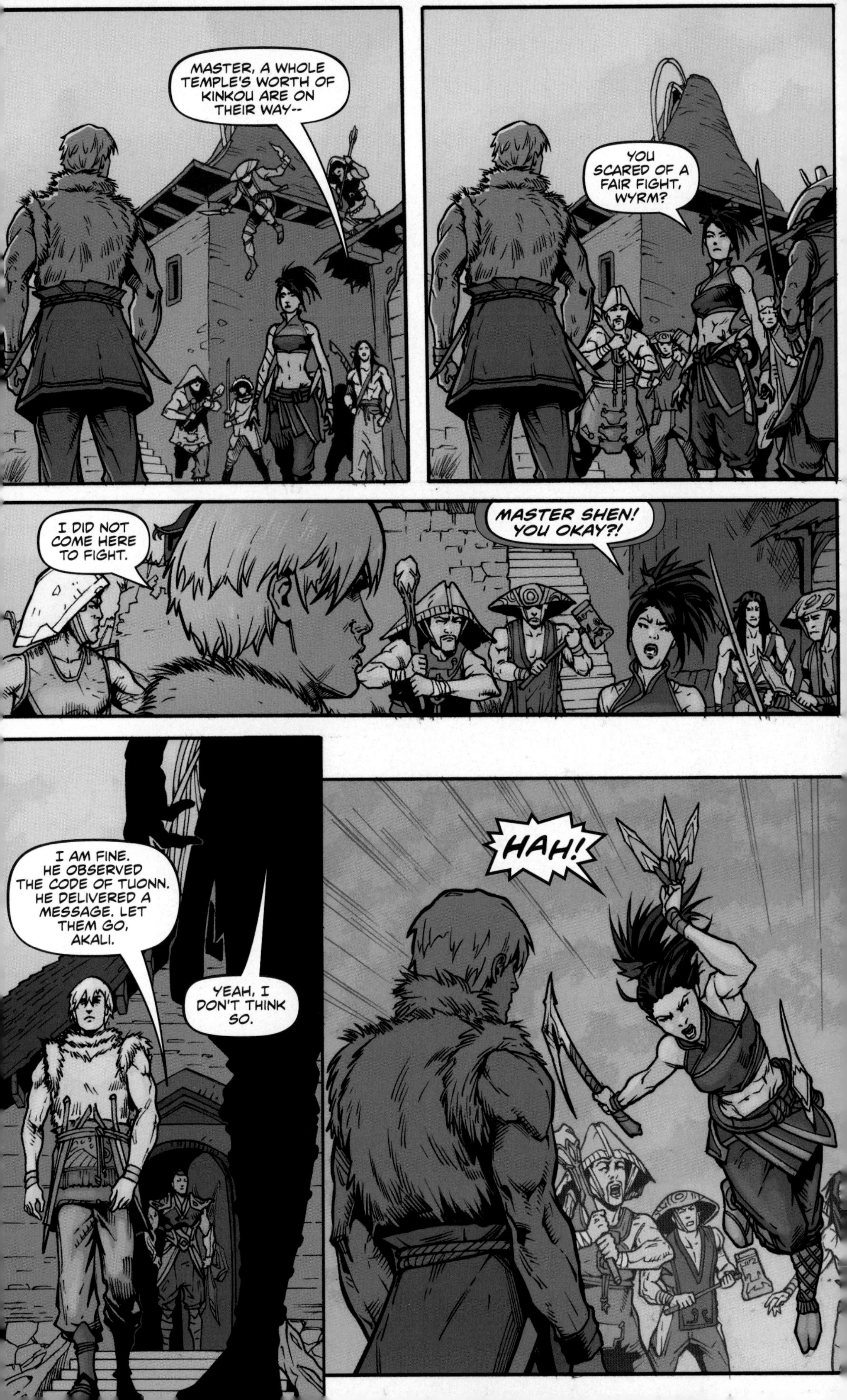
MASTER, A WHOLE TEMPLE'S WORTH OF KINKOU ARE ON THEIR WAY--
YOU SCARED OF A FAIR FIGHT, WYRM?
I DID NOT COME HERE TO FIGHT.
MASTER SHEN! YOU OKAY?!
I AM FINE. HE OBSERVED THE CODE OF TUONN. HE DELIVERED A MESSAGE. LET THEM GO, AKALI.
YEAH, I DON'T THINK SO.
HAH!

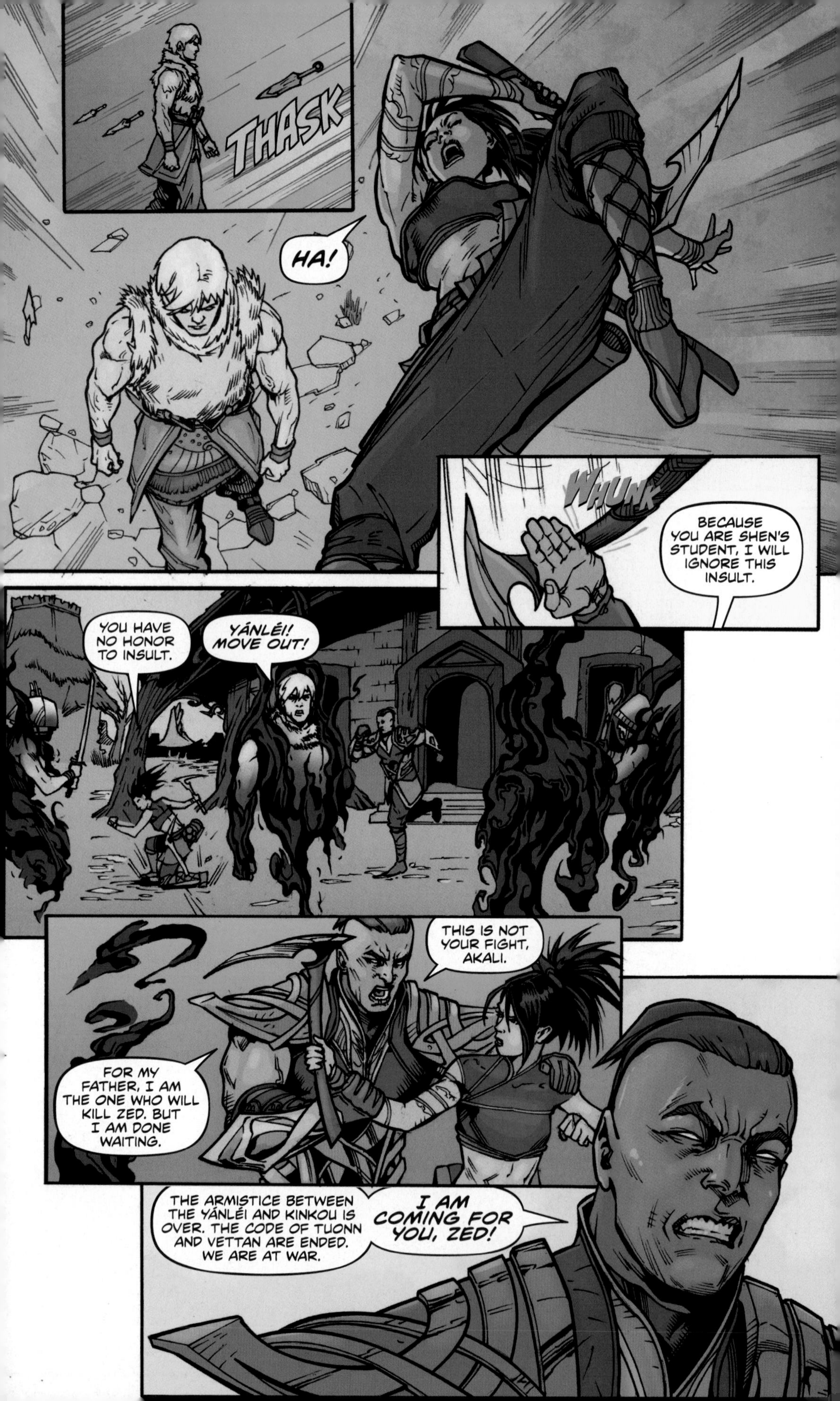
THASK
HA!
WHUNK
BECAUSE YOU ARE SHEN'S STUDENT, I WILL IGNORE THIS INSULT.
YOU HAVE NO HONOR TO INSULT.
YÁNLÉI! MOVE OUT!
THIS IS NOT YOUR FIGHT, AKALI.
FOR MY FATHER, I AM THE ONE WHO WILL KILL ZED. BUT I AM DONE WAITING.
THE ARMISTICE BETWEEN THE YÁNLÉI AND KINKOU IS OVER. THE CODE OF TUONN AND VETTAN ARE ENDED. WE ARE AT WAR.
I AM COMING FOR YOU, ZED!

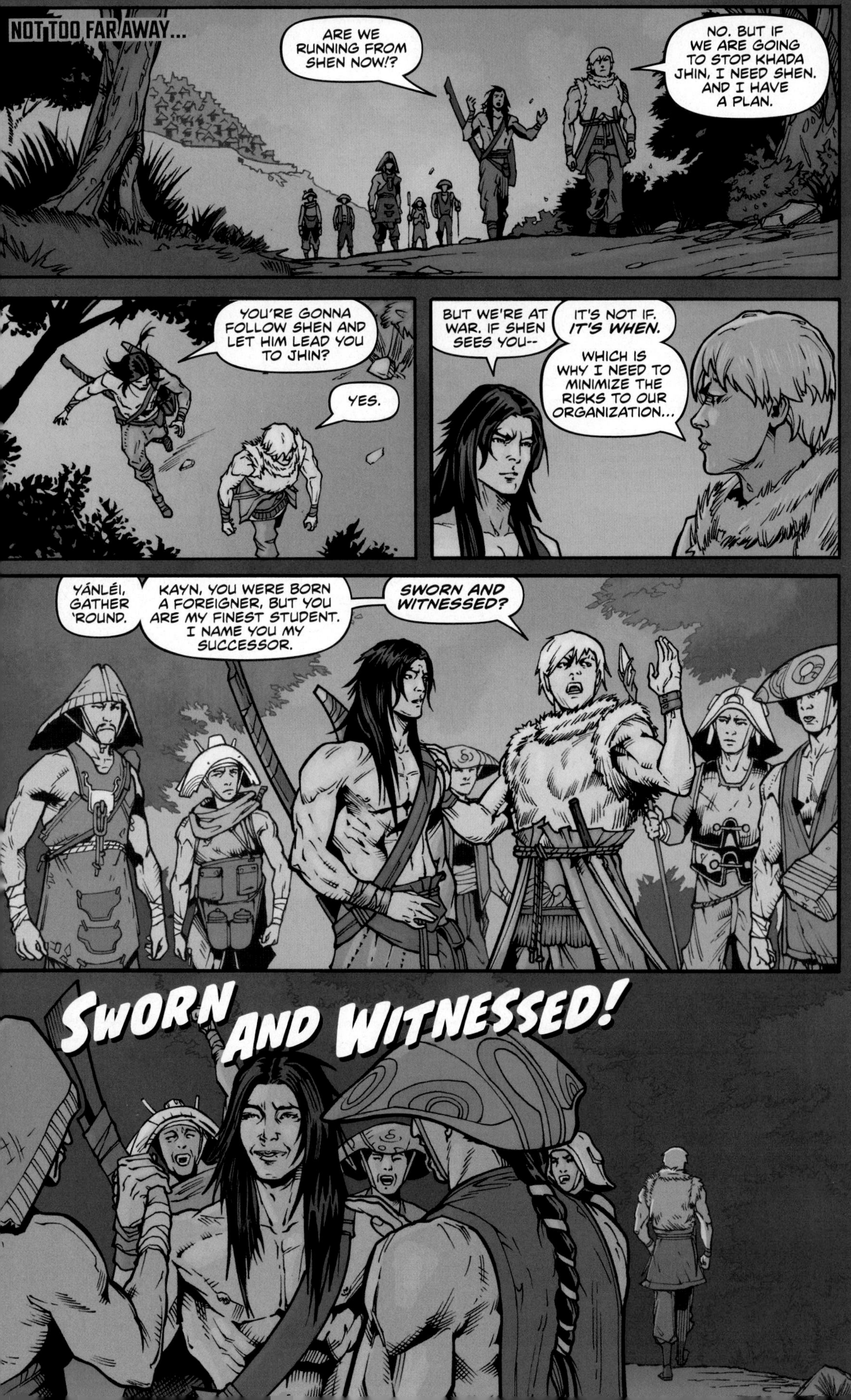
NOT TOO FAR AWAY...
ARE WE RUNNING FROM SHEN NOW!?
NO. BUT IF WE ARE GOING TO STOP KHADA JHIN, I NEED SHEN. AND I HAVE A PLAN.
YOU'RE GONNA FOLLOW SHEN AND LET HIM LEAD YOU TO JHIN?
YES.
BUT WE'RE AT WAR. IF SHEN SEES YOU--
IT'S NOT IF. *IT'S WHEN.*
WHICH IS WHY I NEED TO MINIMIZE THE RISKS TO OUR ORGANIZATION...
YÁNLÉI, GATHER 'ROUND.
KAYN, YOU WERE BORN A FOREIGNER, BUT YOU ARE MY FINEST STUDENT. I NAME YOU MY SUCCESSOR.
SWORN AND WITNESSED?
SWORN AND WITNESSED!

I FOLLOW SHEN AS HE CHASES LEADS ACROSS THE REGION. WHERE OTHERS SEE DEAD ENDS, HE FINDS A TRAIL.

JHIN USED THE DOCKS OVER THERE. IS THAT THE SOTKA RIVER?

YOU'RE GONNA TELL ME THE NAME OF EVERY SHIP THAT TRAVELED UP THE SOTKA RIVER THIS MONTH.

YES, HE DIED WITH ALL THE OTHERS ON THAT SHIP. A DEMON KILLED THEM. LIKE THAT ONE YOUR FATHER SLAYED.

DO YOU KNOW WHERE I COULD GET THE MANIFEST WITH ALL OF THE PASSENGERS' NAMES?

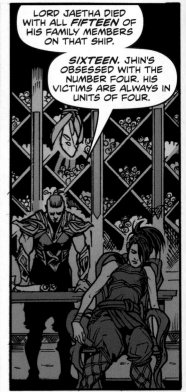

LORD JAETHA DIED WITH ALL *FIFTEEN* OF HIS FAMILY MEMBERS ON THAT SHIP.

SIXTEEN. JHIN'S OBSESSED WITH THE NUMBER FOUR. HIS VICTIMS ARE ALWAYS IN UNITS OF FOUR.

DID LORD JAETHA AND HIS FAMILY HAVE ANY ENEMIES YOU KNEW OF?

HE HATED THOSE DAMN RADICALS. I FIGURE THEY HATED HIM, TOO.

RADICALS?

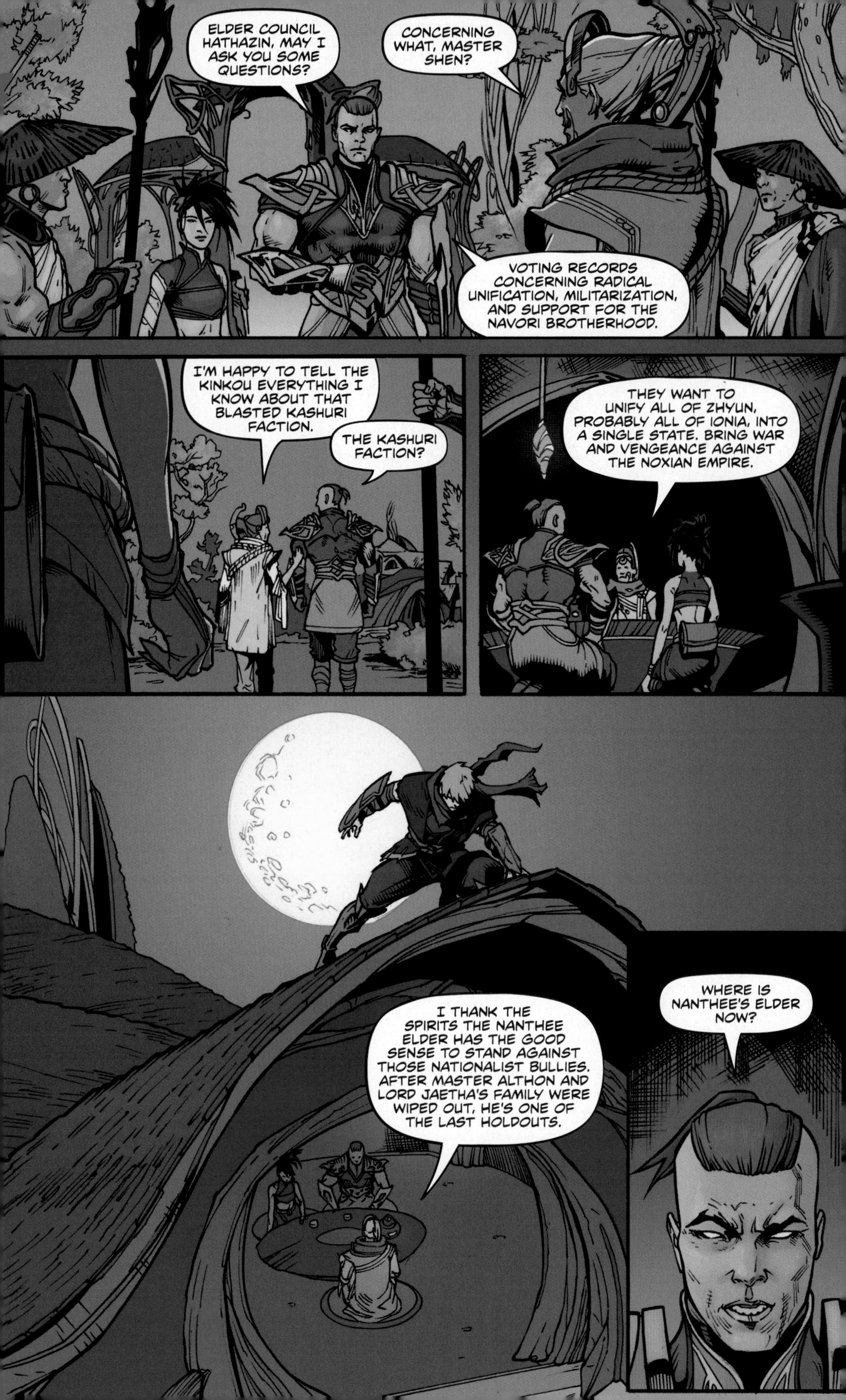
ELDER COUNCIL HATHAZIN, MAY I ASK YOU SOME QUESTIONS?
CONCERNING WHAT, MASTER SHEN?
VOTING RECORDS CONCERNING RADICAL UNIFICATION, MILITARIZATION, AND SUPPORT FOR THE NAVORI BROTHERHOOD.
I'M HAPPY TO TELL THE KINKOU EVERYTHING I KNOW ABOUT THAT BLASTED KASHURI FACTION.
THE KASHURI FACTION?
THEY WANT TO UNIFY ALL OF ZHYUN, PROBABLY ALL OF IONIA, INTO A SINGLE STATE. BRING WAR AND VENGEANCE AGAINST THE NOXIAN EMPIRE.
I THANK THE SPIRITS THE NANTHEE ELDER HAS THE GOOD SENSE TO STAND AGAINST THOSE NATIONALIST BULLIES. AFTER MASTER ALTHON AND LORD JAETHA'S FAMILY WERE WIPED OUT, HE'S ONE OF THE LAST HOLDOUTS.
WHERE IS NANTHEE'S ELDER NOW?

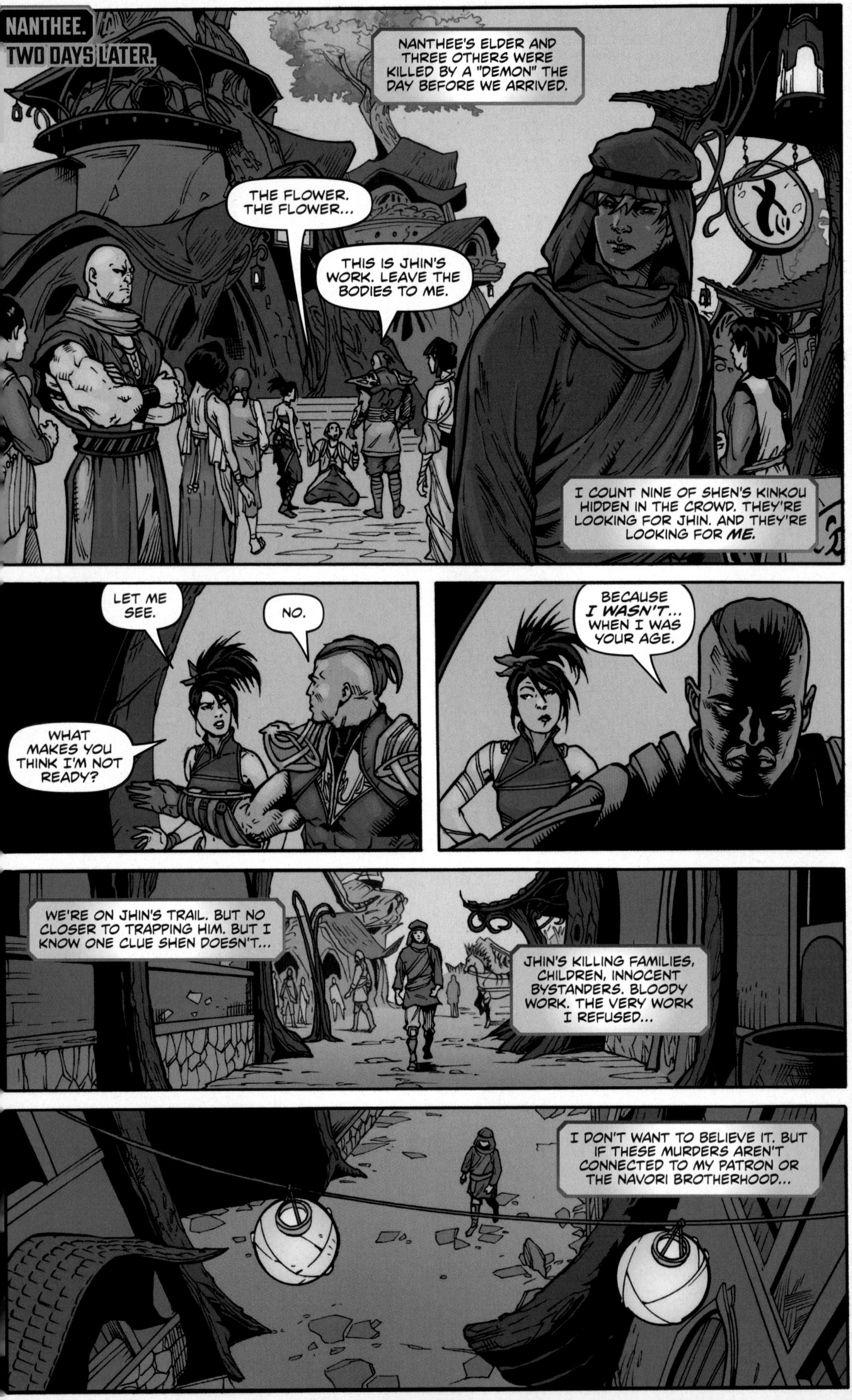
NANTHEE.
TWO DAYS LATER.
NANTHEE'S ELDER AND THREE OTHERS WERE KILLED BY A "DEMON" THE DAY BEFORE WE ARRIVED.
THE FLOWER. THE FLOWER...
THIS IS JHIN'S WORK. LEAVE THE BODIES TO ME.
I COUNT NINE OF SHEN'S KINKOU HIDDEN IN THE CROWD. THEY'RE LOOKING FOR JHIN. AND THEY'RE LOOKING FOR ME.
LET ME SEE.
NO.
WHAT MAKES YOU THINK I'M NOT READY?
BECAUSE I WASN'T... WHEN I WAS YOUR AGE.
WE'RE ON JHIN'S TRAIL. BUT NO CLOSER TO TRAPPING HIM. BUT I KNOW ONE CLUE SHEN DOESN'T...
JHIN'S KILLING FAMILIES, CHILDREN, INNOCENT BYSTANDERS. BLOODY WORK. THE VERY WORK I REFUSED...
I DON'T WANT TO BELIEVE IT. BUT IF THESE MURDERS AREN'T CONNECTED TO MY PATRON OR THE NAVORI BROTHERHOOD...

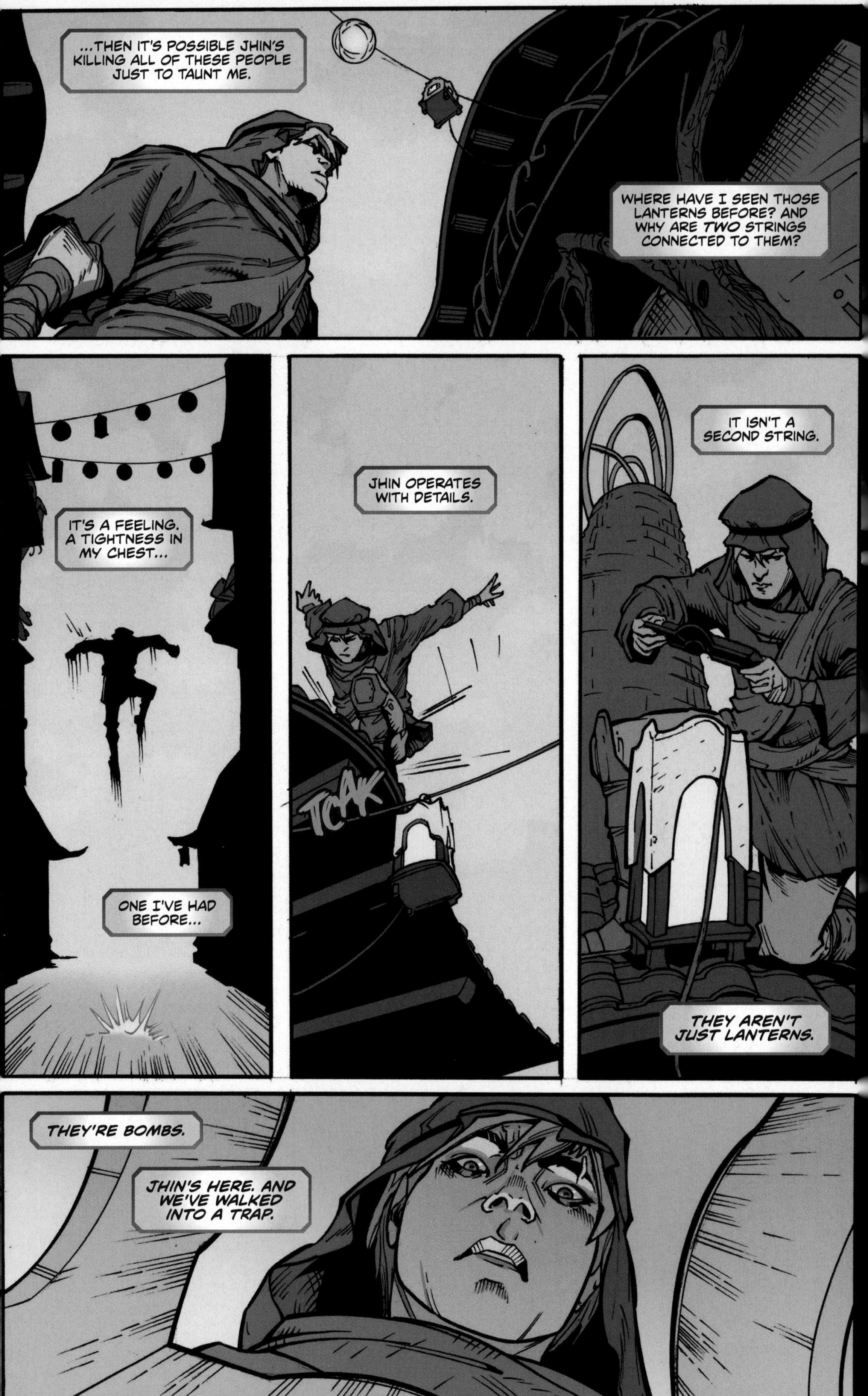
...THEN IT'S POSSIBLE JHIN'S KILLING ALL OF THESE PEOPLE JUST TO TAUNT ME.
WHERE HAVE I SEEN THOSE LANTERNS BEFORE? AND WHY ARE TWO STRINGS CONNECTED TO THEM?
IT'S A FEELING. A TIGHTNESS IN MY CHEST...
ONE I'VE HAD BEFORE...
JHIN OPERATES WITH DETAILS.
TCAK
IT ISN'T A SECOND STRING.
THEY AREN'T JUST LANTERNS.
THEY'RE BOMBS.
JHIN'S HERE. AND WE'VE WALKED INTO A TRAP.

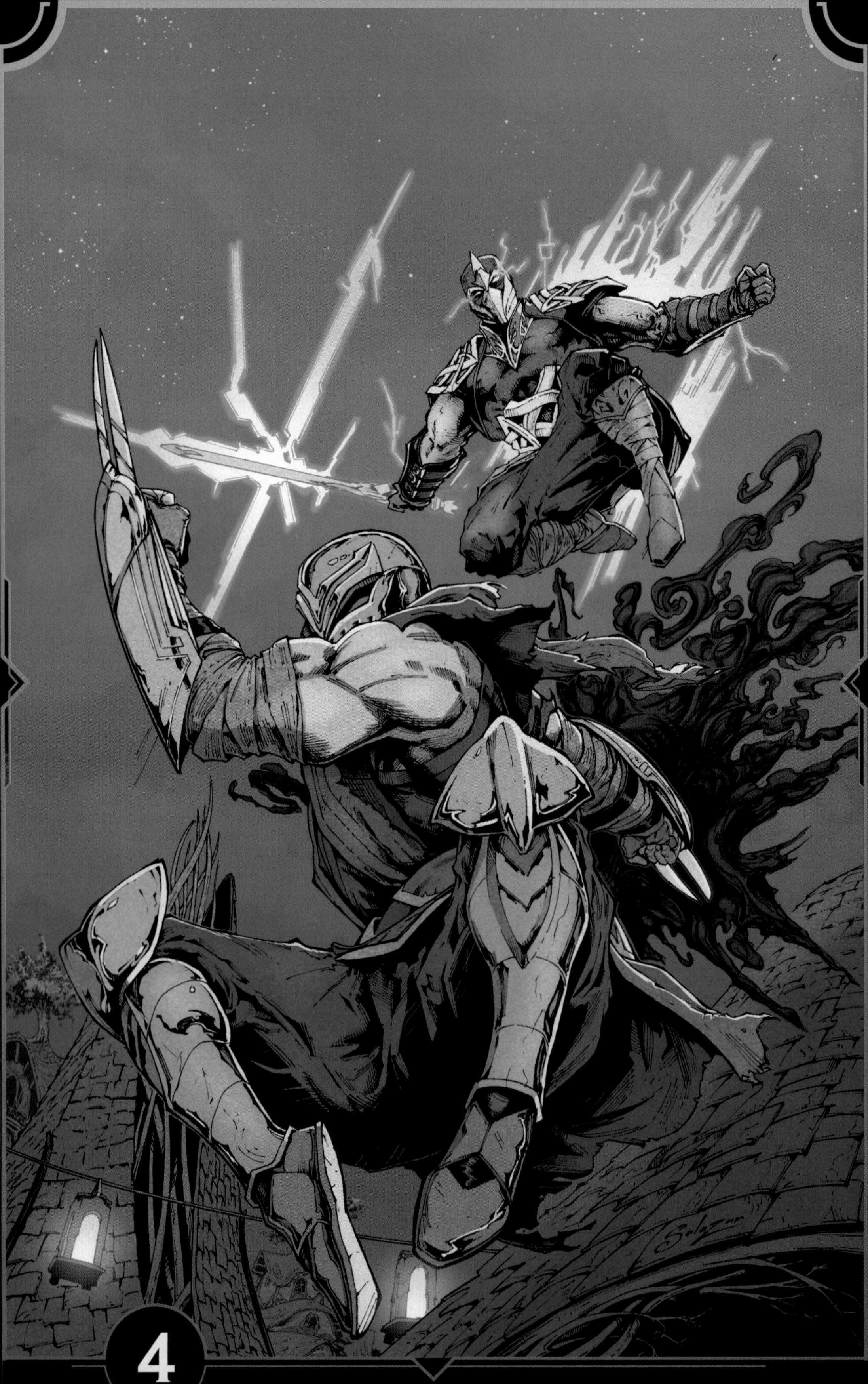

4

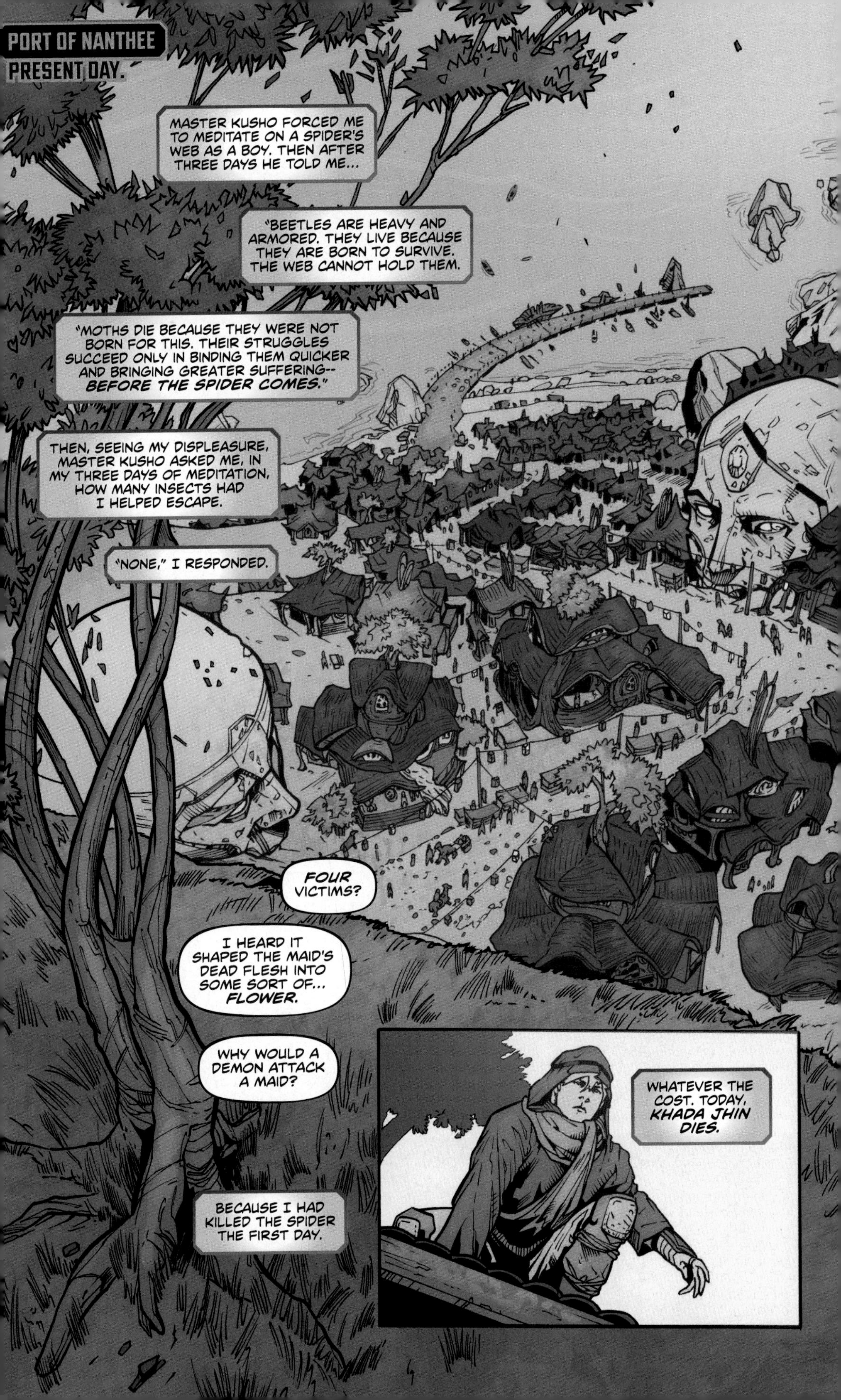
PORT OF NANTHEE
PRESENT DAY.
MASTER KUSHO FORCED ME TO MEDITATE ON A SPIDER'S WEB AS A BOY. THEN AFTER THREE DAYS HE TOLD ME...
"BEETLES ARE HEAVY AND ARMORED. THEY LIVE BECAUSE THEY ARE BORN TO SURVIVE. THE WEB CANNOT HOLD THEM.
"MOTHS DIE BECAUSE THEY WERE NOT BORN FOR THIS. THEIR STRUGGLES SUCCEED ONLY IN BINDING THEM QUICKER AND BRINGING GREATER SUFFERING-- BEFORE THE SPIDER COMES."
THEN, SEEING MY DISPLEASURE, MASTER KUSHO ASKED ME, IN MY THREE DAYS OF MEDITATION, HOW MANY INSECTS HAD I HELPED ESCAPE.
"NONE," I RESPONDED.
FOUR VICTIMS?
I HEARD IT SHAPED THE MAID'S DEAD FLESH INTO SOME SORT OF... FLOWER.
WHY WOULD A DEMON ATTACK A MAID?
BECAUSE I HAD KILLED THE SPIDER THE FIRST DAY.
WHATEVER THE COST. TODAY, KHADA JHIN DIES.

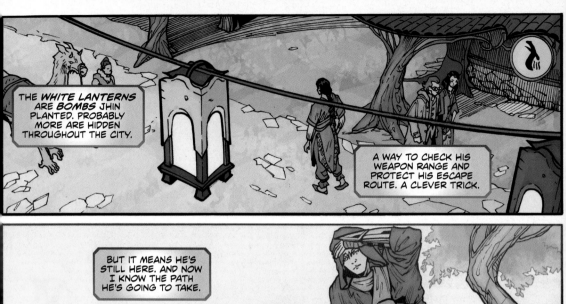

THE *WHITE LANTERNS* ARE *BOMBS* JHIN PLANTED. PROBABLY MORE ARE HIDDEN THROUGHOUT THE CITY.

A WAY TO CHECK HIS WEAPON RANGE AND PROTECT HIS ESCAPE ROUTE. A CLEVER TRICK.

BUT IT MEANS HE'S STILL HERE. AND NOW I KNOW THE PATH HE'S GOING TO TAKE.

GONG

DAMMIT!

AS KUSHO'S STUDENT, I MEMORIZED THE CUSTOMS AND DETAILS OF DOZENS OF TOWNS. AND SUDDENLY I REMEMBER...

...BEFORE SHIPS DEPART NANTHEE, THEY RING A BELL FOR THE PASSENGERS.

THEY RING IT *FOUR* TIMES.

JHIN'S *OBSESSED* WITH THAT NUMBER. FOUR KNIVES, FOUR SHOTS, VICTIMS IN UNITS OF FOUR.

WHICH MEANS ON THAT FOURTH RING, HE'S GOING TO DETONATE THESE BOMBS.

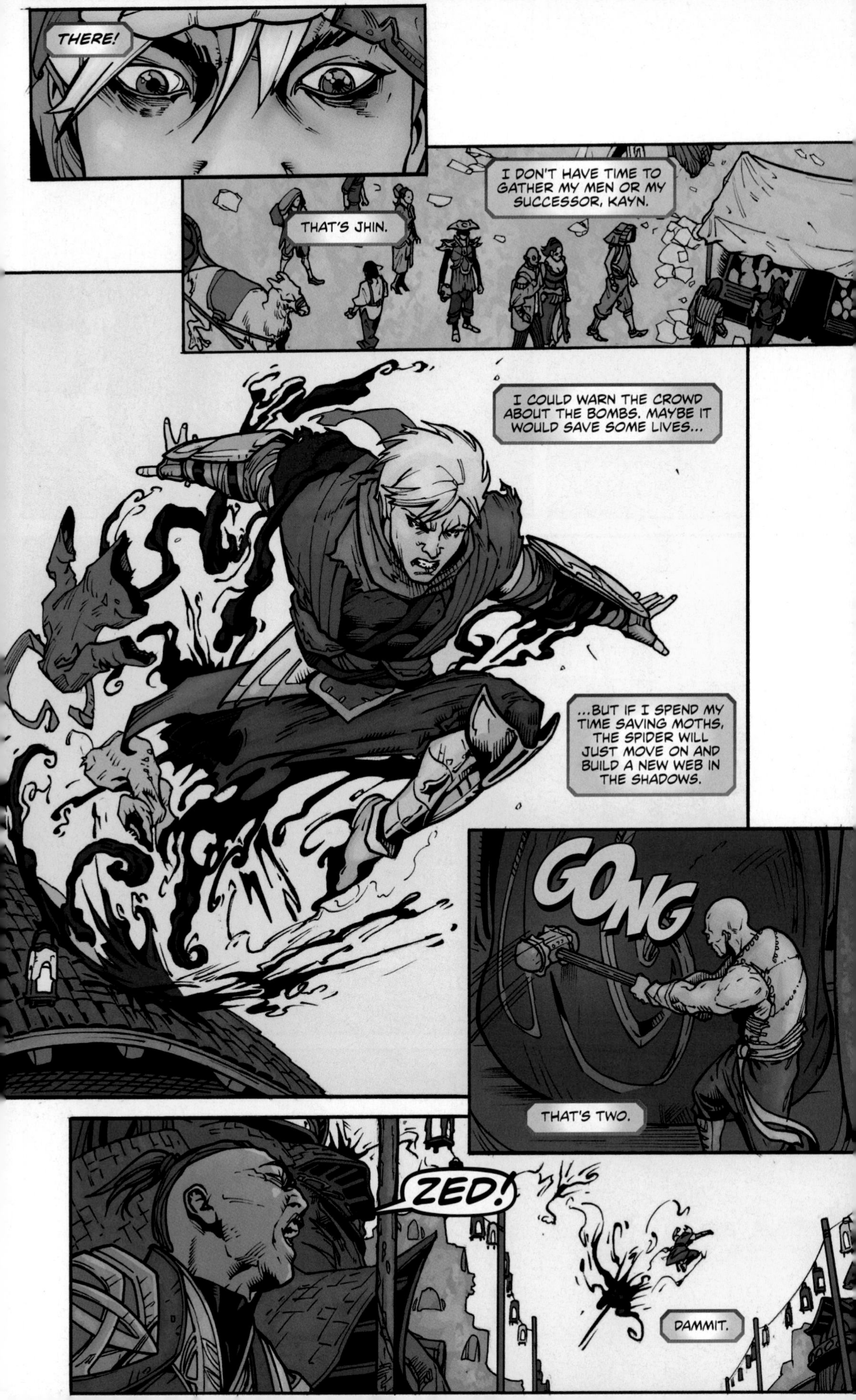
THERE!
THAT'S JHIN.
I DON'T HAVE TIME TO GATHER MY MEN OR MY SUCCESSOR, KAYN.
I COULD WARN THE CROWD ABOUT THE BOMBS. MAYBE IT WOULD SAVE SOME LIVES...
...BUT IF I SPEND MY TIME SAVING MOTHS, THE SPIDER WILL JUST MOVE ON AND BUILD A NEW WEB IN THE SHADOWS.
GONG
THAT'S TWO.
ZED!
DAMMIT.

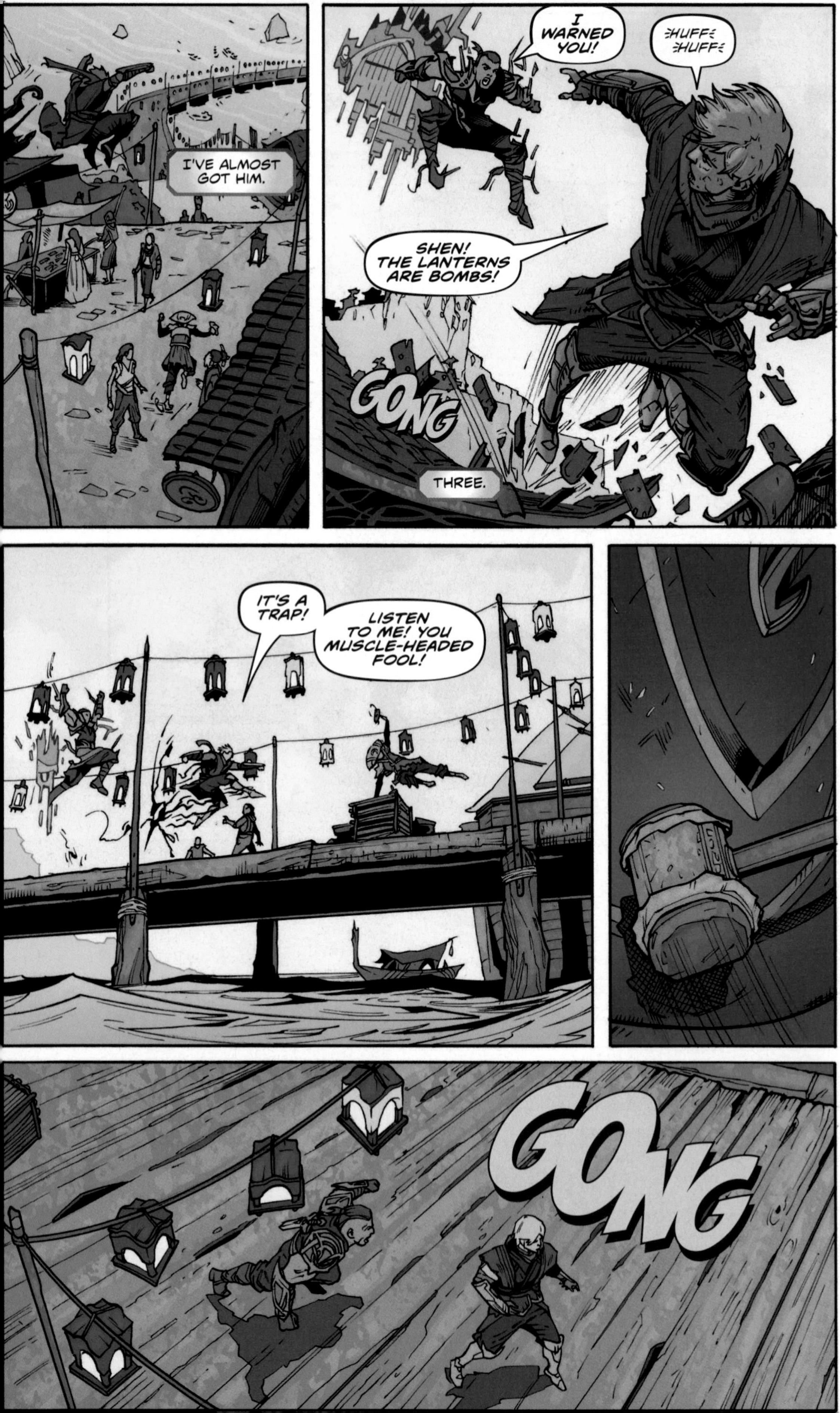
I'VE ALMOST GOT HIM.
I WARNED YOU!
HUFF HUFF
SHEN! THE LANTERNS ARE BOMBS!
GONG
THREE.
IT'S A TRAP!
LISTEN TO ME! YOU MUSCLE-HEADED FOOL!
GONG

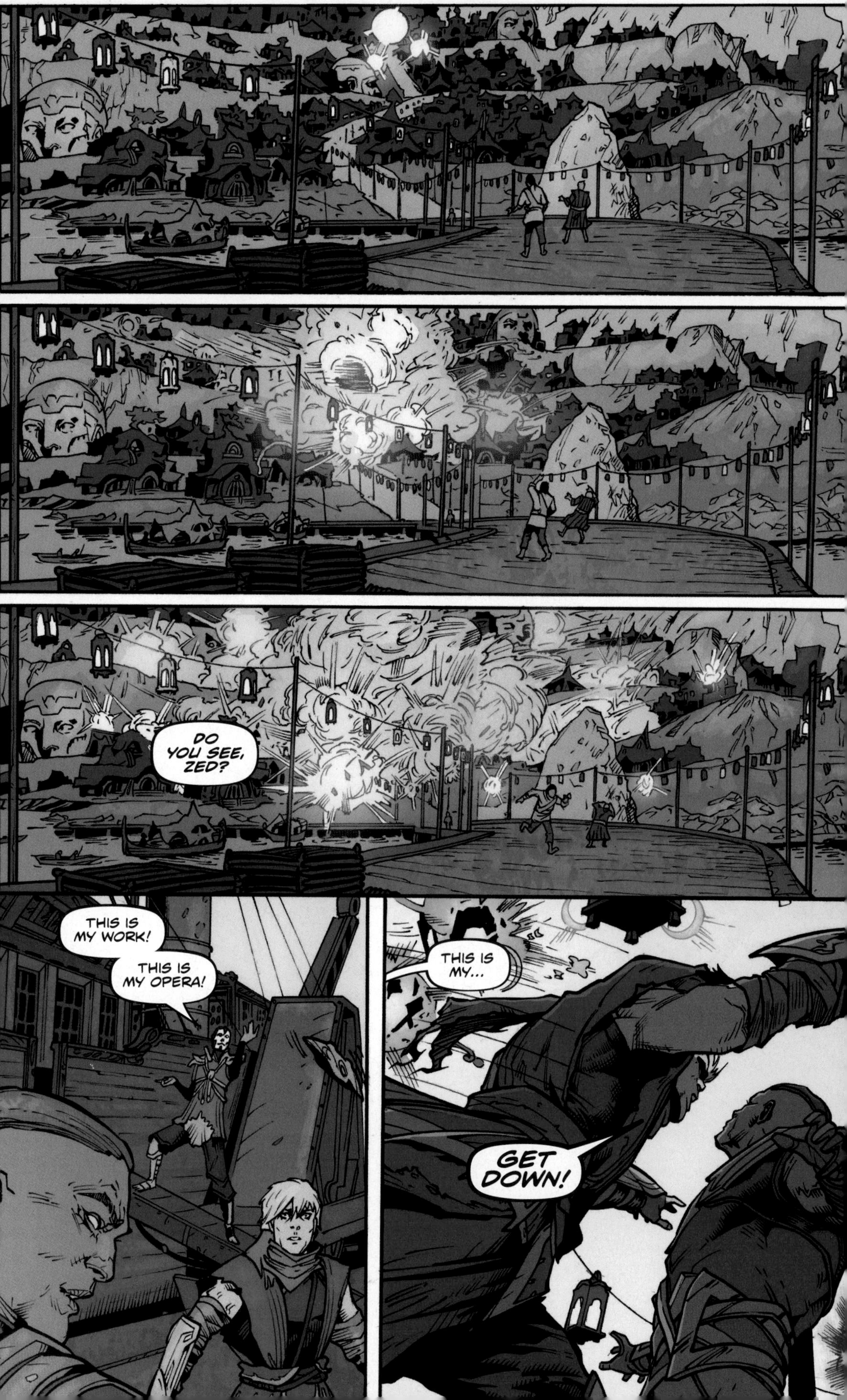

DO YOU SEE, ZED?
THIS IS MY WORK!
THIS IS MY OPERA!
THIS IS MY...
GET DOWN!

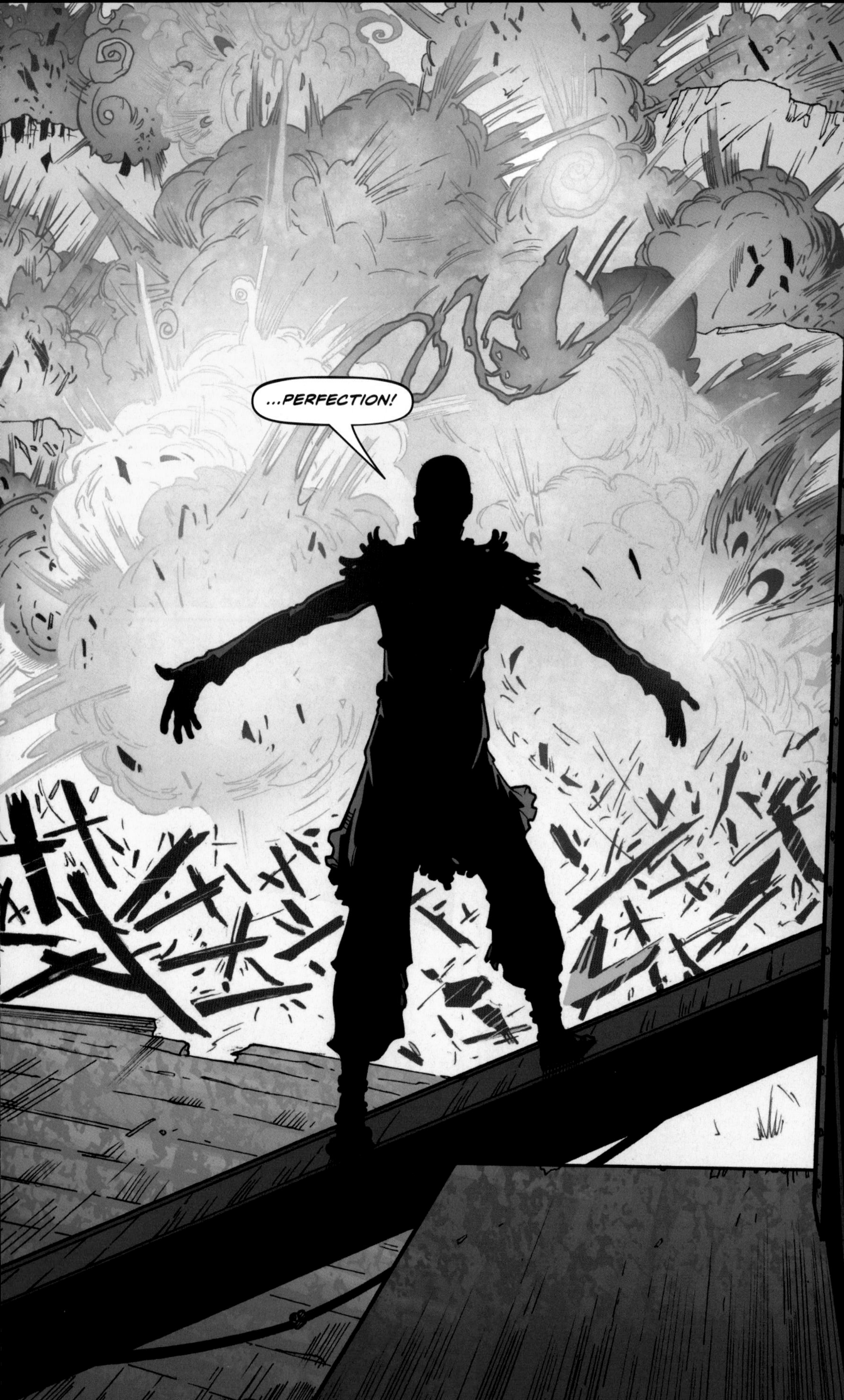
...PERFECTION!

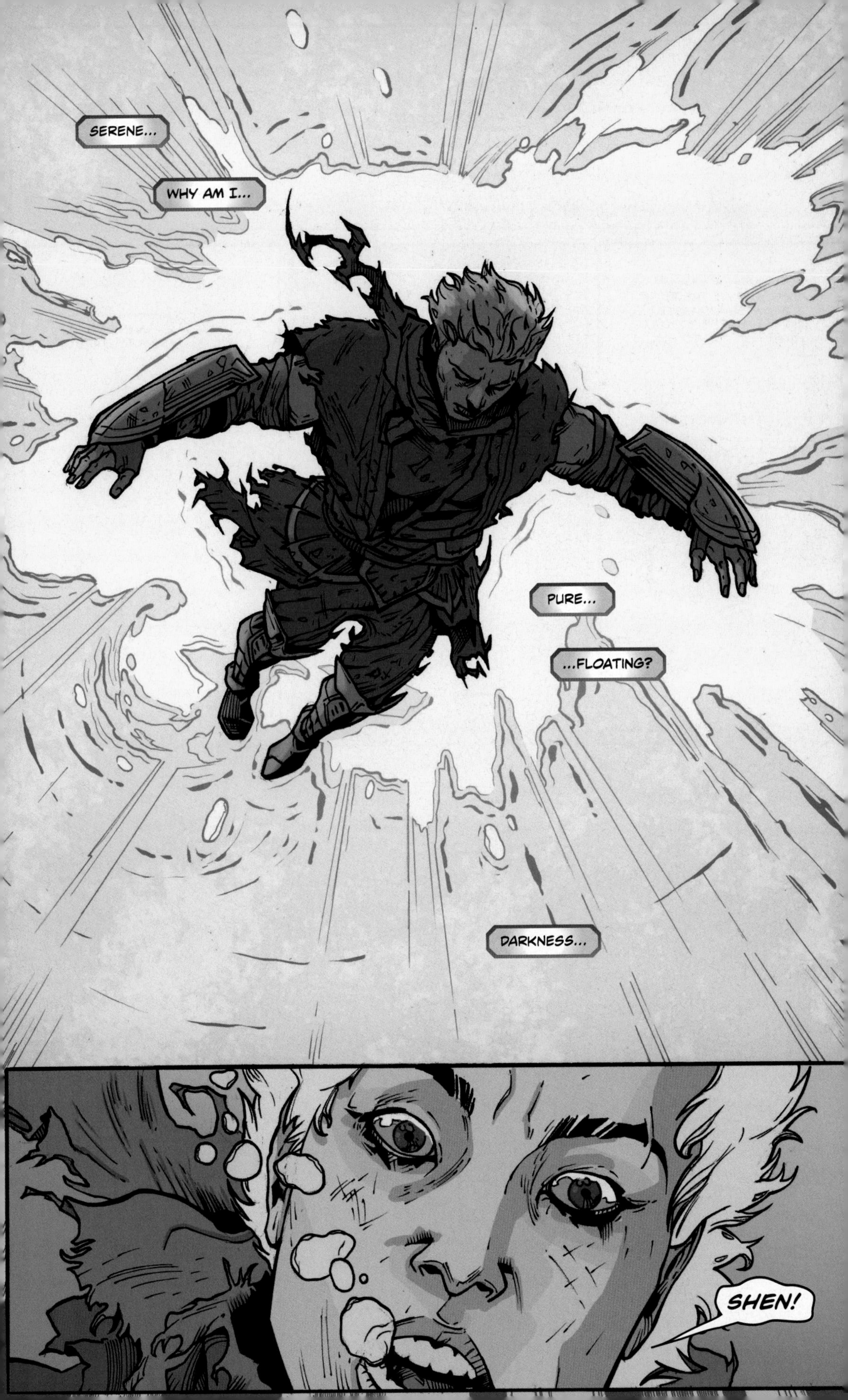
SERENE...
WHY AM I...
PURE...
...FLOATING?
DARKNESS...
SHEN!

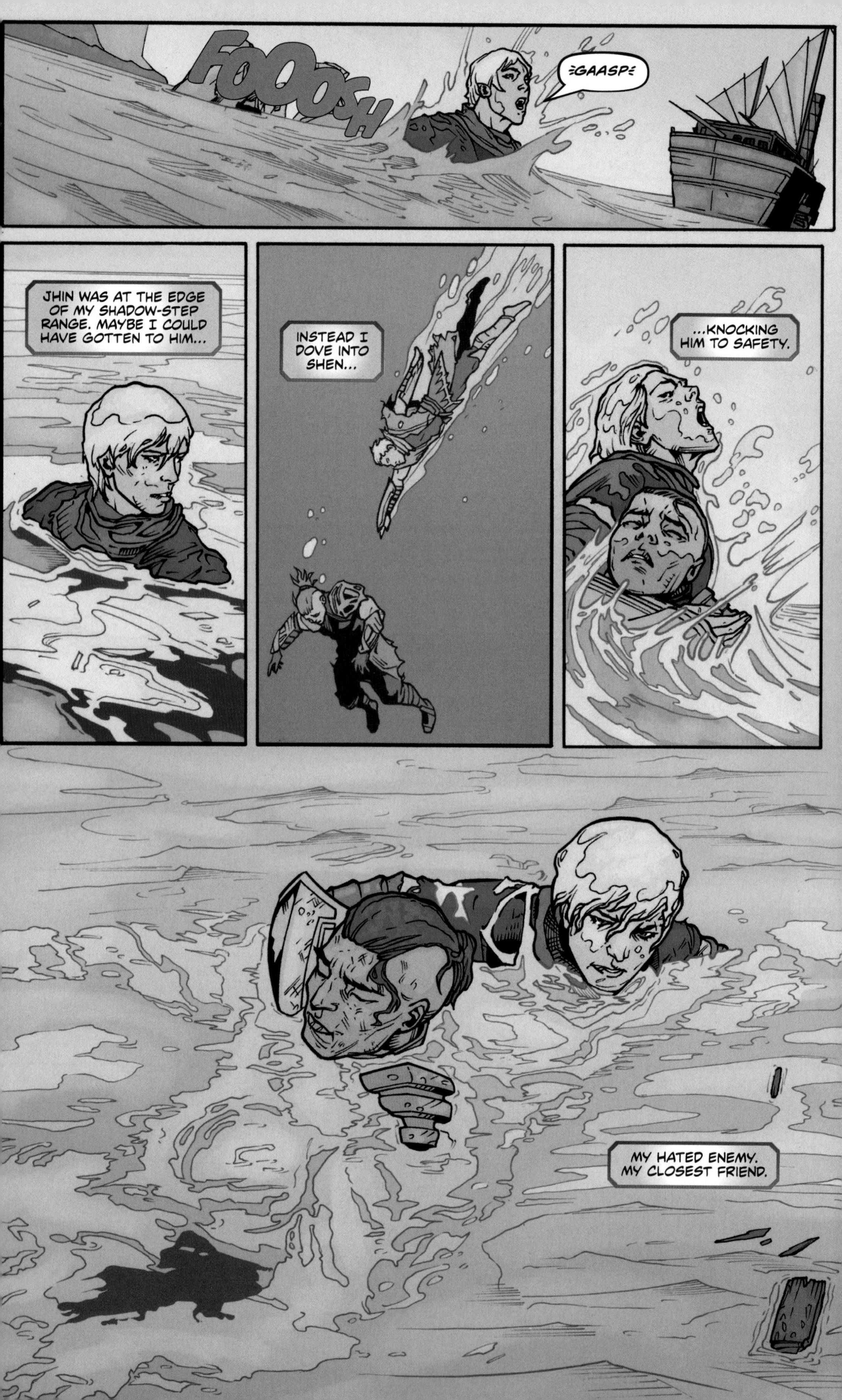
FOOOSH
GAASP
JHIN WAS AT THE EDGE OF MY SHADOW-STEP RANGE. MAYBE I COULD HAVE GOTTEN TO HIM...
INSTEAD I DOVE INTO SHEN...
...KNOCKING HIM TO SAFETY.
MY HATED ENEMY. MY CLOSEST FRIEND.

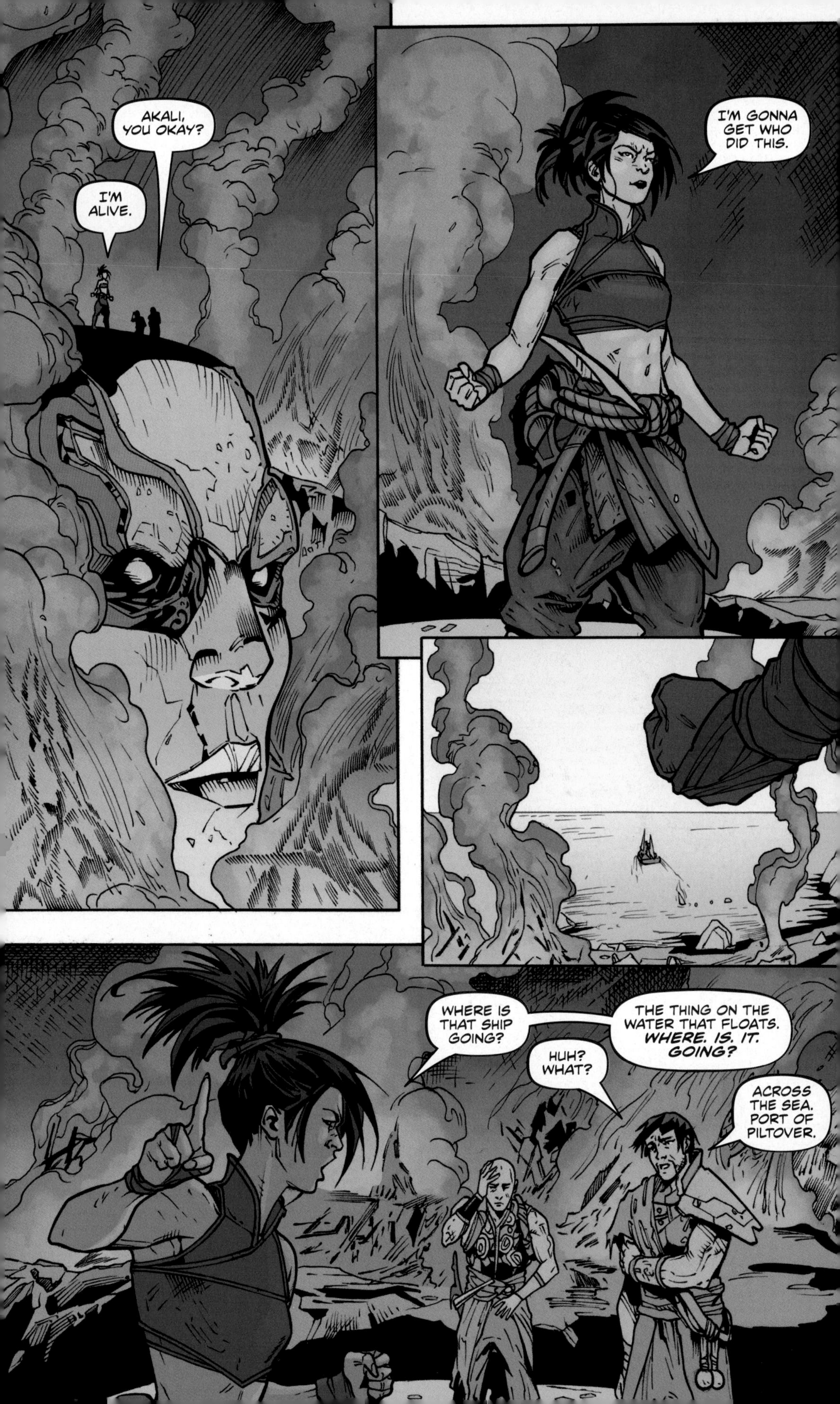
AKALI, YOU OKAY?
I'M ALIVE.
I'M GONNA GET WHO DID THIS.
WHERE IS THAT SHIP GOING?
THE THING ON THE WATER THAT FLOATS. *WHERE. IS. IT. GOING?*
HUH? WHAT?
ACROSS THE SEA. PORT OF PILTOVER.

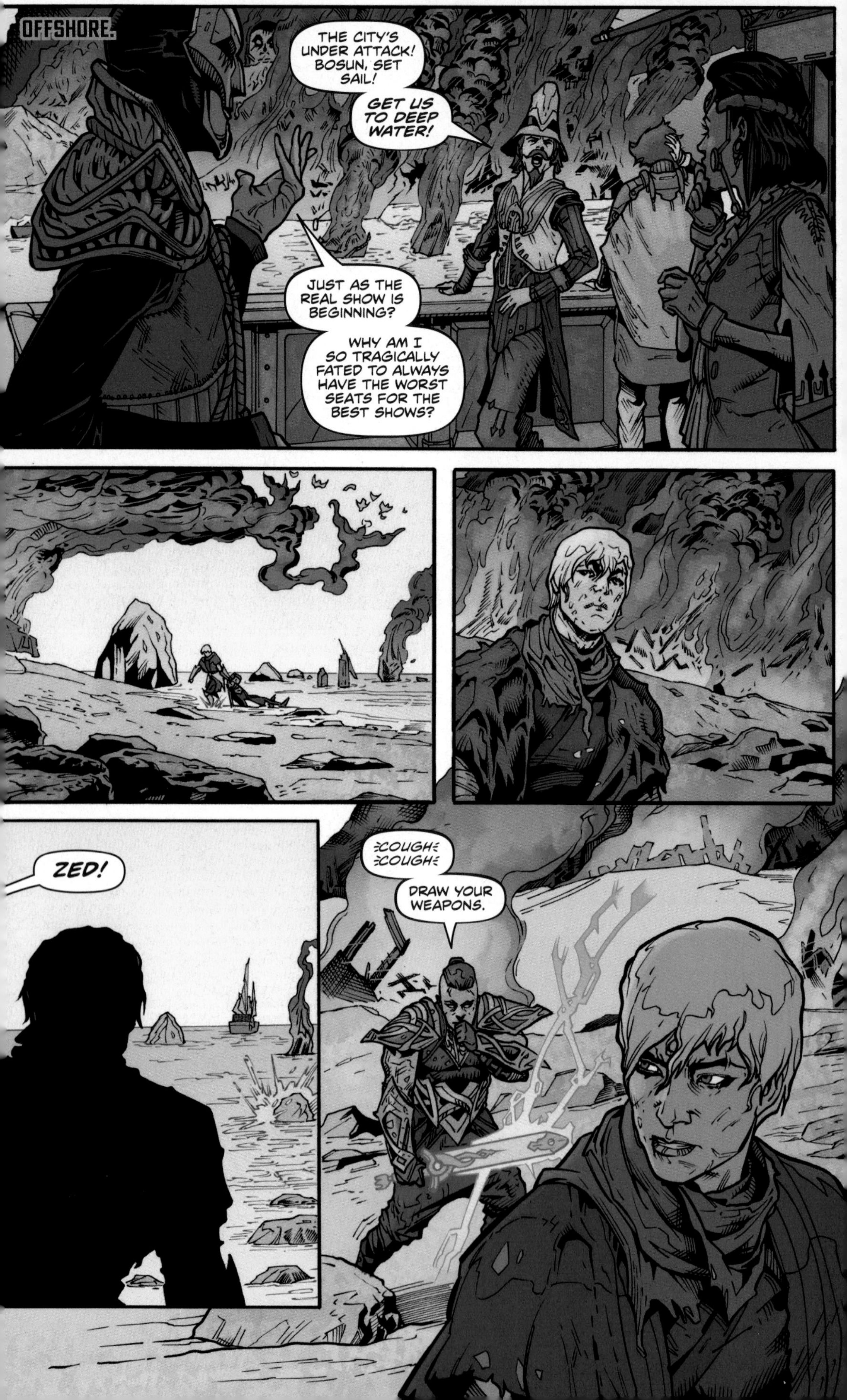
OFFSHORE.
THE CITY'S UNDER ATTACK! BOSUN, SET SAIL!
GET US TO DEEP WATER!
JUST AS THE REAL SHOW IS BEGINNING?
WHY AM I SO TRAGICALLY FATED TO ALWAYS HAVE THE WORST SEATS FOR THE BEST SHOWS?
ZED!
COUGH
COUGH
DRAW YOUR WEAPONS.

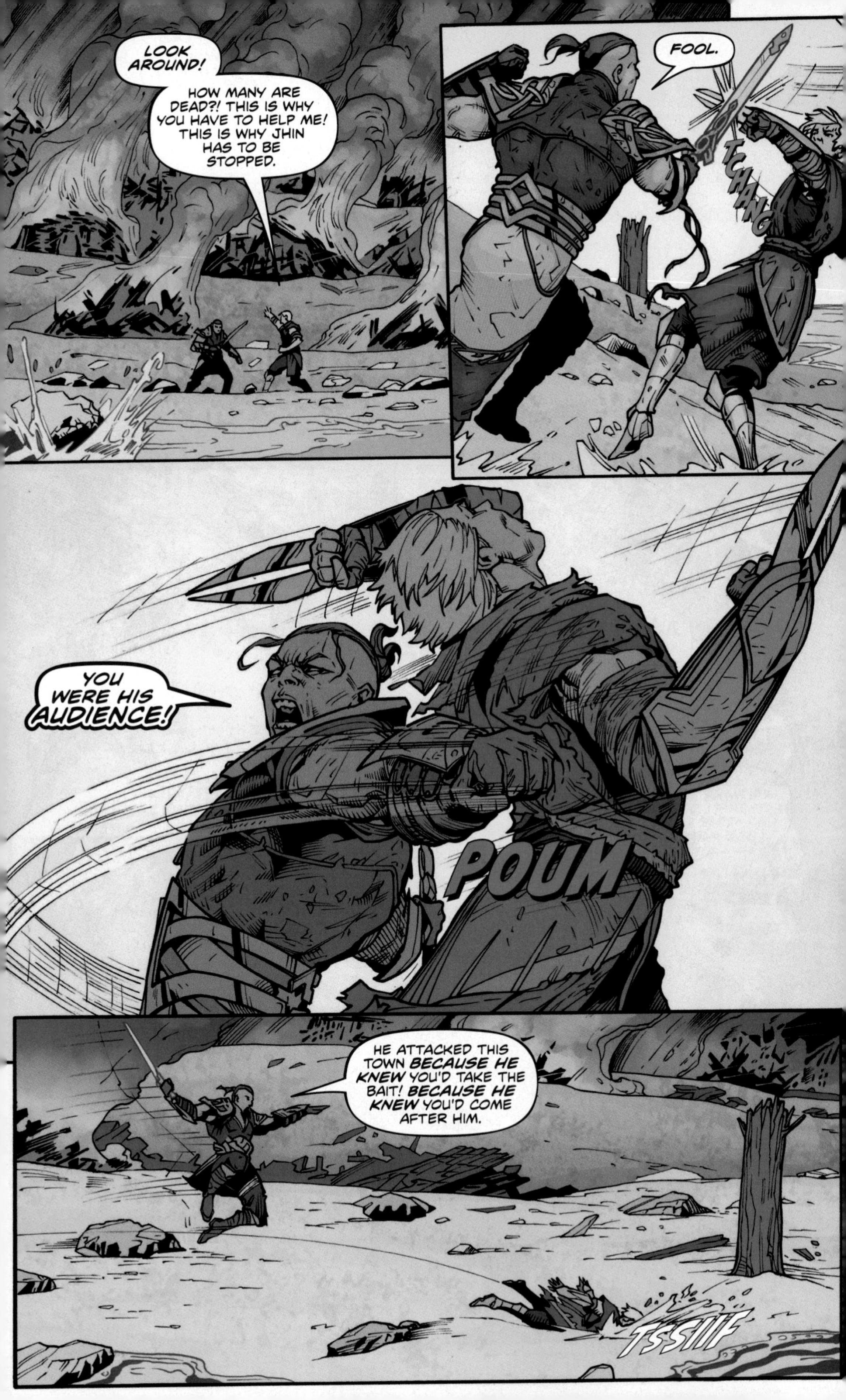
LOOK AROUND!
HOW MANY ARE DEAD?! THIS IS WHY YOU HAVE TO HELP ME! THIS IS WHY JHIN HAS TO BE STOPPED.
FOOL.
TCHANG
YOU WERE HIS AUDIENCE!
POUM
HE ATTACKED THIS TOWN **BECAUSE HE KNEW** YOU'D TAKE THE BAIT! **BECAUSE HE KNEW** YOU'D COME AFTER HIM.
TSSIIF

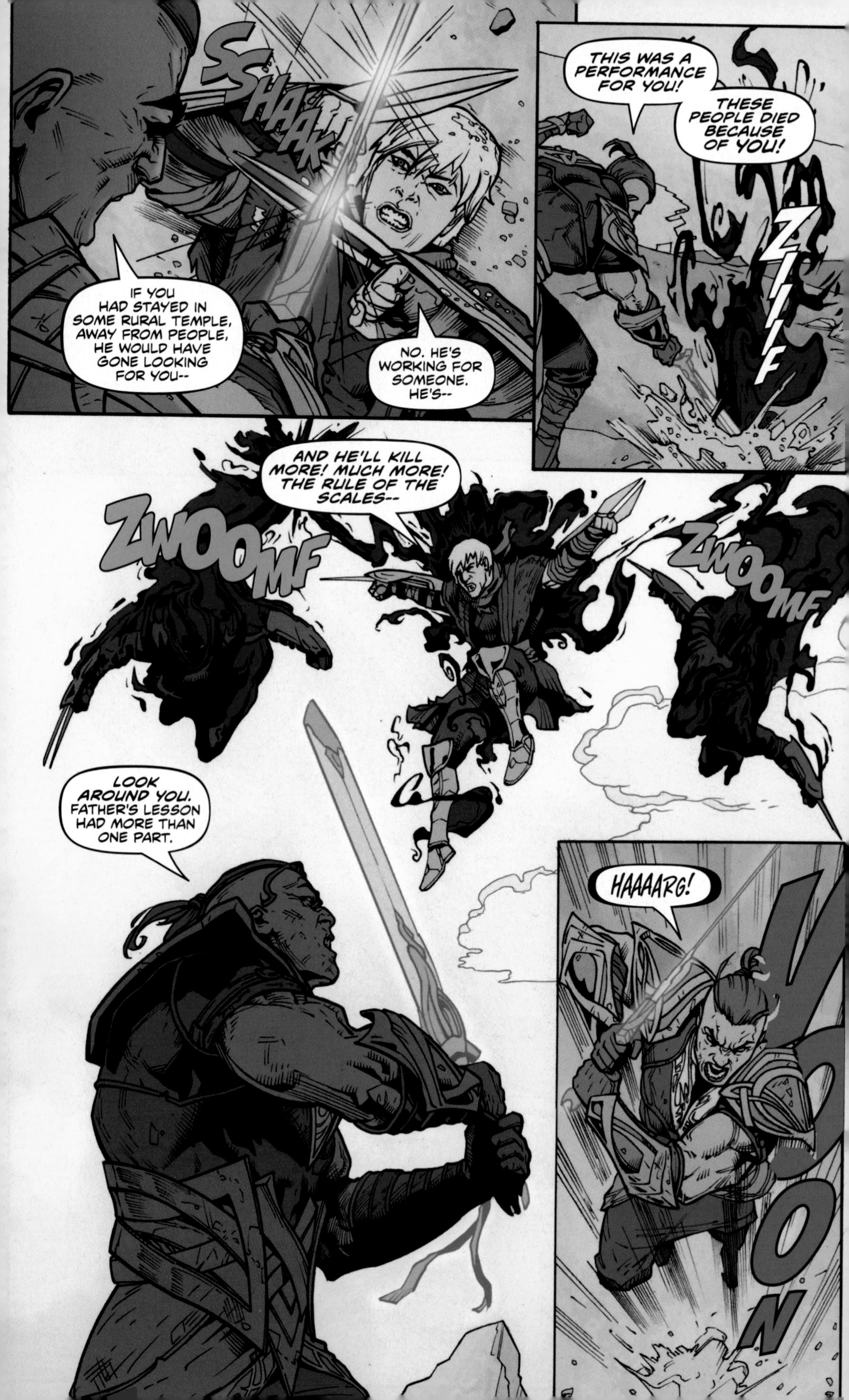
SSHAAK
IF YOU HAD STAYED IN SOME RURAL TEMPLE, AWAY FROM PEOPLE, HE WOULD HAVE GONE LOOKING FOR YOU--
NO. HE'S WORKING FOR SOMEONE. HE'S--
THIS WAS A PERFORMANCE FOR YOU!
THESE PEOPLE DIED BECAUSE OF YOU!
ZIIIF
AND HE'LL KILL MORE! MUCH MORE! THE RULE OF THE SCALES--
ZWOOMF
ZWOOMF
LOOK AROUND YOU. FATHER'S LESSON HAD MORE THAN ONE PART.
HAAAARG!

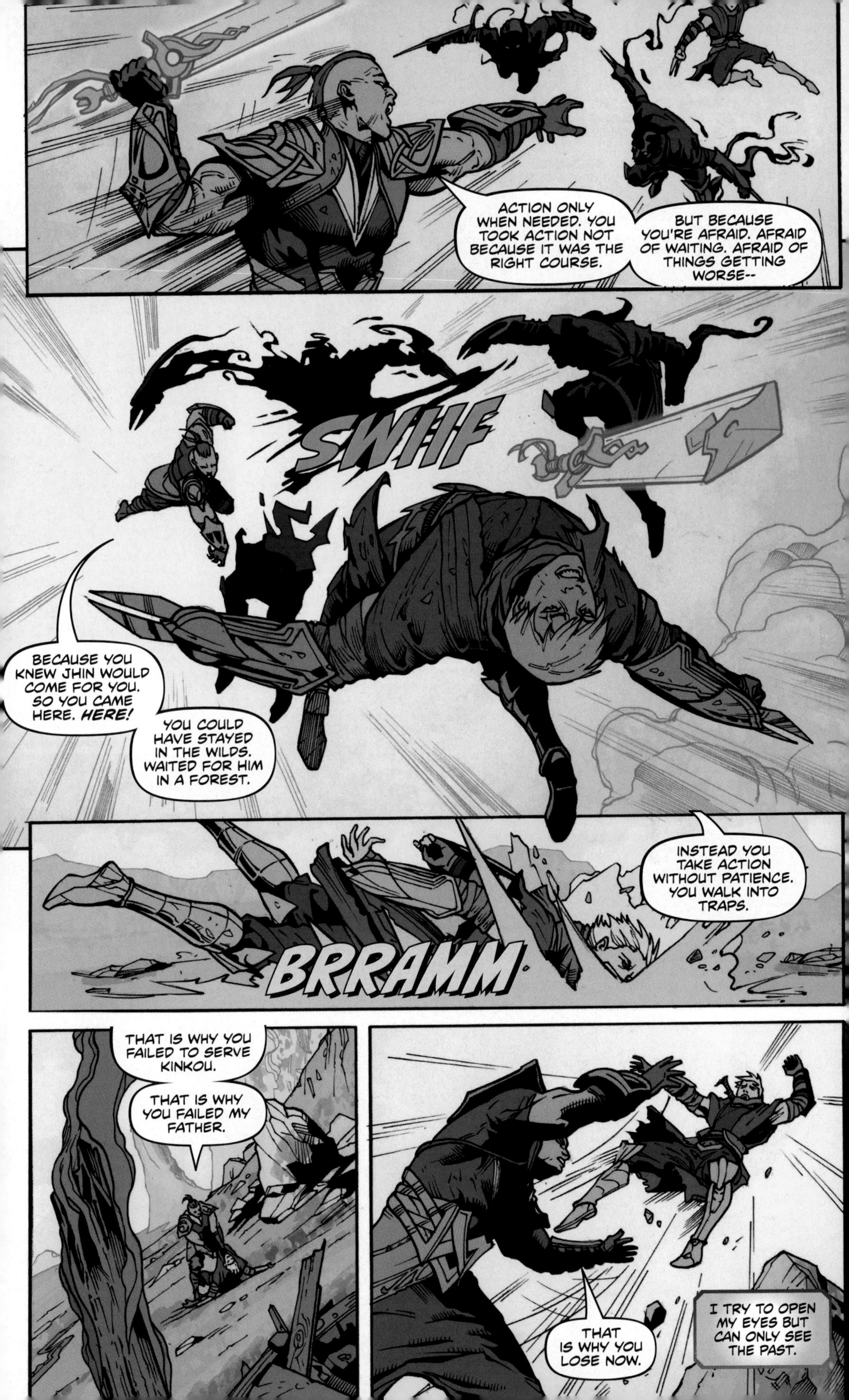
ACTION ONLY WHEN NEEDED. YOU TOOK ACTION NOT BECAUSE IT WAS THE RIGHT COURSE.
BUT BECAUSE YOU'RE AFRAID. AFRAID OF WAITING. AFRAID OF THINGS GETTING WORSE--
SWHF
BECAUSE YOU KNEW JHIN WOULD COME FOR YOU. SO YOU CAME HERE. *HERE!*
YOU COULD HAVE STAYED IN THE WILDS. WAITED FOR HIM IN A FOREST.
INSTEAD YOU TAKE ACTION WITHOUT PATIENCE. YOU WALK INTO TRAPS.
BRRAMM
THAT IS WHY YOU FAILED TO SERVE KINKOU.
THAT IS WHY YOU FAILED MY FATHER.
THAT IS WHY YOU LOSE NOW.
I TRY TO OPEN MY EYES BUT CAN ONLY SEE THE PAST.

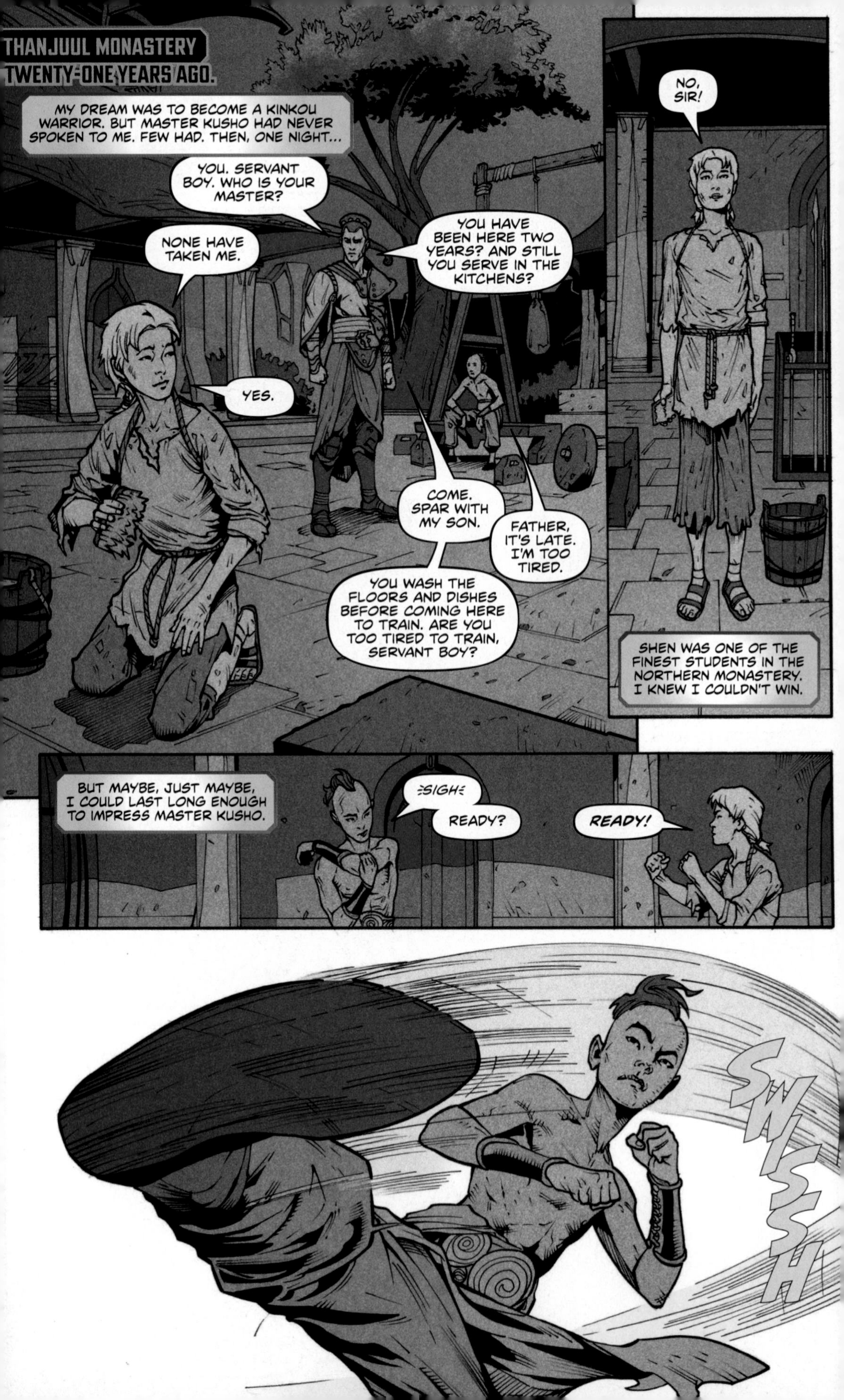

THANJUUL MONASTERY
TWENTY-ONE YEARS AGO.
MY DREAM WAS TO BECOME A KINKOU WARRIOR. BUT MASTER KUSHO HAD NEVER SPOKEN TO ME. FEW HAD. THEN, ONE NIGHT...
YOU. SERVANT BOY. WHO IS YOUR MASTER?
NONE HAVE TAKEN ME.
YOU HAVE BEEN HERE TWO YEARS? AND STILL YOU SERVE IN THE KITCHENS?
YES.
COME. SPAR WITH MY SON.
FATHER, IT'S LATE. I'M TOO TIRED.
YOU WASH THE FLOORS AND DISHES BEFORE COMING HERE TO TRAIN. ARE YOU TOO TIRED TO TRAIN, SERVANT BOY?
NO, SIR!
SHEN WAS ONE OF THE FINEST STUDENTS IN THE NORTHERN MONASTERY. I KNEW I COULDN'T WIN.
BUT MAYBE, JUST MAYBE, I COULD LAST LONG ENOUGH TO IMPRESS MASTER KUSHO.
SIGH
READY?
READY!
SWISH

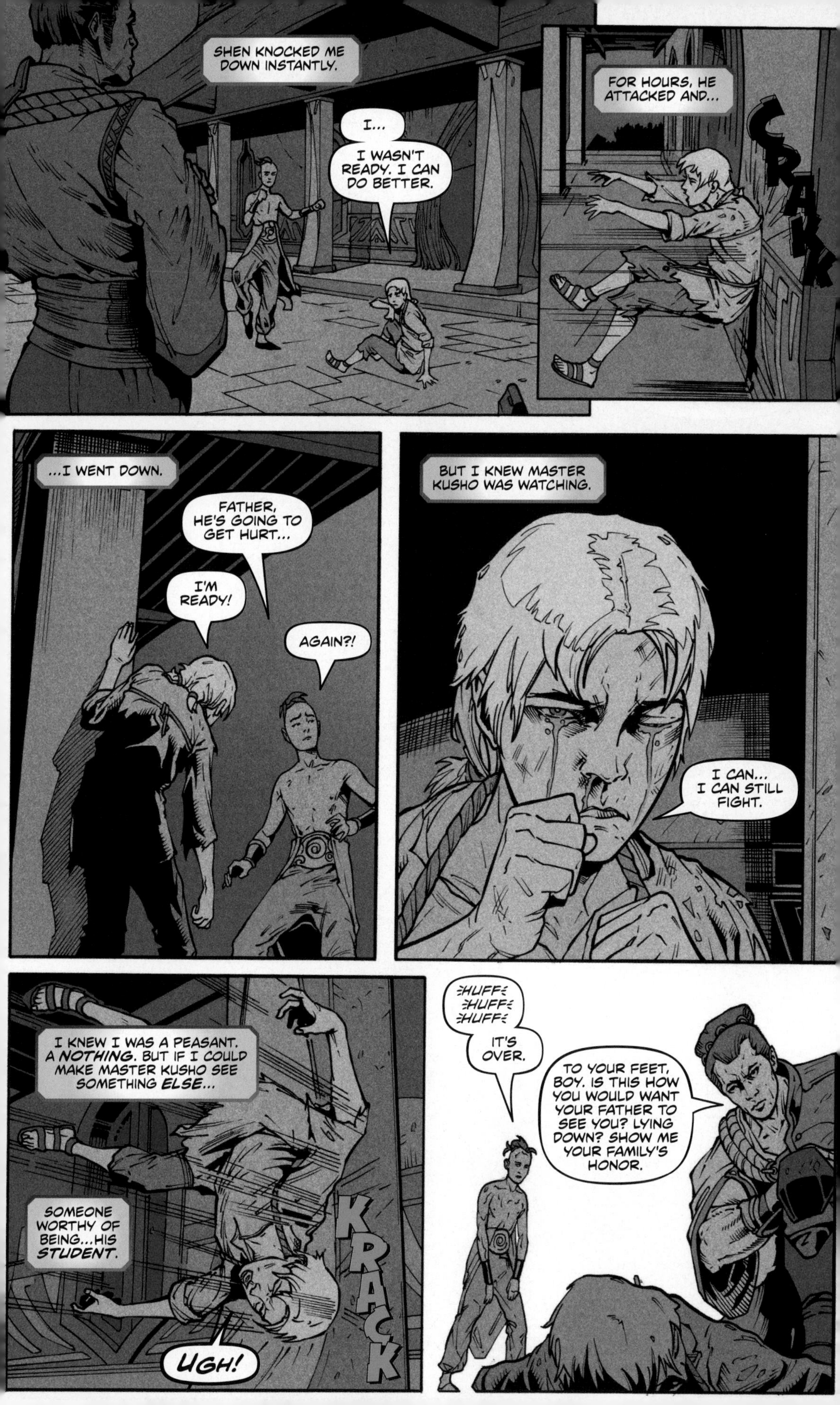
SHEN KNOCKED ME DOWN INSTANTLY.
I...
I WASN'T READY. I CAN DO BETTER.
FOR HOURS, HE ATTACKED AND...
CRAK
...I WENT DOWN.
FATHER, HE'S GOING TO GET HURT...
I'M READY!
AGAIN?!
BUT I KNEW MASTER KUSHO WAS WATCHING.
I CAN... I CAN STILL FIGHT.
I KNEW I WAS A PEASANT. A NOTHING. BUT IF I COULD MAKE MASTER KUSHO SEE SOMETHING ELSE...
SOMEONE WORTHY OF BEING...HIS STUDENT.
KRACK
UGH!
HUFF HUFF HUFF
IT'S OVER.
TO YOUR FEET, BOY. IS THIS HOW YOU WOULD WANT YOUR FATHER TO SEE YOU? LYING DOWN? SHOW ME YOUR FAMILY'S HONOR.

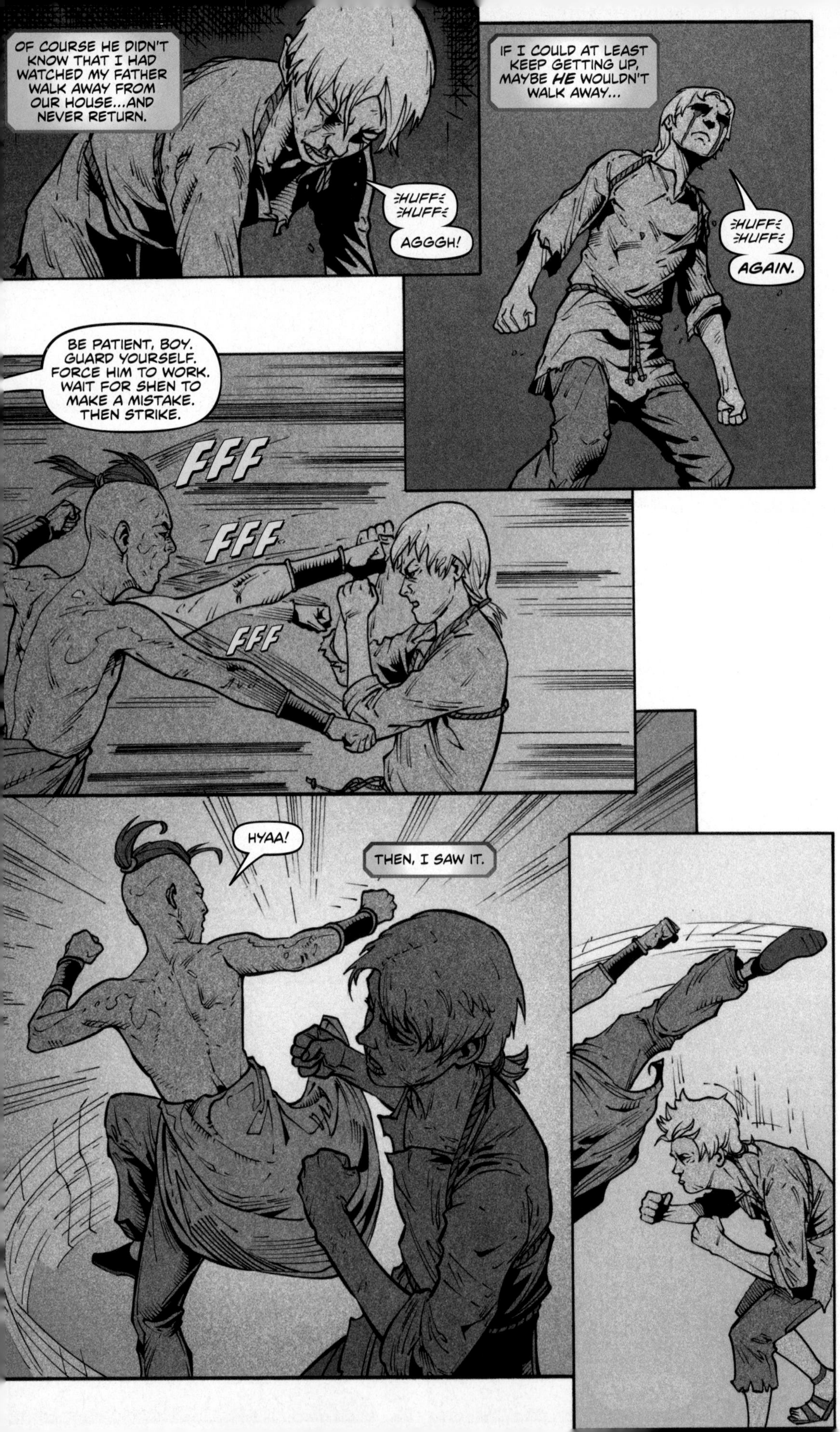
OF COURSE HE DIDN'T KNOW THAT I HAD WATCHED MY FATHER WALK AWAY FROM OUR HOUSE...AND NEVER RETURN.
HUFF HUFF
AGGGH!
IF I COULD AT LEAST KEEP GETTING UP, MAYBE HE WOULDN'T WALK AWAY...
HUFF HUFF
AGAIN.
BE PATIENT, BOY. GUARD YOURSELF. FORCE HIM TO WORK. WAIT FOR SHEN TO MAKE A MISTAKE. THEN STRIKE.
FFF
FFF
FFF
HYAA!
THEN, I SAW IT.

POW

WHOA.

TAK

I TOLD YOU YOUR KICKS WERE PREDICTABLE, SHEN.

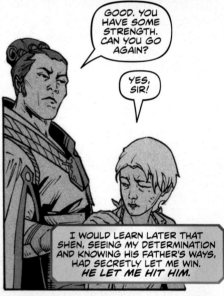

GOOD. YOU HAVE SOME STRENGTH. CAN YOU GO AGAIN?

YES, SIR!

I WOULD LEARN LATER THAT SHEN, SEEING MY DETERMINATION AND KNOWING HIS FATHER'S WAYS, HAD SECRETLY LET ME WIN. *HE LET ME HIT HIM.*

THEN I WILL TAKE YOU AS MY STUDENT.

ALL THAT I ACHIEVED AND BECAME...WAS FROM THAT MOMENT OF SHEN'S KINDNESS.

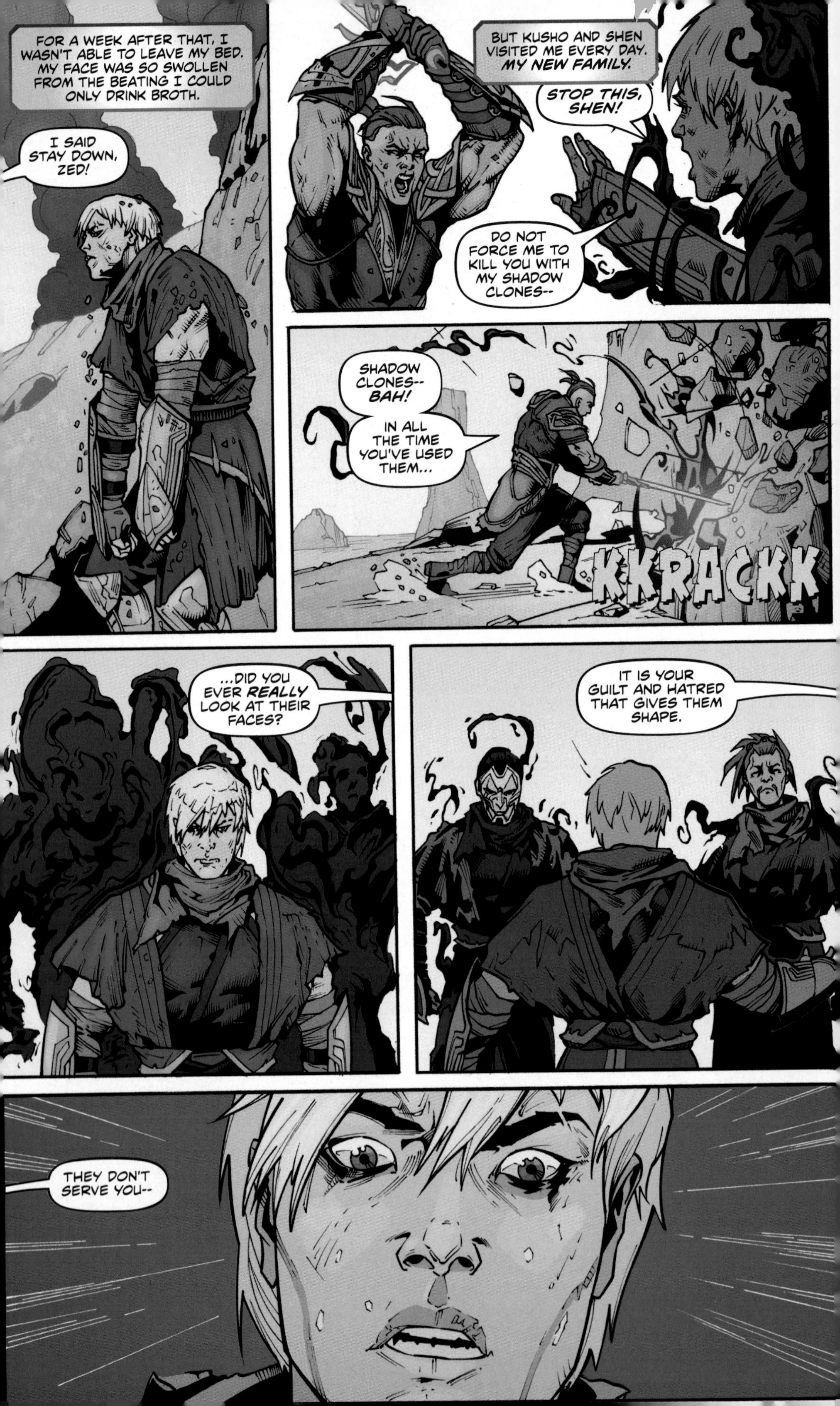
FOR A WEEK AFTER THAT, I WASN'T ABLE TO LEAVE MY BED. MY FACE WAS SO SWOLLEN FROM THE BEATING I COULD ONLY DRINK BROTH.
I SAID STAY DOWN, ZED!
BUT KUSHO AND SHEN VISITED ME EVERY DAY. MY NEW FAMILY.
STOP THIS, SHEN!
DO NOT FORCE ME TO KILL YOU WITH MY SHADOW CLONES--
SHADOW CLONES-- BAH!
IN ALL THE TIME YOU'VE USED THEM...
KKRACKK
...DID YOU EVER REALLY LOOK AT THEIR FACES?
IT IS YOUR GUILT AND HATRED THAT GIVES THEM SHAPE.
THEY DON'T SERVE YOU--

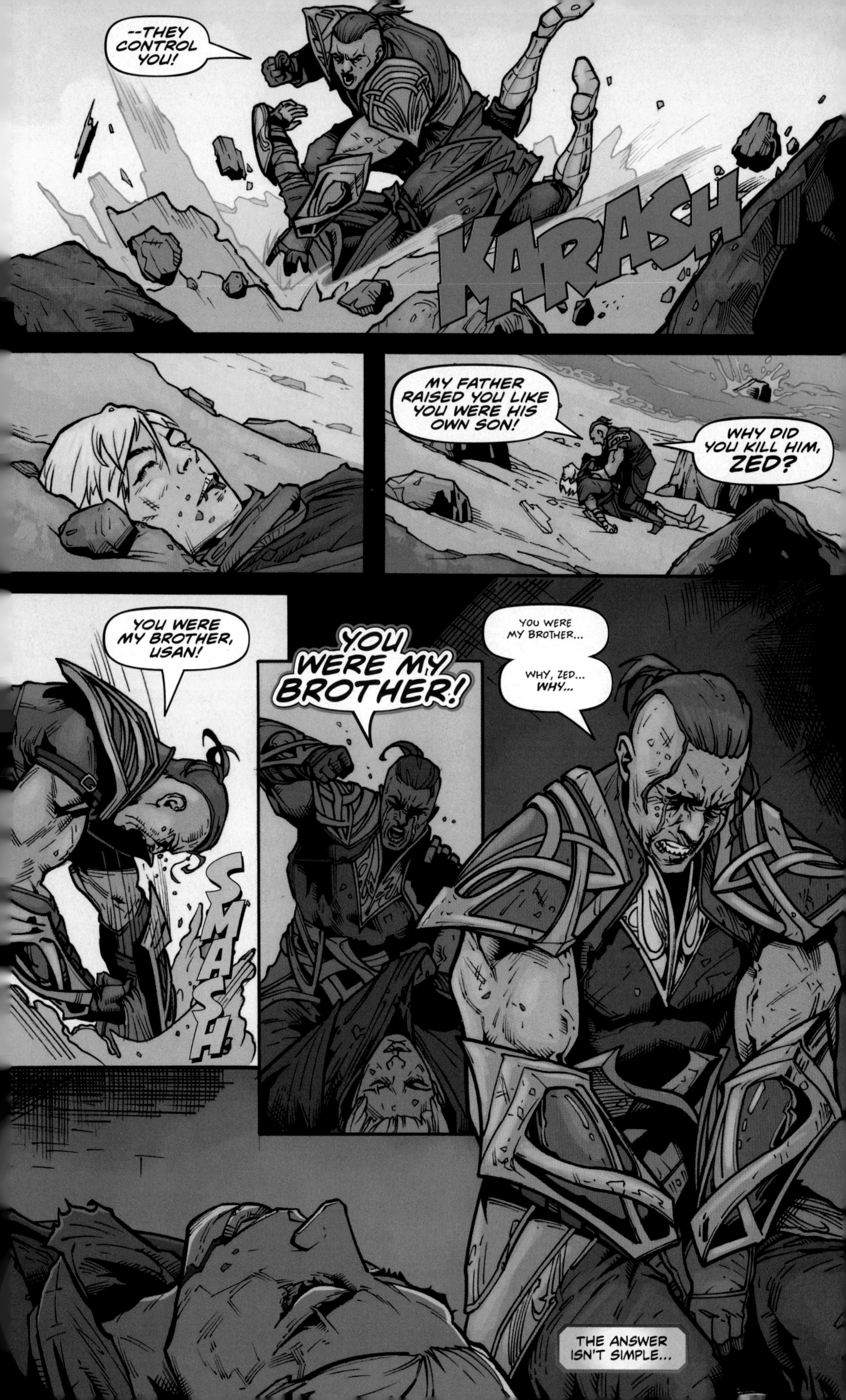
--THEY CONTROL YOU!
KARASH
MY FATHER RAISED YOU LIKE YOU WERE HIS OWN SON!
WHY DID YOU KILL HIM, ZED?
YOU WERE MY BROTHER, USAN!
SMASH
YOU WERE MY BROTHER!
YOU WERE MY BROTHER...
WHY, ZED... WHY...
THE ANSWER ISN'T SIMPLE...

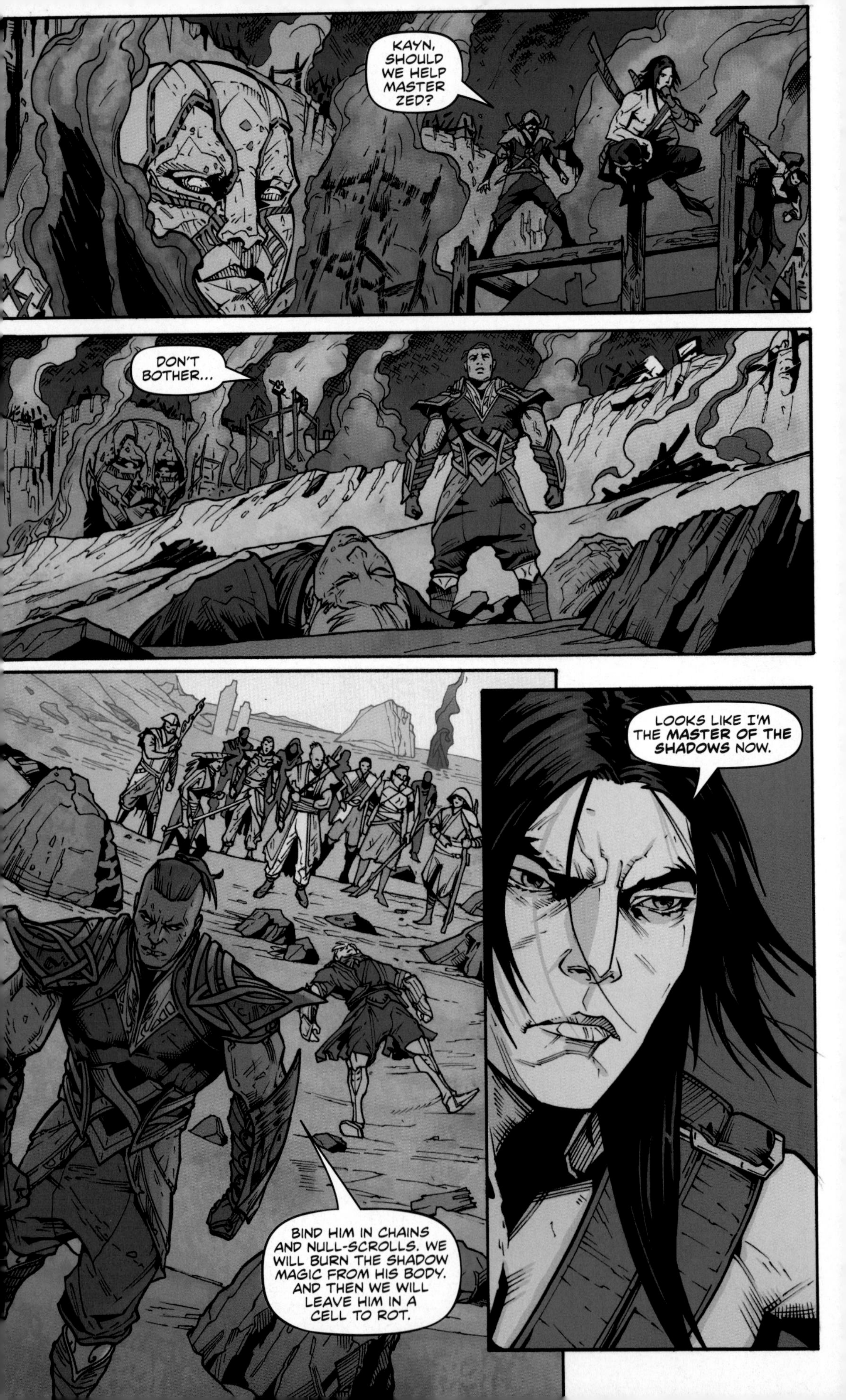
KAYN, SHOULD WE HELP MASTER ZED?
DON'T BOTHER...
LOOKS LIKE I'M THE MASTER OF THE SHADOWS NOW.
BIND HIM IN CHAINS AND NULL-SCROLLS. WE WILL BURN THE SHADOW MAGIC FROM HIS BODY. AND THEN WE WILL LEAVE HIM IN A CELL TO ROT.

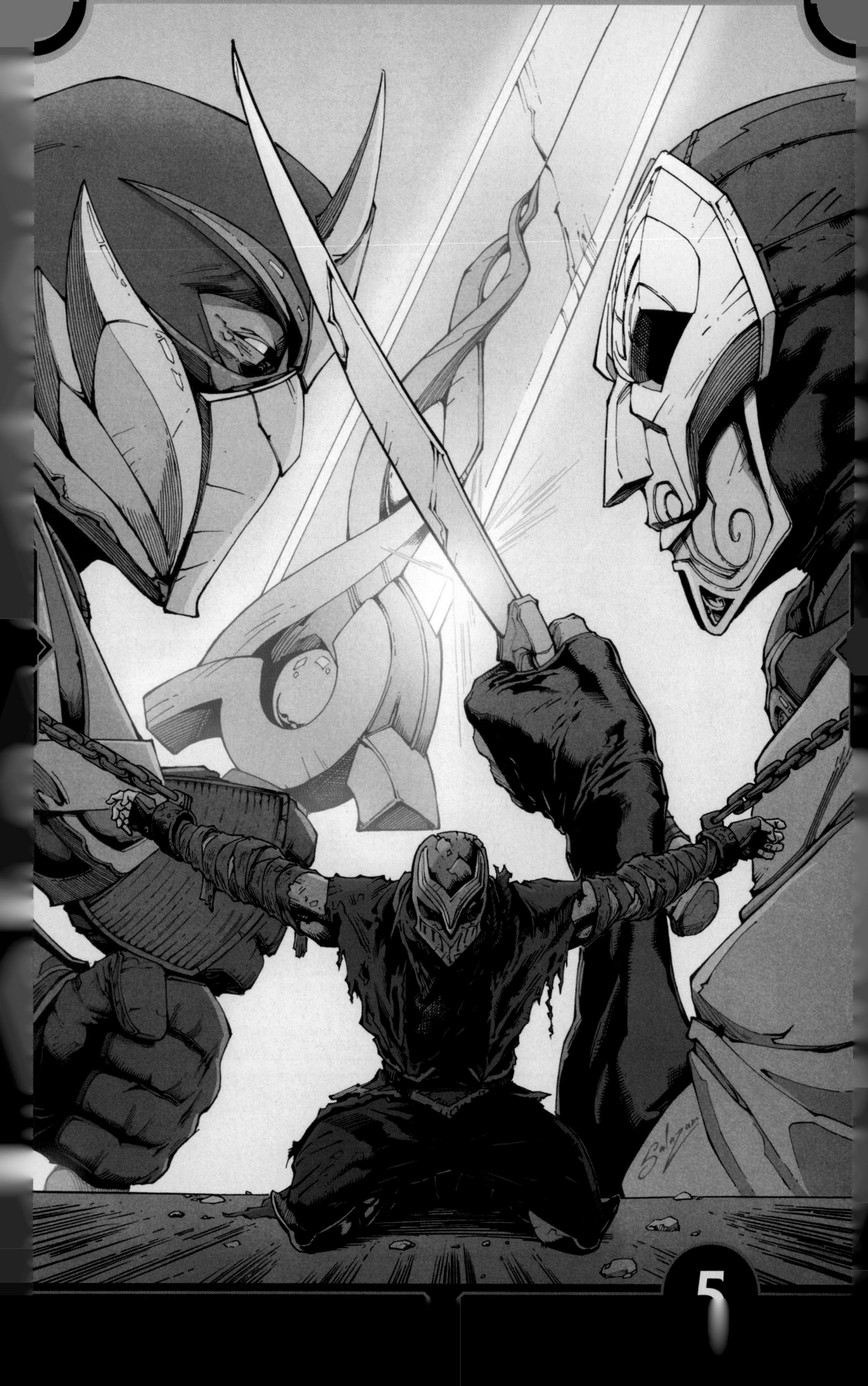

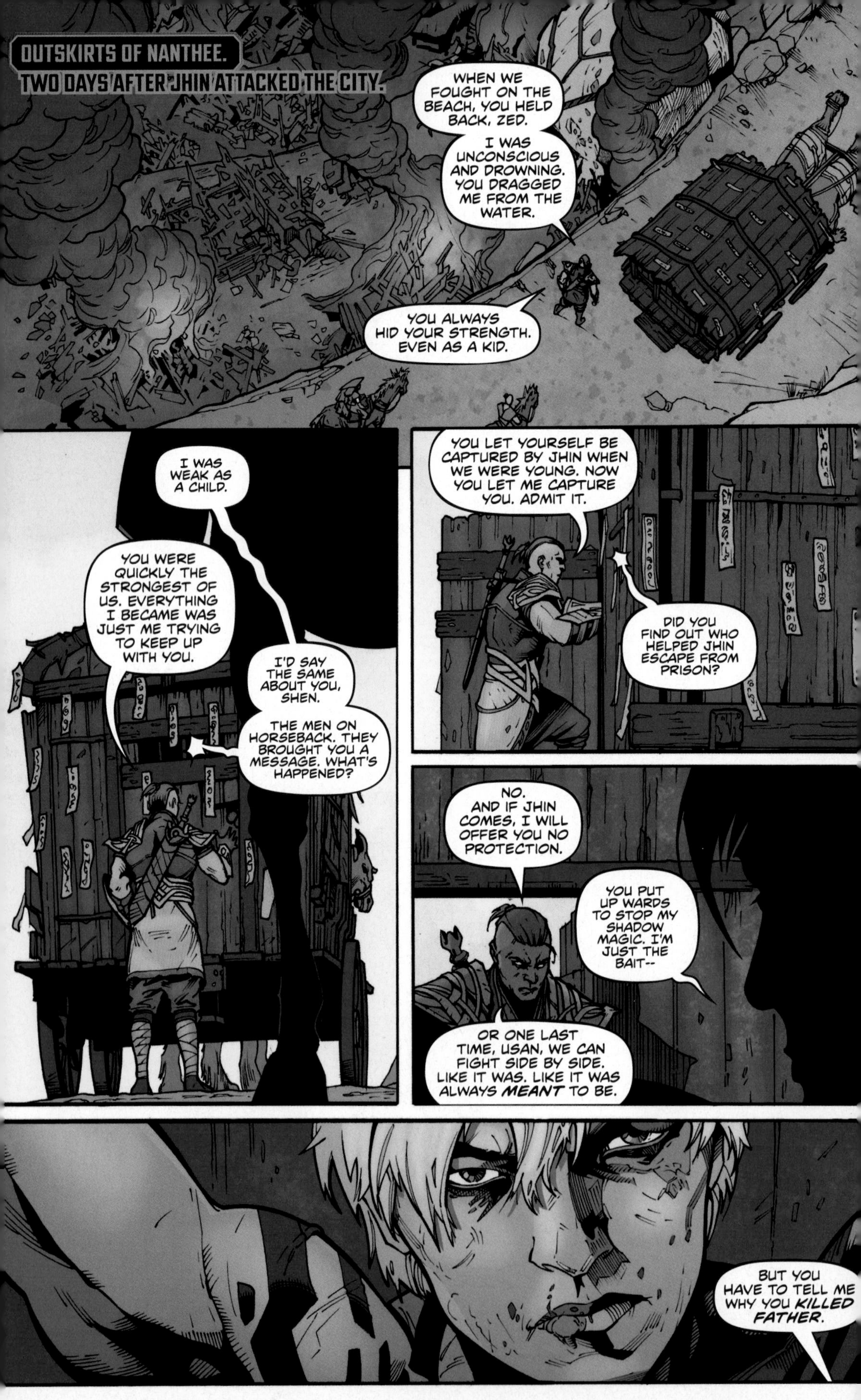
OUTSKIRTS OF NANTHEE.
TWO DAYS AFTER JHIN ATTACKED THE CITY.
WHEN WE FOUGHT ON THE BEACH, YOU HELD BACK, ZED.
I WAS UNCONSCIOUS AND DROWNING. YOU DRAGGED ME FROM THE WATER.
YOU ALWAYS HID YOUR STRENGTH. EVEN AS A KID.
I WAS WEAK AS A CHILD.
YOU WERE QUICKLY THE STRONGEST OF US. EVERYTHING I BECAME WAS JUST ME TRYING TO KEEP UP WITH YOU.
I'D SAY THE SAME ABOUT YOU, SHEN.
THE MEN ON HORSEBACK. THEY BROUGHT YOU A MESSAGE. WHAT'S HAPPENED?
YOU LET YOURSELF BE CAPTURED BY JHIN WHEN WE WERE YOUNG. NOW YOU LET ME CAPTURE YOU. ADMIT IT.
DID YOU FIND OUT WHO HELPED JHIN ESCAPE FROM PRISON?
NO. AND IF JHIN COMES, I WILL OFFER YOU NO PROTECTION.
YOU PUT UP WARDS TO STOP MY SHADOW MAGIC. I'M JUST THE BAIT--
OR ONE LAST TIME, USAN, WE CAN FIGHT SIDE BY SIDE. LIKE IT WAS. LIKE IT WAS ALWAYS MEANT TO BE.
BUT YOU HAVE TO TELL ME WHY YOU KILLED FATHER.

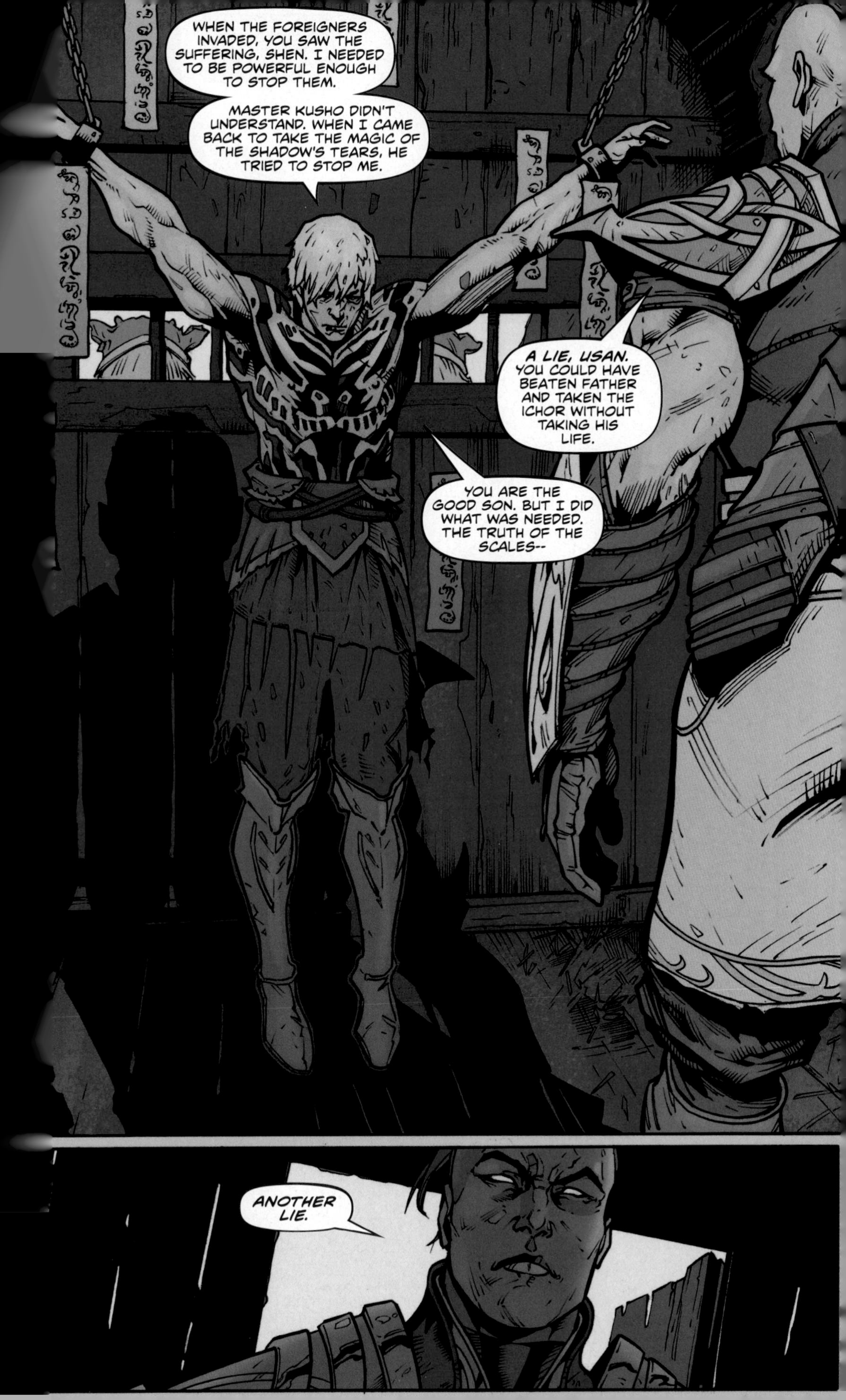
WHEN THE FOREIGNERS INVADED, YOU SAW THE SUFFERING, SHEN. I NEEDED TO BE POWERFUL ENOUGH TO STOP THEM.
MASTER KUSHO DIDN'T UNDERSTAND. WHEN I CAME BACK TO TAKE THE MAGIC OF THE SHADOW'S TEARS, HE TRIED TO STOP ME.
A LIE, USAN. YOU COULD HAVE BEATEN FATHER AND TAKEN THE ICHOR WITHOUT TAKING HIS LIFE.
YOU ARE THE GOOD SON. BUT I DID WHAT WAS NEEDED. THE TRUTH OF THE SCALES--
ANOTHER LIE.

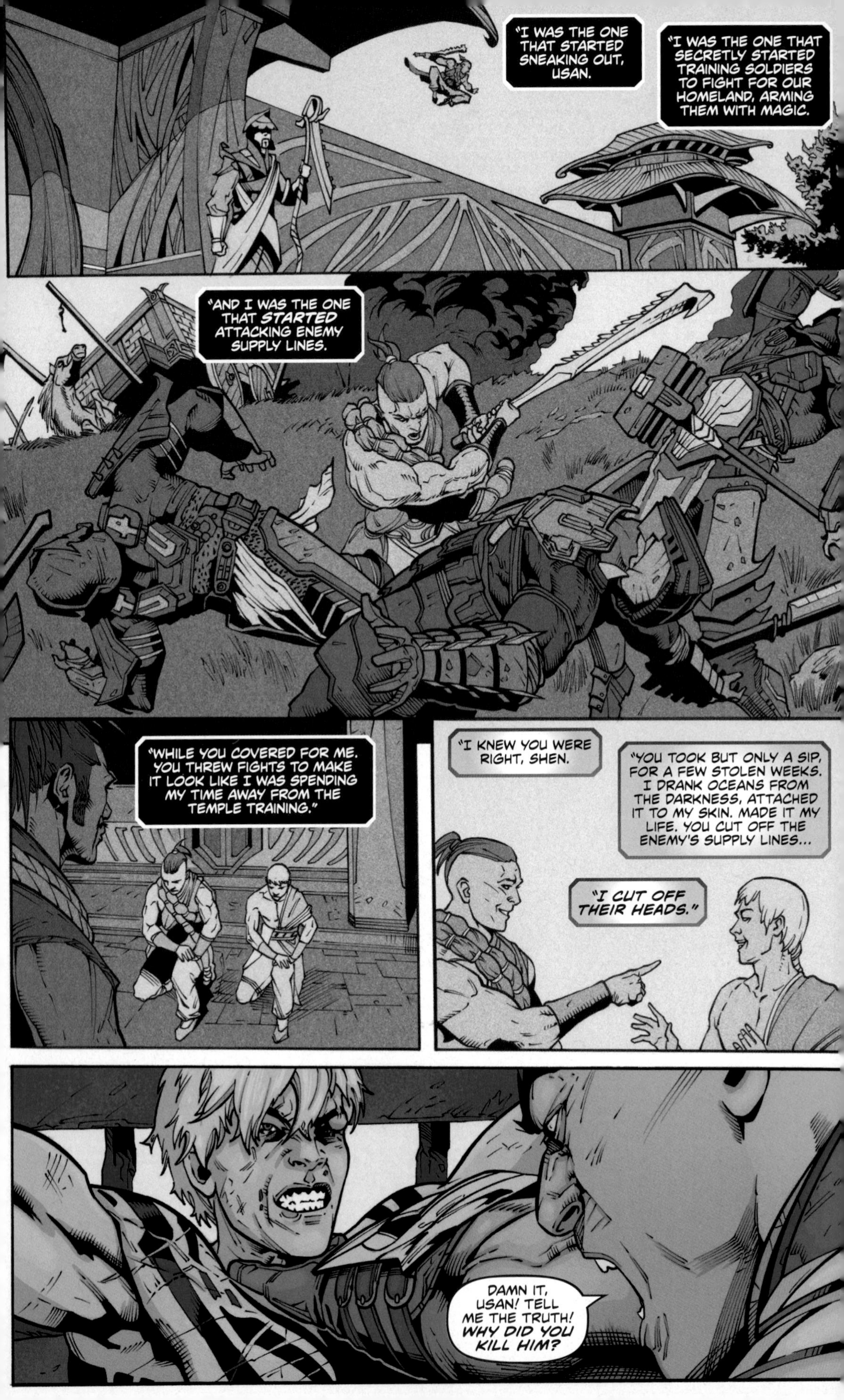
"I WAS THE ONE THAT STARTED SNEAKING OUT, USAN.
"I WAS THE ONE THAT SECRETLY STARTED TRAINING SOLDIERS TO FIGHT FOR OUR HOMELAND, ARMING THEM WITH MAGIC.
"AND I WAS THE ONE THAT *STARTED* ATTACKING ENEMY SUPPLY LINES.
"WHILE YOU COVERED FOR ME. YOU THREW FIGHTS TO MAKE IT LOOK LIKE I WAS SPENDING MY TIME AWAY FROM THE TEMPLE TRAINING."
"I KNEW YOU WERE RIGHT, SHEN.
"YOU TOOK BUT ONLY A SIP, FOR A FEW STOLEN WEEKS. I DRANK OCEANS FROM THE DARKNESS, ATTACHED IT TO MY SKIN. MADE IT MY LIFE. YOU CUT OFF THE ENEMY'S SUPPLY LINES...
"*I CUT OFF THEIR HEADS.*"
DAMN IT, USAN! TELL ME THE TRUTH! *WHY DID YOU KILL HIM?*

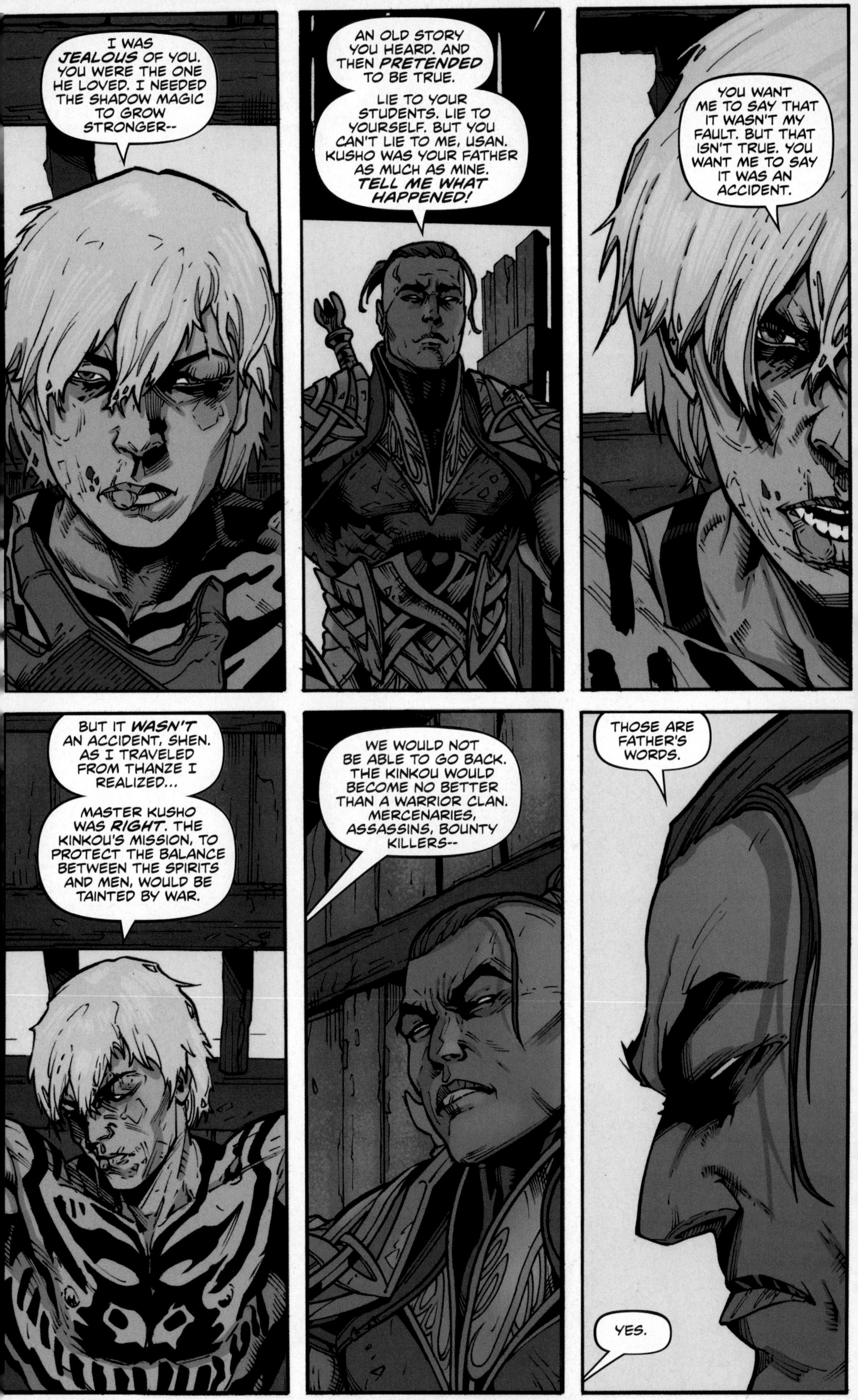
I WAS *JEALOUS* OF YOU. YOU WERE THE ONE HE LOVED. I NEEDED THE SHADOW MAGIC TO GROW STRONGER--
AN OLD STORY YOU HEARD. AND THEN *PRETENDED* TO BE TRUE.
LIE TO YOUR STUDENTS. LIE TO YOURSELF. BUT YOU CAN'T LIE TO ME, USAN. KUSHO WAS YOUR FATHER AS MUCH AS MINE. *TELL ME WHAT HAPPENED!*
YOU WANT ME TO SAY THAT IT WASN'T MY FAULT. BUT THAT ISN'T TRUE. YOU WANT ME TO SAY IT WAS AN ACCIDENT.
BUT IT *WASN'T* AN ACCIDENT, SHEN. AS I TRAVELED FROM THANZE I REALIZED...
MASTER KUSHO WAS *RIGHT*. THE KINKOU'S MISSION, TO PROTECT THE BALANCE BETWEEN THE SPIRITS AND MEN, WOULD BE TAINTED BY WAR.
WE WOULD NOT BE ABLE TO GO BACK. THE KINKOU WOULD BECOME NO BETTER THAN A WARRIOR CLAN. MERCENARIES, ASSASSINS, BOUNTY KILLERS--
THOSE ARE FATHER'S WORDS.
YES.

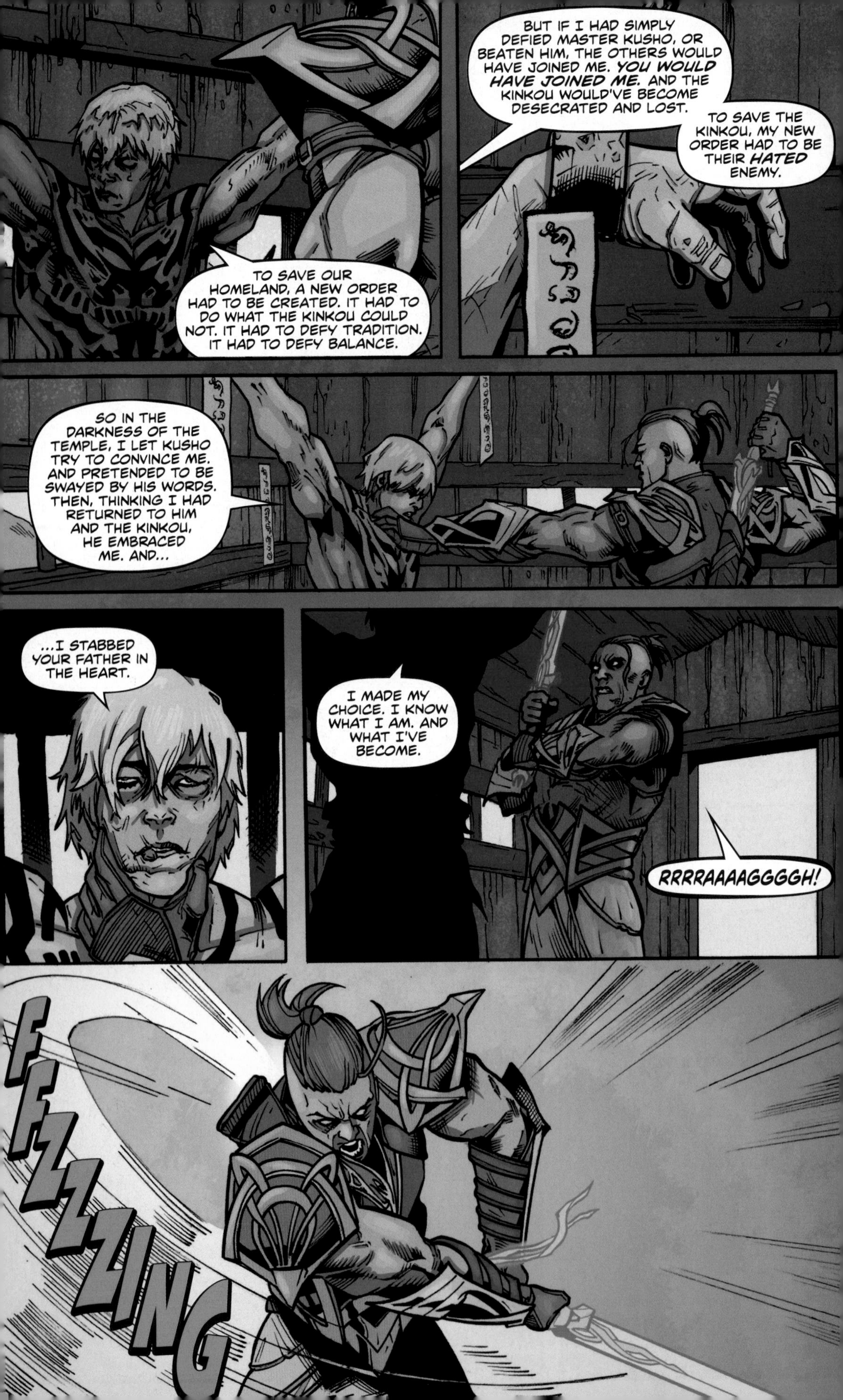
TO SAVE OUR HOMELAND, A NEW ORDER HAD TO BE CREATED. IT HAD TO DO WHAT THE KINKOU COULD NOT. IT HAD TO DEFY TRADITION. IT HAD TO DEFY BALANCE.
BUT IF I HAD SIMPLY DEFIED MASTER KUSHO, OR BEATEN HIM, THE OTHERS WOULD HAVE JOINED ME. ***YOU WOULD HAVE JOINED ME.*** AND THE KINKOU WOULD'VE BECOME DESECRATED AND LOST.
TO SAVE THE KINKOU, MY NEW ORDER HAD TO BE THEIR ***HATED*** ENEMY.
SO IN THE DARKNESS OF THE TEMPLE, I LET KUSHO TRY TO CONVINCE ME. AND PRETENDED TO BE SWAYED BY HIS WORDS. THEN, THINKING I HAD RETURNED TO HIM AND THE KINKOU, HE EMBRACED ME. AND...
...I STABBED YOUR FATHER IN THE HEART.
I MADE MY CHOICE. I KNOW WHAT I AM. AND WHAT I'VE BECOME.
RRRRAAAAGGGGH!
FFZZZING

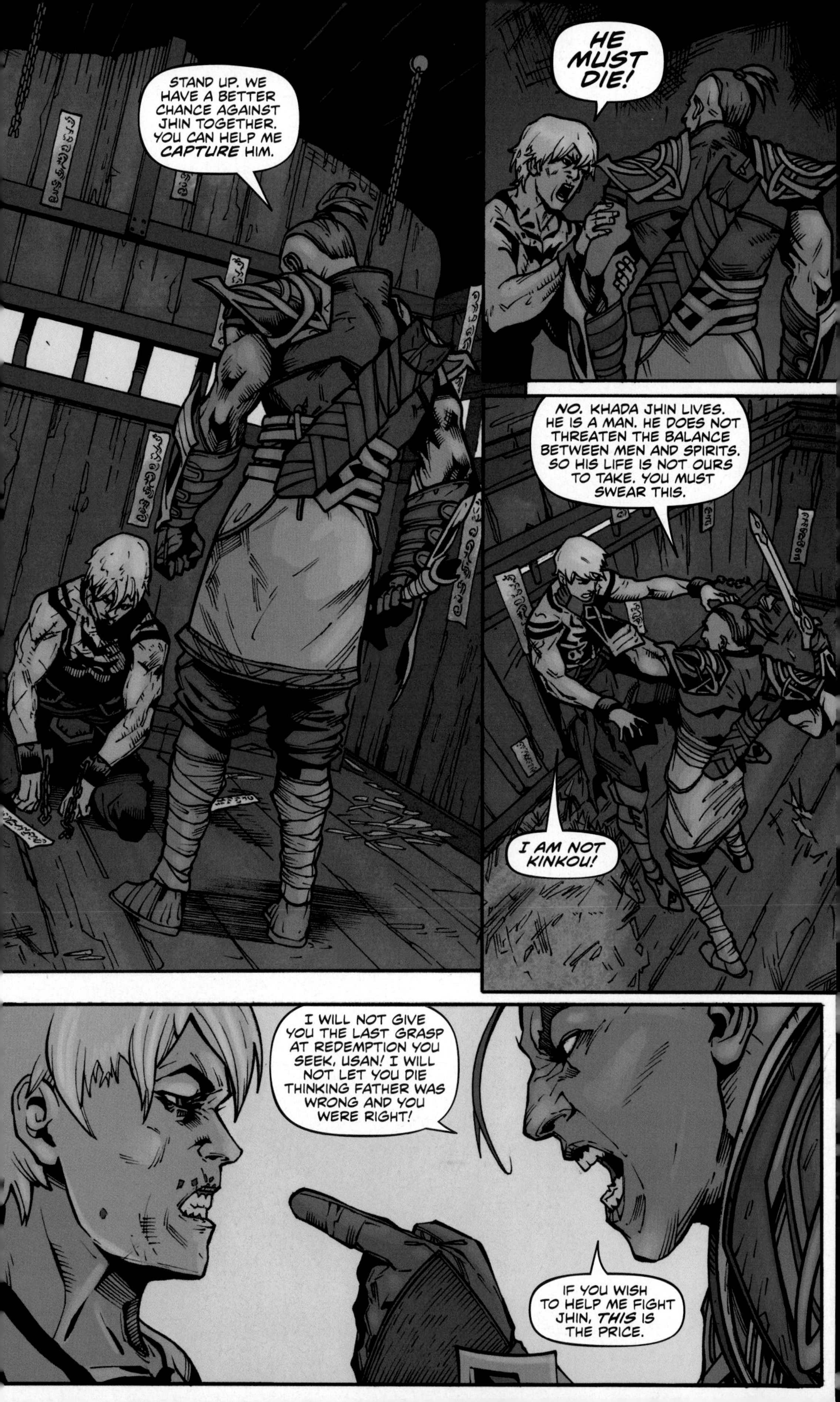
STAND UP. WE HAVE A BETTER CHANCE AGAINST JHIN TOGETHER. YOU CAN HELP ME *CAPTURE* HIM.
HE MUST DIE!
NO. KHADA JHIN LIVES. HE IS A MAN. HE DOES NOT THREATEN THE BALANCE BETWEEN MEN AND SPIRITS. SO HIS LIFE IS NOT OURS TO TAKE. YOU MUST SWEAR THIS.
I AM NOT KINKOU!
I WILL NOT GIVE YOU THE LAST GRASP AT REDEMPTION YOU SEEK, USAN! I WILL NOT LET YOU DIE THINKING FATHER WAS WRONG AND YOU WERE RIGHT!
IF YOU WISH TO HELP ME FIGHT JHIN, *THIS* IS THE PRICE.

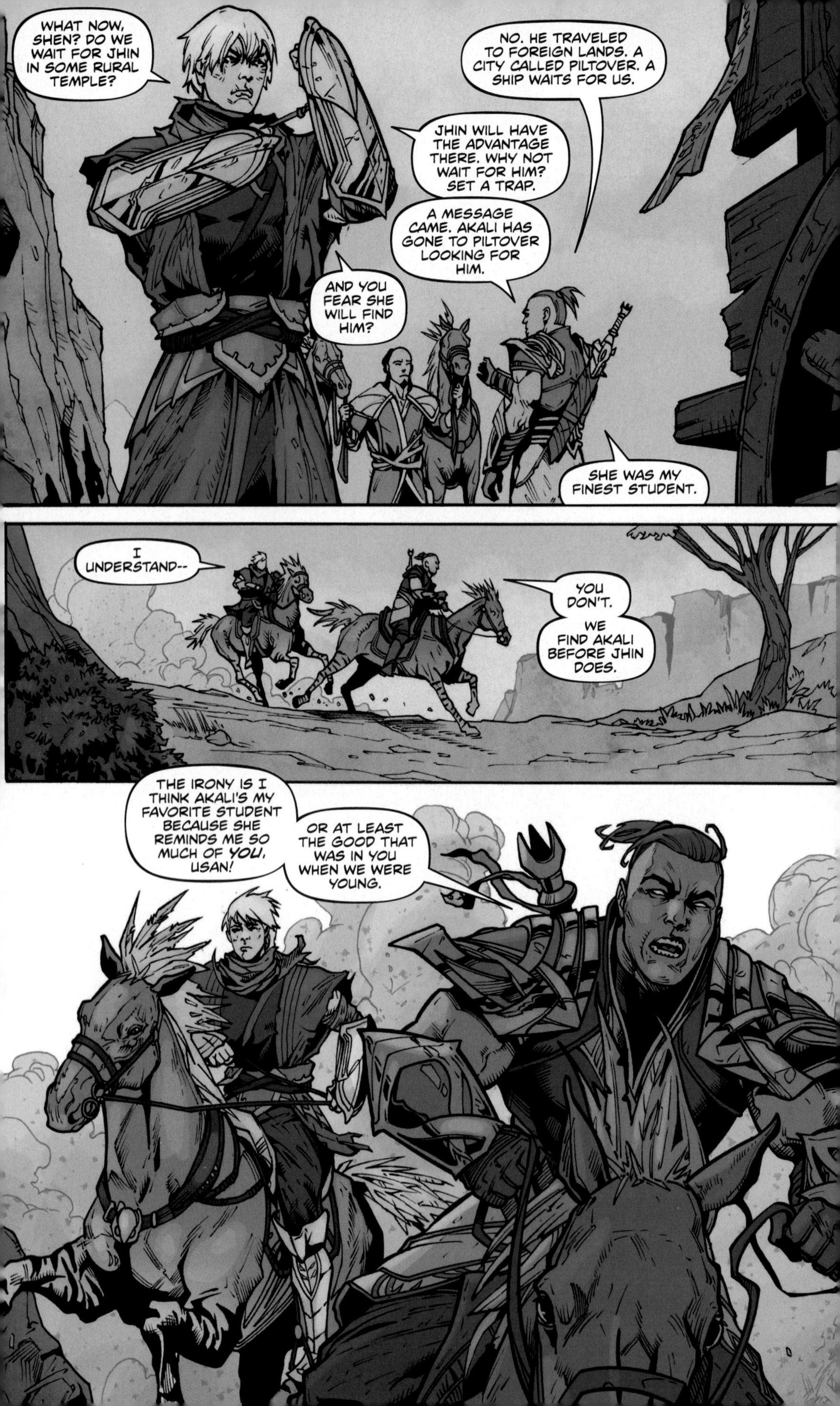
WHAT NOW, SHEN? DO WE WAIT FOR JHIN IN SOME RURAL TEMPLE?
NO. HE TRAVELED TO FOREIGN LANDS. A CITY CALLED PILTOVER. A SHIP WAITS FOR US.
JHIN WILL HAVE THE ADVANTAGE THERE. WHY NOT WAIT FOR HIM? SET A TRAP.
A MESSAGE CAME. AKALI HAS GONE TO PILTOVER LOOKING FOR HIM.
AND YOU FEAR SHE WILL FIND HIM?
SHE WAS MY FINEST STUDENT.
I UNDERSTAND--
YOU DON'T.
WE FIND AKALI BEFORE JHIN DOES.
THE IRONY IS I THINK AKALI'S MY FAVORITE STUDENT BECAUSE SHE REMINDS ME SO MUCH OF *YOU*, USAN!
OR AT LEAST THE GOOD THAT WAS IN YOU WHEN WE WERE YOUNG.

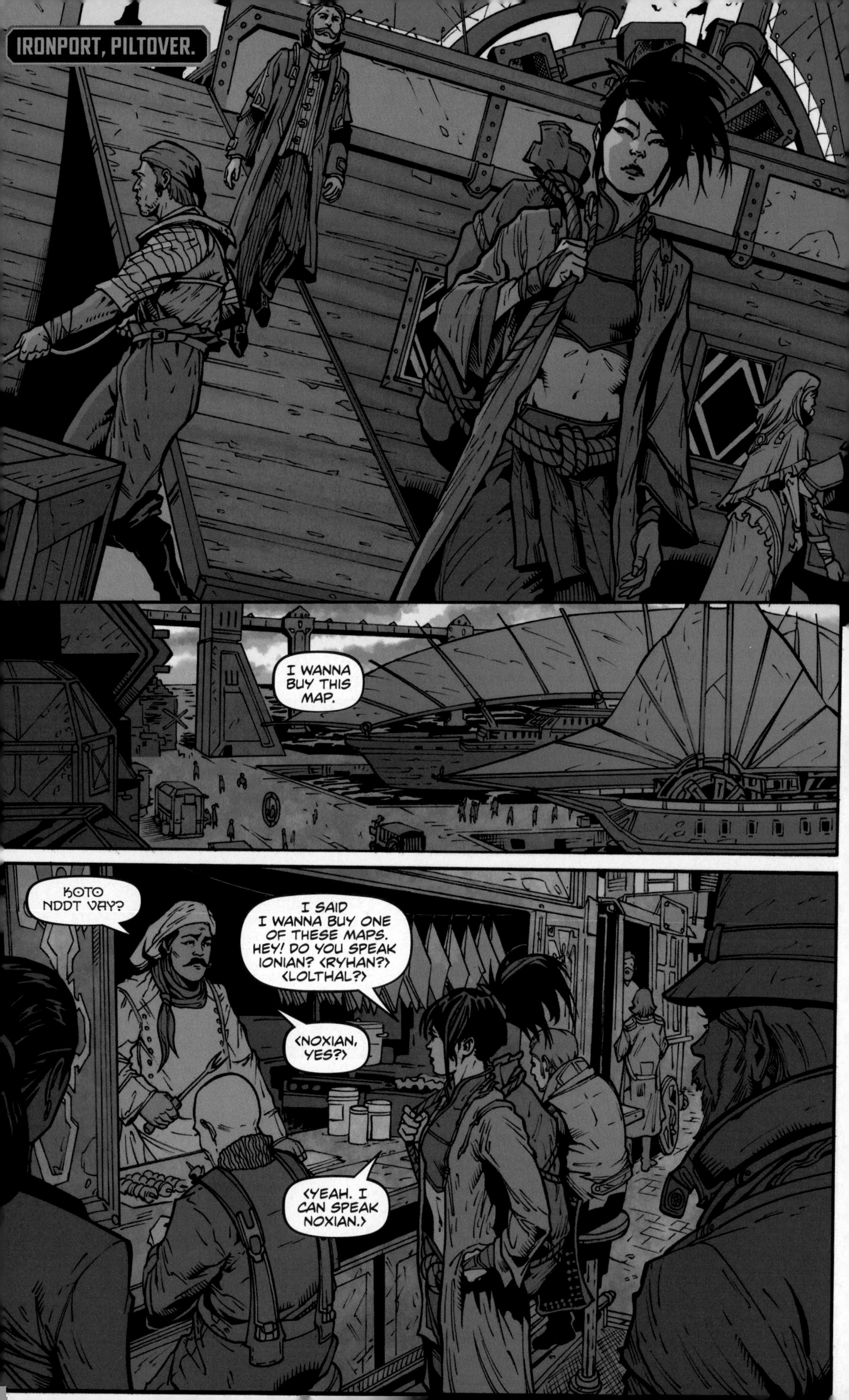
IRONPORT, PILTOVER.
I WANNA BUY THIS MAP.
KOTO NDDT VAY?
I SAID I WANNA BUY ONE OF THESE MAPS. HEY! DO YOU SPEAK IONIAN? <RYHAN?> <LOLTHAL?>
<NOXIAN, YES?>
<YEAH. I CAN SPEAK NOXIAN.>

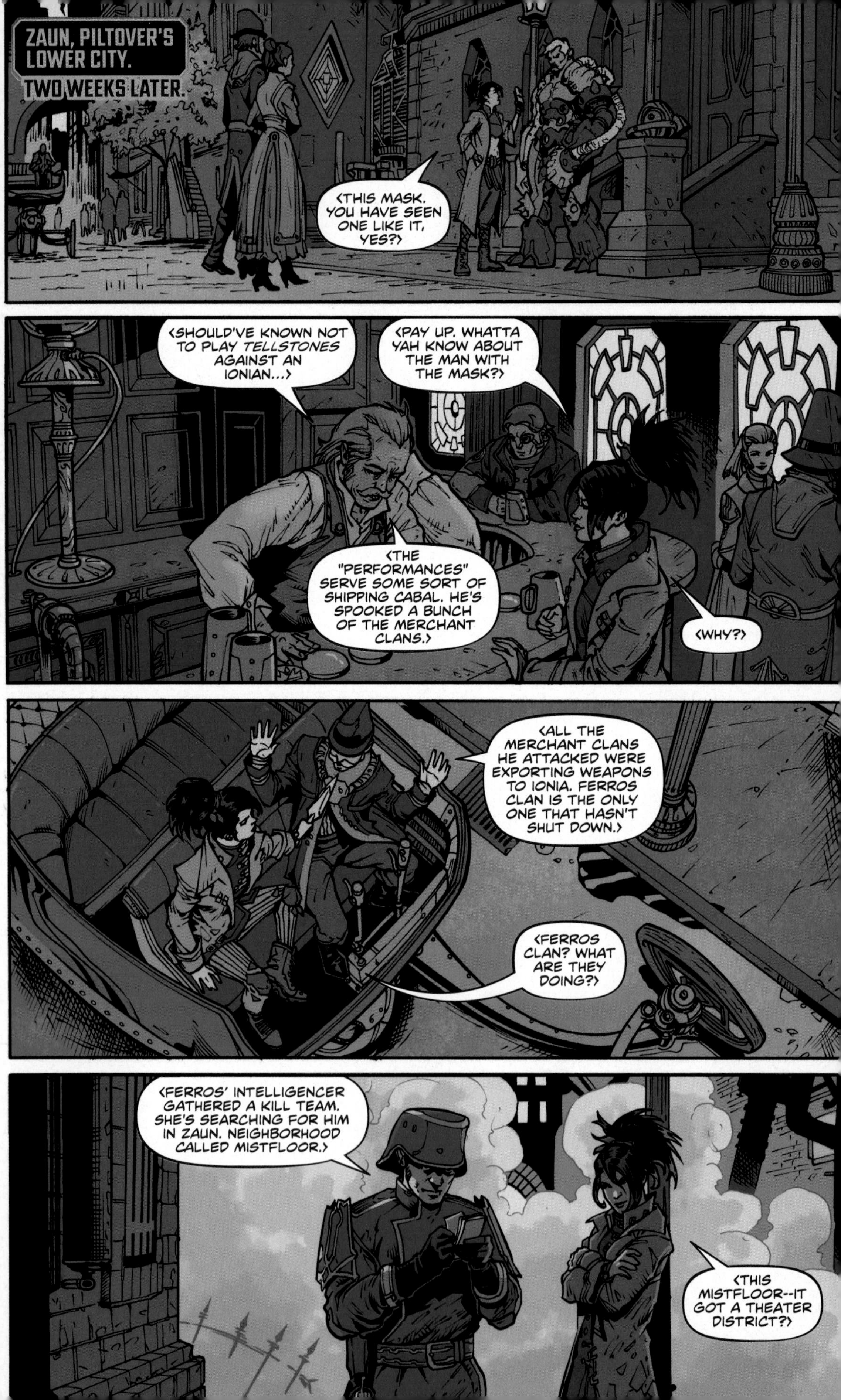
ZAUN, PILTOVER'S LOWER CITY.
TWO WEEKS LATER.
<THIS MASK. YOU HAVE SEEN ONE LIKE IT, YES?>
<SHOULD'VE KNOWN NOT TO PLAY *TELLSTONES* AGAINST AN IONIAN...>
<PAY UP. WHATTA YAH KNOW ABOUT THE MAN WITH THE MASK?>
<THE "PERFORMANCES" SERVE SOME SORT OF SHIPPING CABAL. HE'S SPOOKED A BUNCH OF THE MERCHANT CLANS.>
<WHY?>
<ALL THE MERCHANT CLANS HE ATTACKED WERE EXPORTING WEAPONS TO IONIA. FERROS CLAN IS THE ONLY ONE THAT HASN'T SHUT DOWN.>
<FERROS CLAN? WHAT ARE THEY DOING?>
<FERROS' INTELLIGENCER GATHERED A KILL TEAM. SHE'S SEARCHING FOR HIM IN ZAUN. NEIGHBORHOOD CALLED MISTFLOOR.>
<THIS MISTFLOOR--IT GOT A THEATER DISTRICT?>

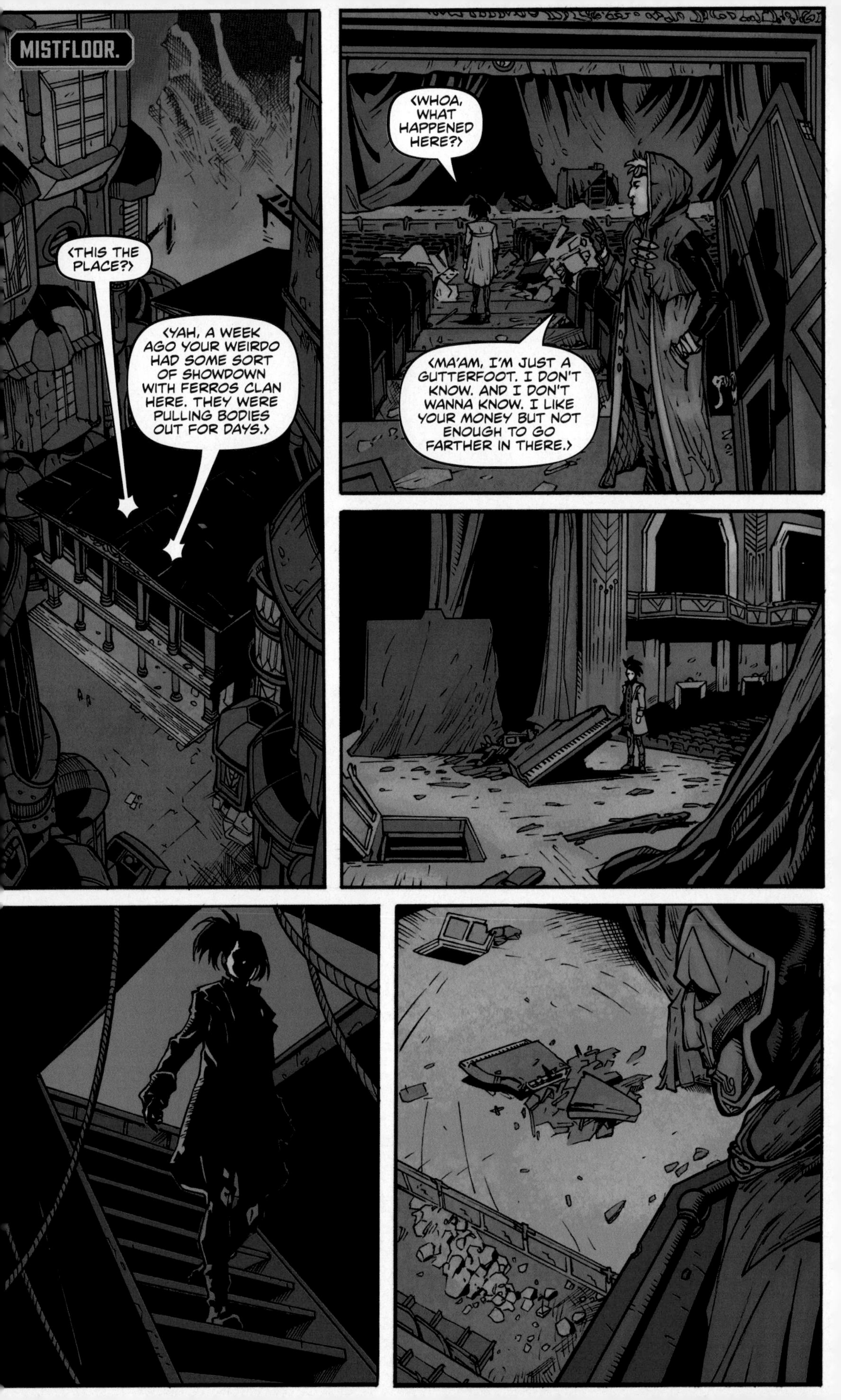
MISTFLOOR.
‹THIS THE PLACE?›
‹YAH, A WEEK AGO YOUR WEIRDO HAD SOME SORT OF SHOWDOWN WITH FERROS CLAN HERE. THEY WERE PULLING BODIES OUT FOR DAYS.›
‹WHOA, WHAT HAPPENED HERE?›
‹MA'AM, I'M JUST A GUTTERFOOT. I DON'T KNOW. AND I DON'T WANNA KNOW. I LIKE YOUR MONEY BUT NOT ENOUGH TO GO FARTHER IN THERE.›

WHAT'D HE SAY?

MY PILTOVERIAN'S RUSTY, BUT HE SAW HER ABOUT A MONTH AGO. SOUNDS LIKE SHE WAS GONNA START BY CHECKING THE THEATER DISTRICTS.

YOU HAVE CONTACTS YOU CAN TRUST HERE?

THAT I CAN *TRUST?*

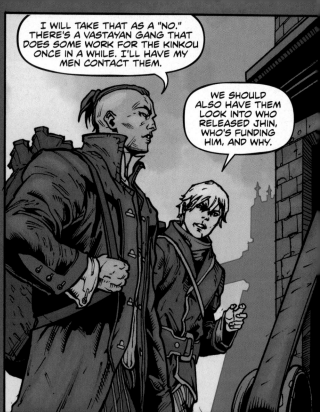

I WILL TAKE THAT AS A "NO." THERE'S A VASTAYAN GANG THAT DOES SOME WORK FOR THE KINKOU ONCE IN A WHILE. I'LL HAVE MY MEN CONTACT THEM.

WE SHOULD ALSO HAVE THEM LOOK INTO WHO RELEASED JHIN, WHO'S FUNDING HIM, AND WHY.

YOU'VE ASKED ME THAT QUESTION MANY TIMES. AS IF THAT WOULD REVEAL SOMETHING.

BUT IT'S *YOU* WHO SHOULD PONDER WHO LET JHIN OUT, NOT *ME.*

AS FAR AS I KNOW, ONLY FOUR PEOPLE IN THE WORLD KNEW WHERE KHADA JHIN WAS IMPRISONED: YEVNAI, YOU, ME, AND FATHER.

SO THE *REAL QUESTION* IS WHO YOU *TOLD,* ZED...

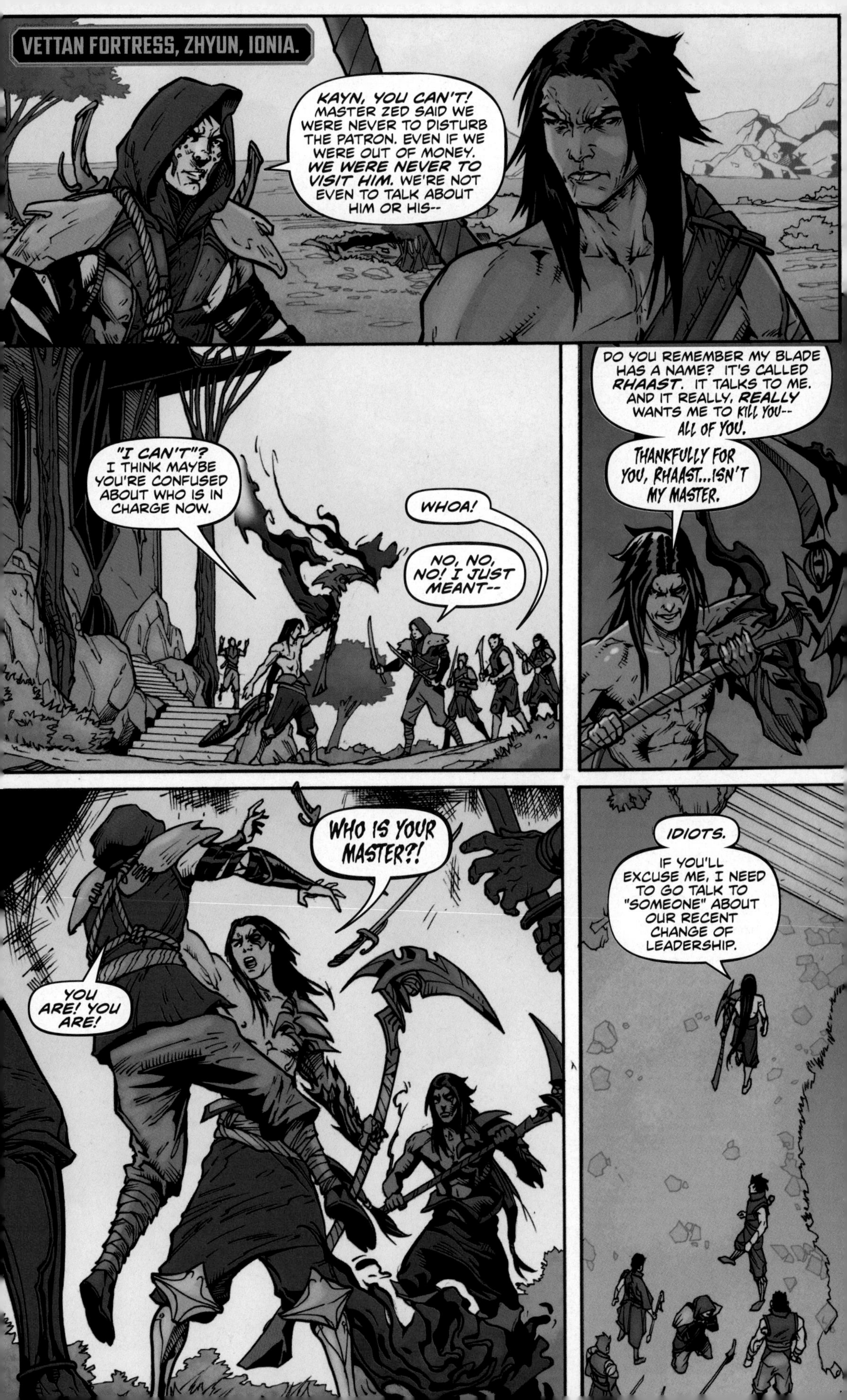
VETTAN FORTRESS, ZHYUN, IONIA.
KAYN, YOU CAN'T! MASTER ZED SAID WE WERE NEVER TO DISTURB THE PATRON. EVEN IF WE WERE OUT OF MONEY. WE WERE NEVER TO VISIT HIM. WE'RE NOT EVEN TO TALK ABOUT HIM OR HIS--
"I CAN'T"? I THINK MAYBE YOU'RE CONFUSED ABOUT WHO IS IN CHARGE NOW.
WHOA!
NO, NO, NO! I JUST MEANT--
DO YOU REMEMBER MY BLADE HAS A NAME? IT'S CALLED RHAAST. IT TALKS TO ME. AND IT REALLY, REALLY WANTS ME TO KILL YOU-- ALL OF YOU.
THANKFULLY FOR YOU, RHAAST...ISN'T MY MASTER.
WHO IS YOUR MASTER?!
YOU ARE! YOU ARE!
IDIOTS.
IF YOU'LL EXCUSE ME, I NEED TO GO TALK TO "SOMEONE" ABOUT OUR RECENT CHANGE OF LEADERSHIP.

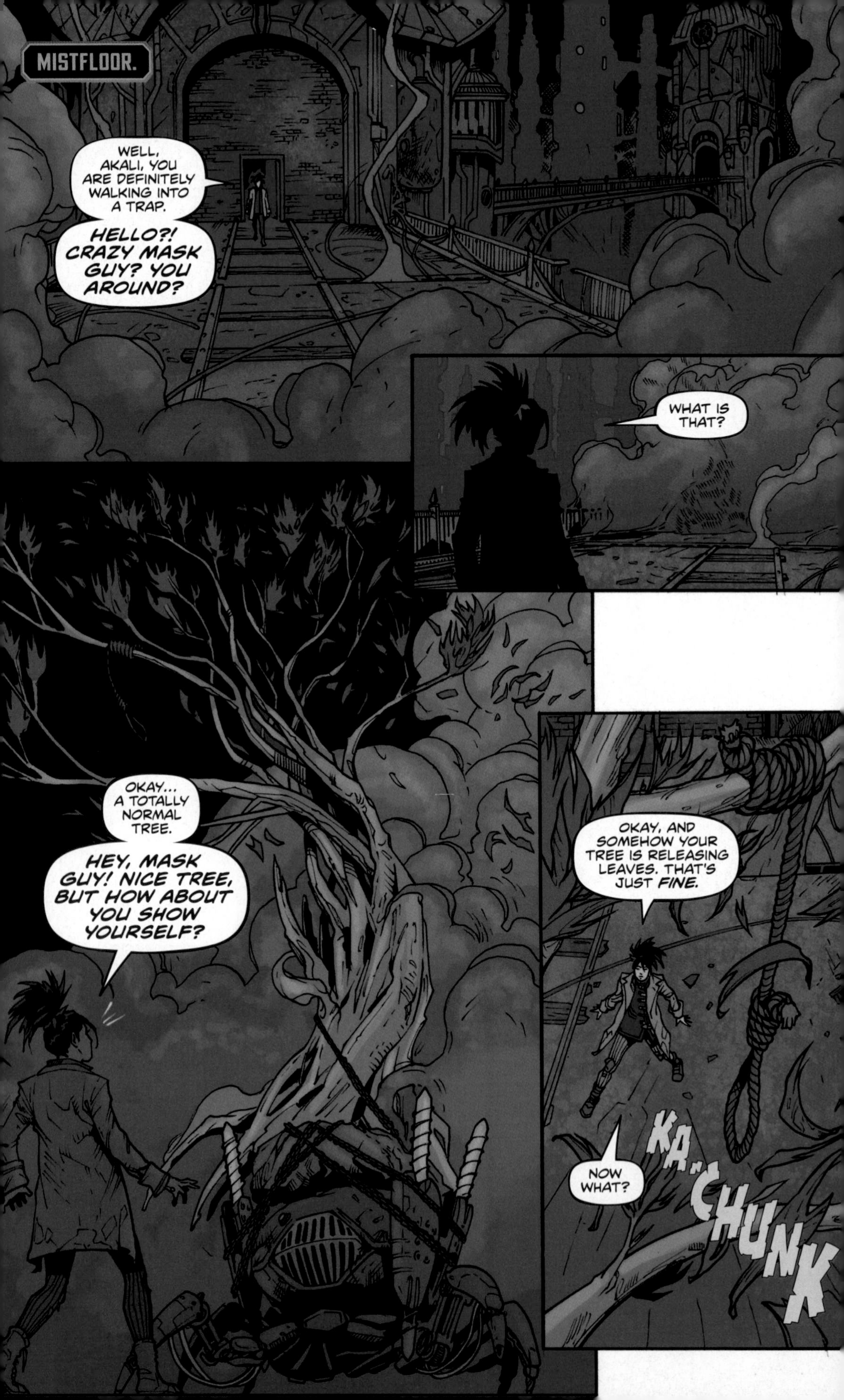
MISTFLOOR.
WELL, AKALI, YOU ARE DEFINITELY WALKING INTO A TRAP.
HELLO?! CRAZY MASK GUY? YOU AROUND?
WHAT IS THAT?
OKAY... A TOTALLY NORMAL TREE.
HEY, MASK GUY! NICE TREE, BUT HOW ABOUT YOU SHOW YOURSELF?
OKAY, AND SOMEHOW YOUR TREE IS RELEASING LEAVES. THAT'S JUST FINE.
NOW WHAT?
KA-CHUNK

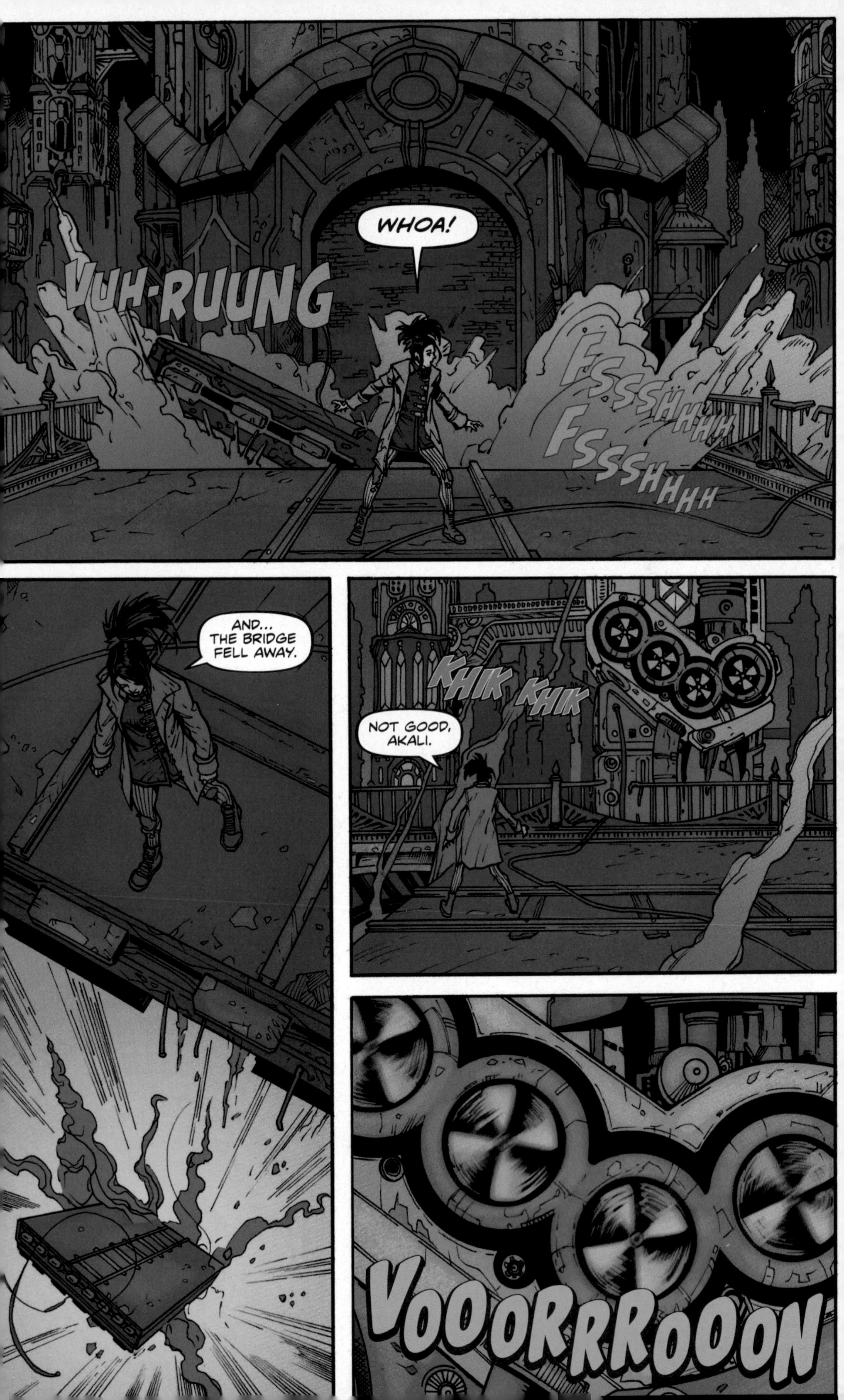
VUH-RUUNG
WHOA!
FSSSHHHHH
FSSSHHHHH
AND... THE BRIDGE FELL AWAY.
KHIK KHIK
NOT GOOD, AKALI.
VOOORRROOON

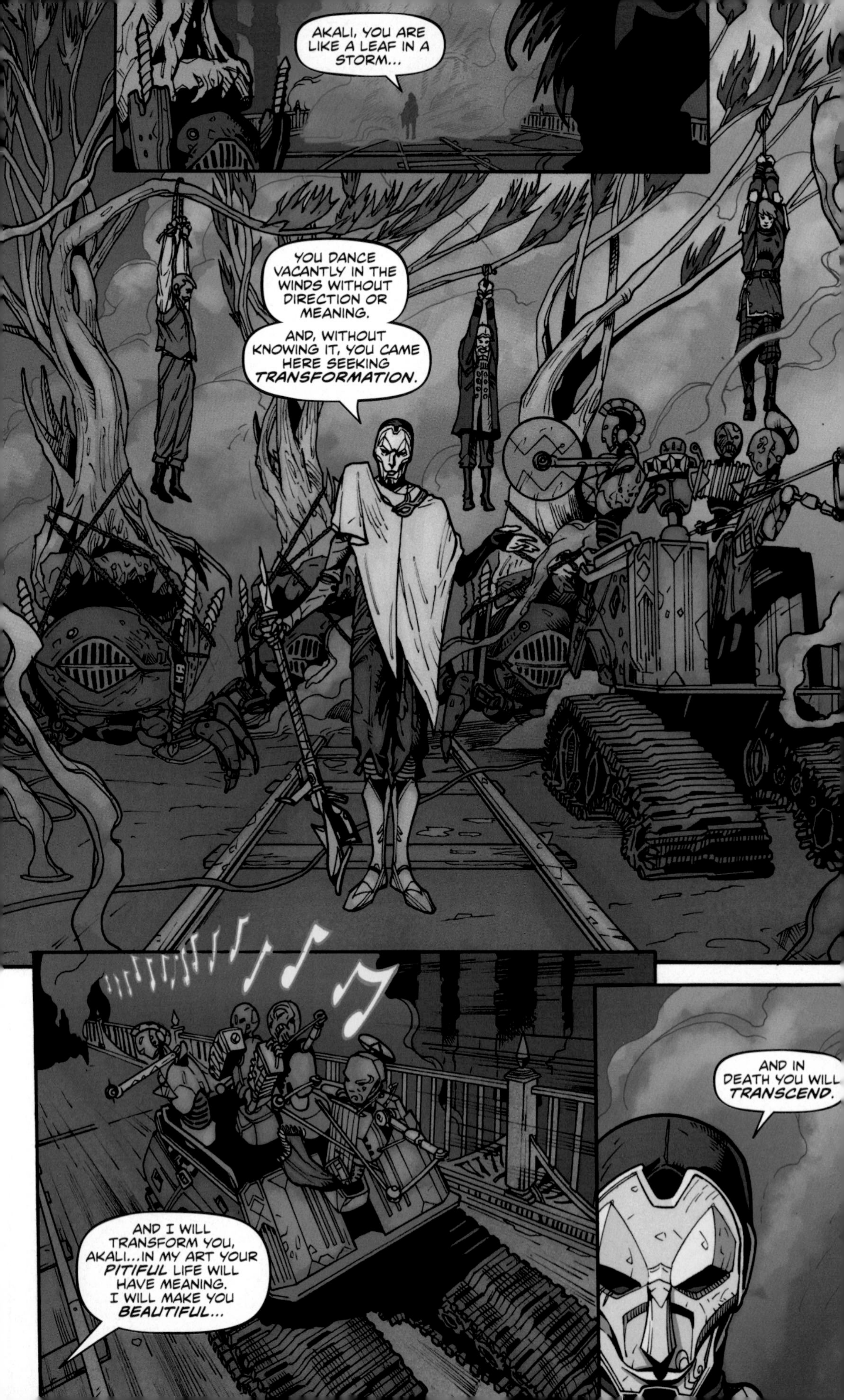
AKALI, YOU ARE LIKE A LEAF IN A STORM...
YOU DANCE VACANTLY IN THE WINDS WITHOUT DIRECTION OR MEANING.
AND, WITHOUT KNOWING IT, YOU CAME HERE SEEKING *TRANSFORMATION*.
AND I WILL TRANSFORM YOU, AKALI...IN MY ART YOUR *PITIFUL* LIFE WILL HAVE MEANING. I WILL MAKE YOU *BEAUTIFUL*...
AND IN DEATH YOU WILL *TRANSCEND*.

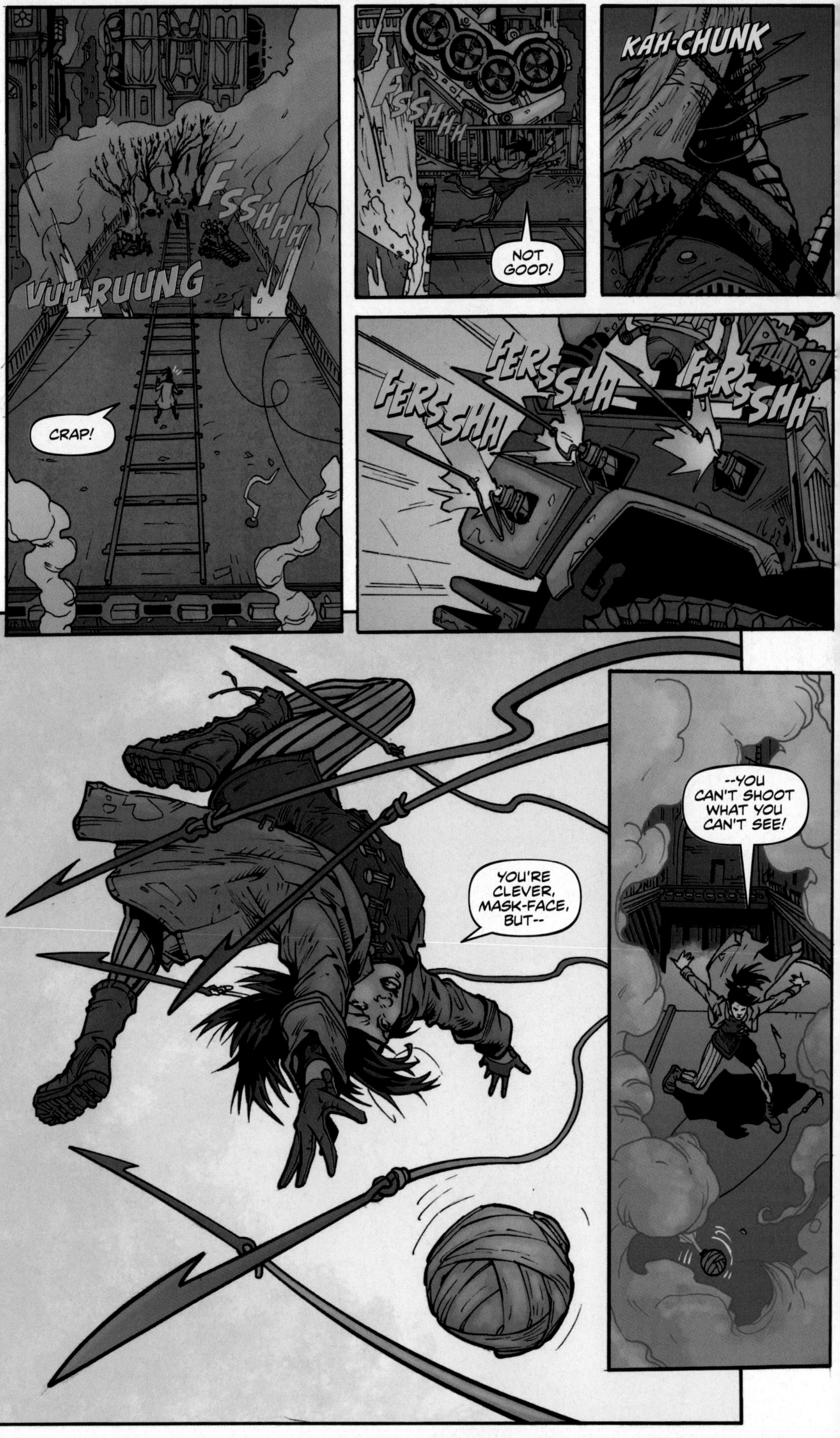
VUH-RUUNG
FSSHHH
CRAP!
FSSHHH
NOT GOOD!
KAH-CHUNK
FERSSHH
FERSSHH
FERSSHH
YOU'RE CLEVER, MASK-FACE, BUT--
--YOU CAN'T SHOOT WHAT YOU CAN'T SEE!

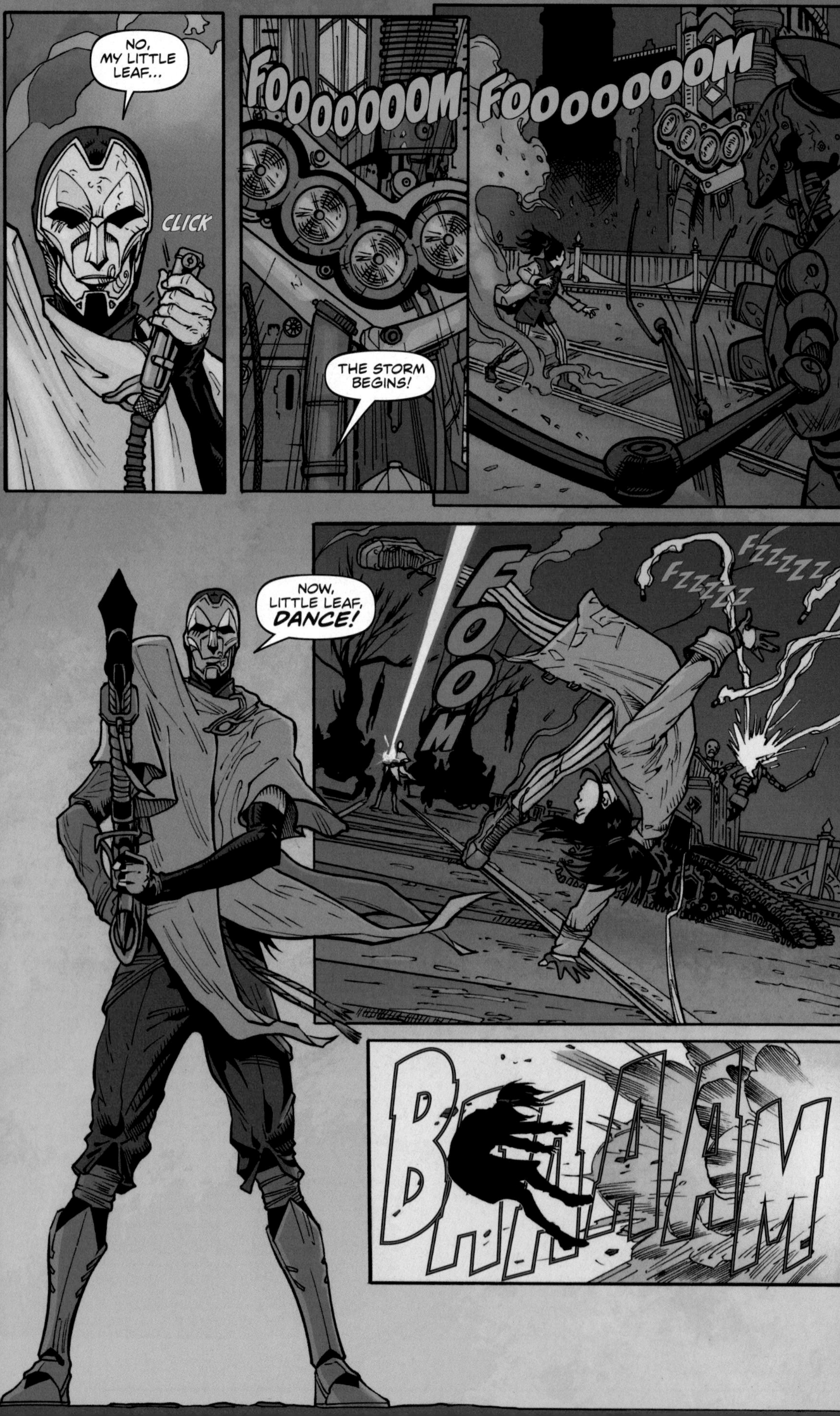
NO, MY LITTLE LEAF...
CLICK
FOOOOOOOM
THE STORM BEGINS!
FOOOOOOOOM
NOW, LITTLE LEAF, DANCE!
FOOOM
FZZZZZ
FZZZZZ
BRAAAM

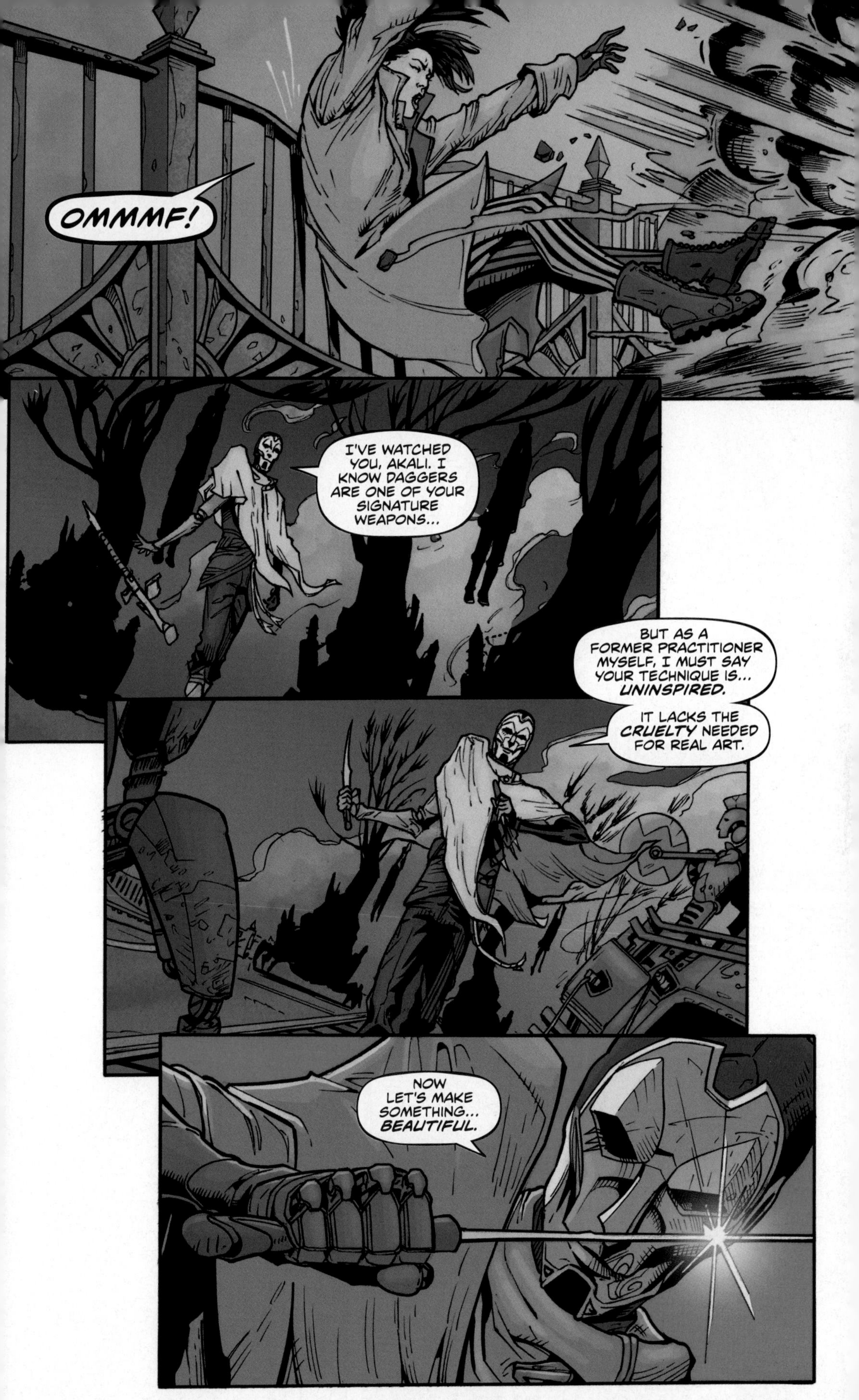
OMMMF!
I'VE WATCHED YOU, AKALI. I KNOW DAGGERS ARE ONE OF YOUR SIGNATURE WEAPONS...
BUT AS A FORMER PRACTITIONER MYSELF, I MUST SAY YOUR TECHNIQUE IS... UNINSPIRED.
IT LACKS THE CRUELTY NEEDED FOR REAL ART.
NOW LET'S MAKE SOMETHING... BEAUTIFUL.

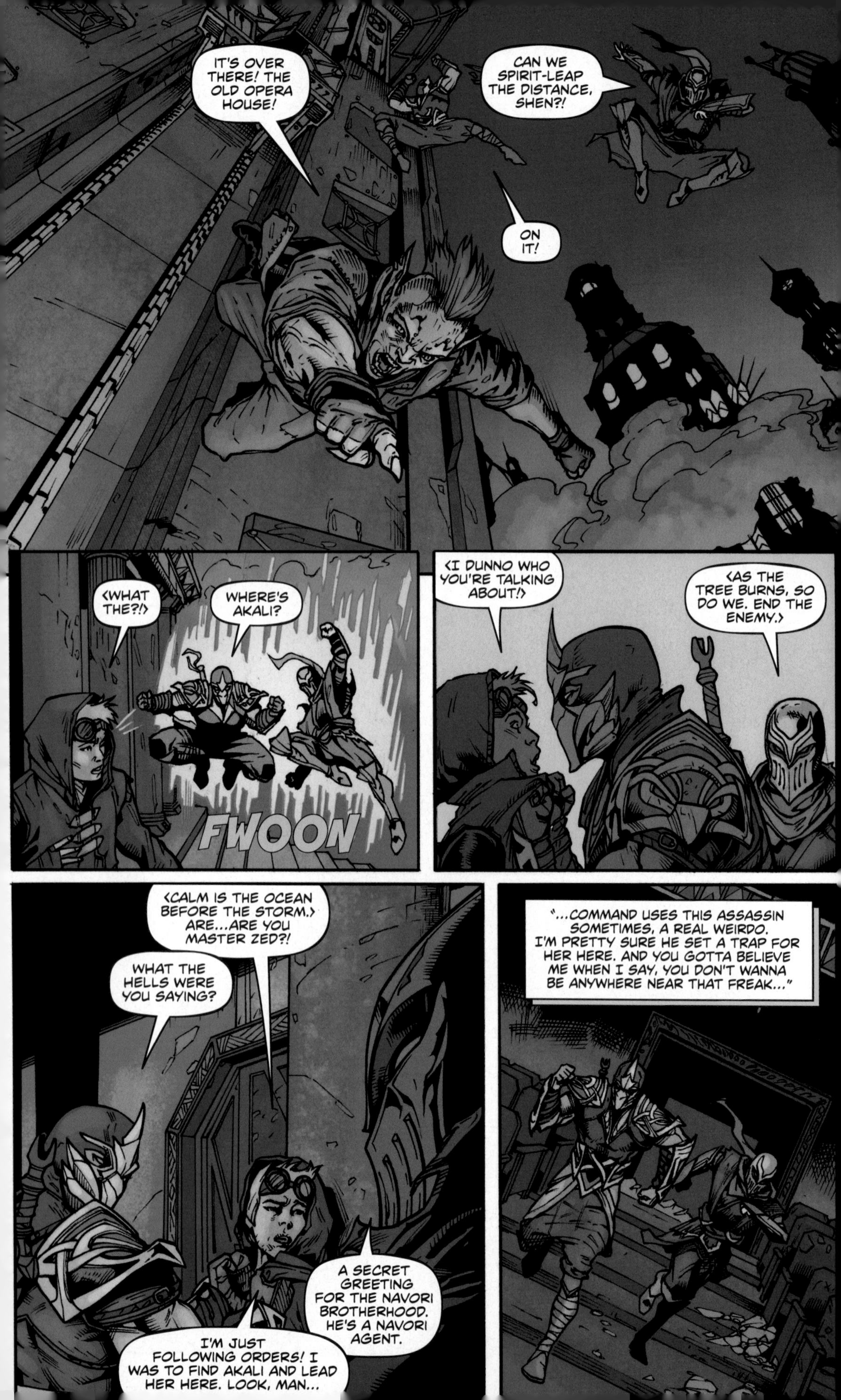
IT'S OVER THERE! THE OLD OPERA HOUSE!
CAN WE SPIRIT-LEAP THE DISTANCE, SHEN?!
ON IT!
‹WHAT THE?!›
WHERE'S AKALI?
FWOON
‹I DUNNO WHO YOU'RE TALKING ABOUT!›
‹AS THE TREE BURNS, SO DO WE. END THE ENEMY.›
‹CALM IS THE OCEAN BEFORE THE STORM.› ARE...ARE YOU MASTER ZED?!
WHAT THE HELLS WERE YOU SAYING?
A SECRET GREETING FOR THE NAVORI BROTHERHOOD. HE'S A NAVORI AGENT.
I'M JUST FOLLOWING ORDERS! I WAS TO FIND AKALI AND LEAD HER HERE. LOOK, MAN...
"...COMMAND USES THIS ASSASSIN SOMETIMES, A REAL WEIRDO. I'M PRETTY SURE HE SET A TRAP FOR HER HERE. AND YOU GOTTA BELIEVE ME WHEN I SAY, YOU DON'T WANNA BE ANYWHERE NEAR THAT FREAK..."

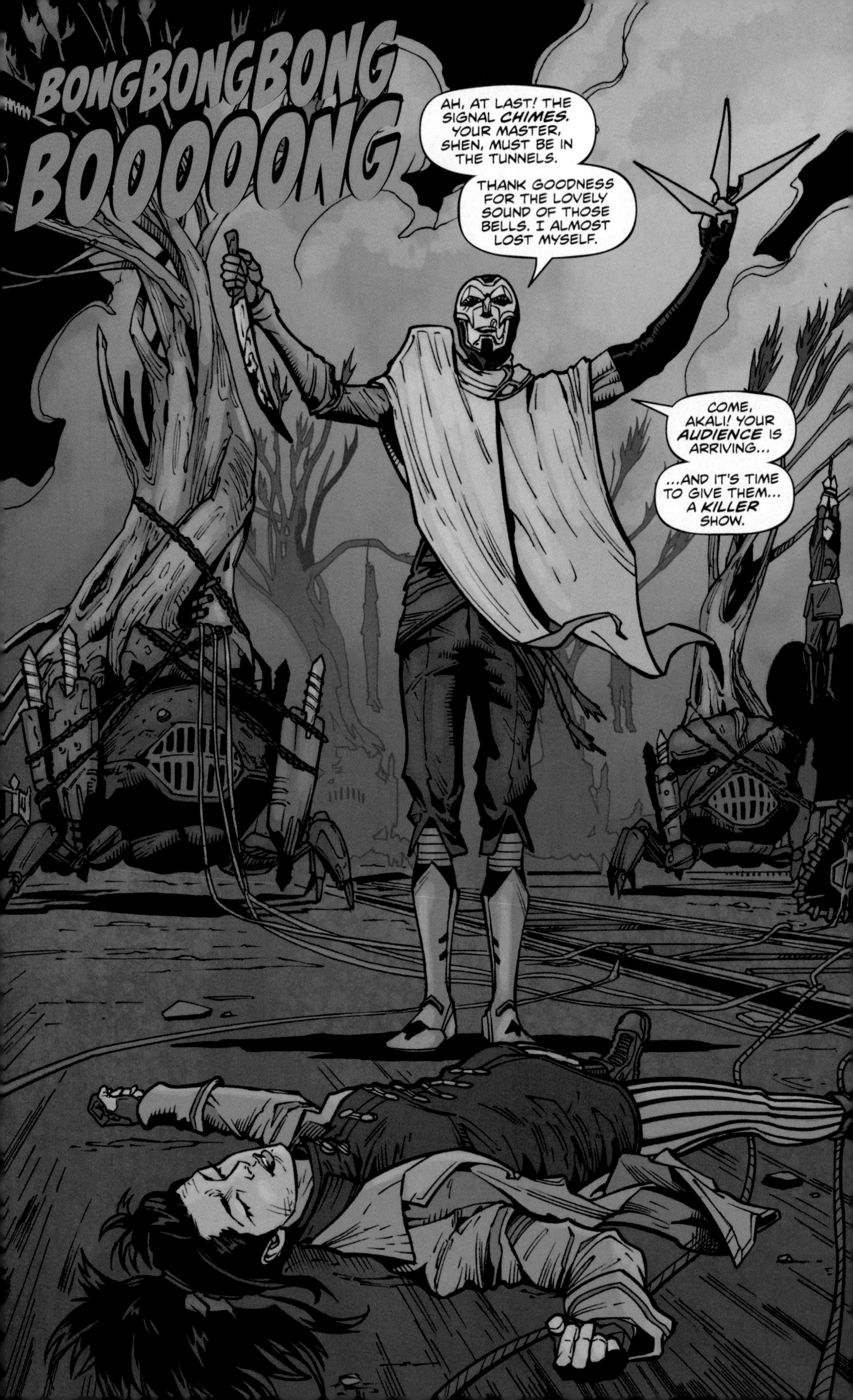
BONGBONGBONG
BOOOOONG
AH, AT LAST! THE SIGNAL CHIMES. YOUR MASTER, SHEN, MUST BE IN THE TUNNELS.
THANK GOODNESS FOR THE LOVELY SOUND OF THOSE BELLS. I ALMOST LOST MYSELF.
COME, AKALI! YOUR AUDIENCE IS ARRIVING...
...AND IT'S TIME TO GIVE THEM... A KILLER SHOW.

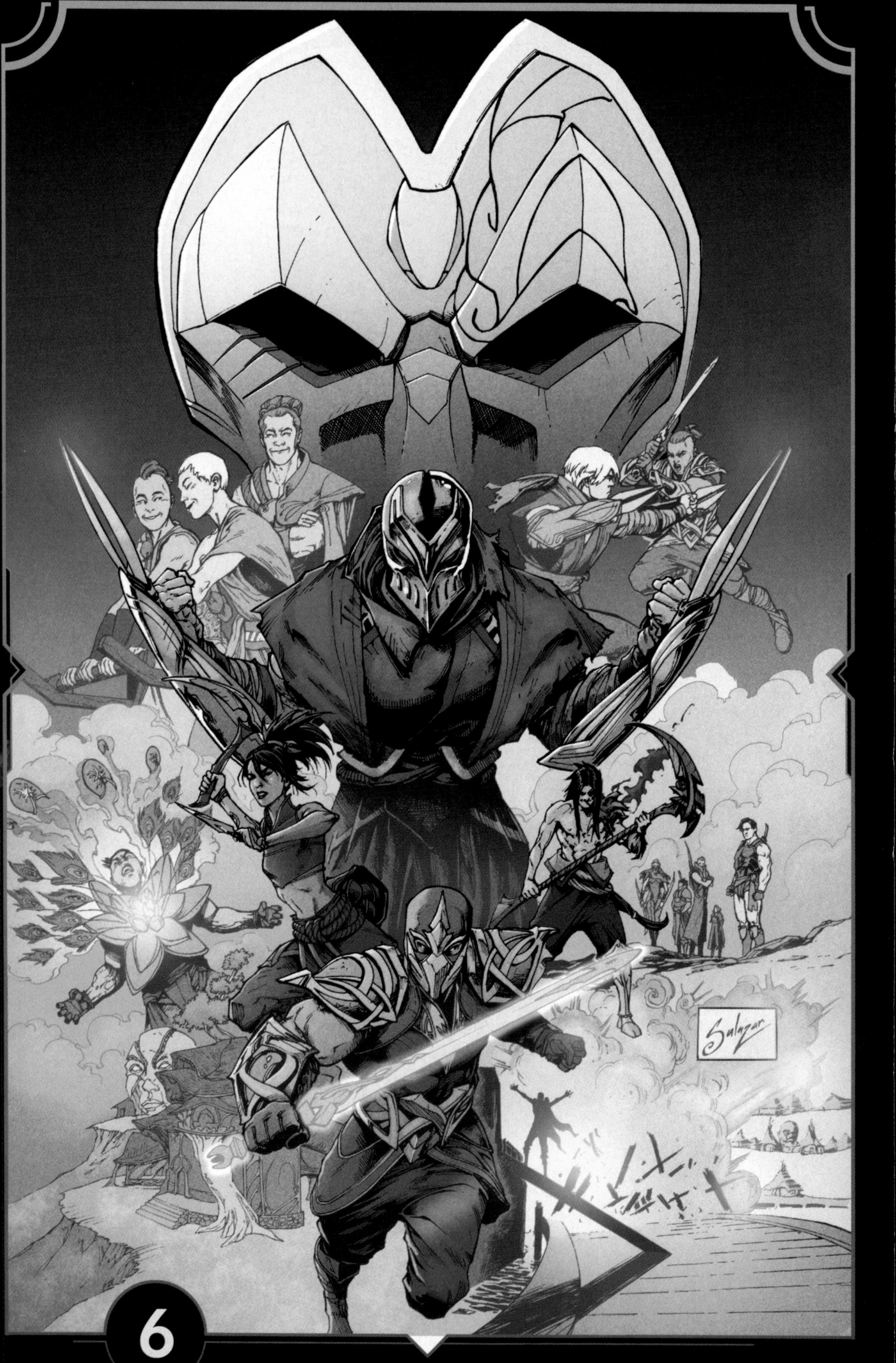
Salazar
6

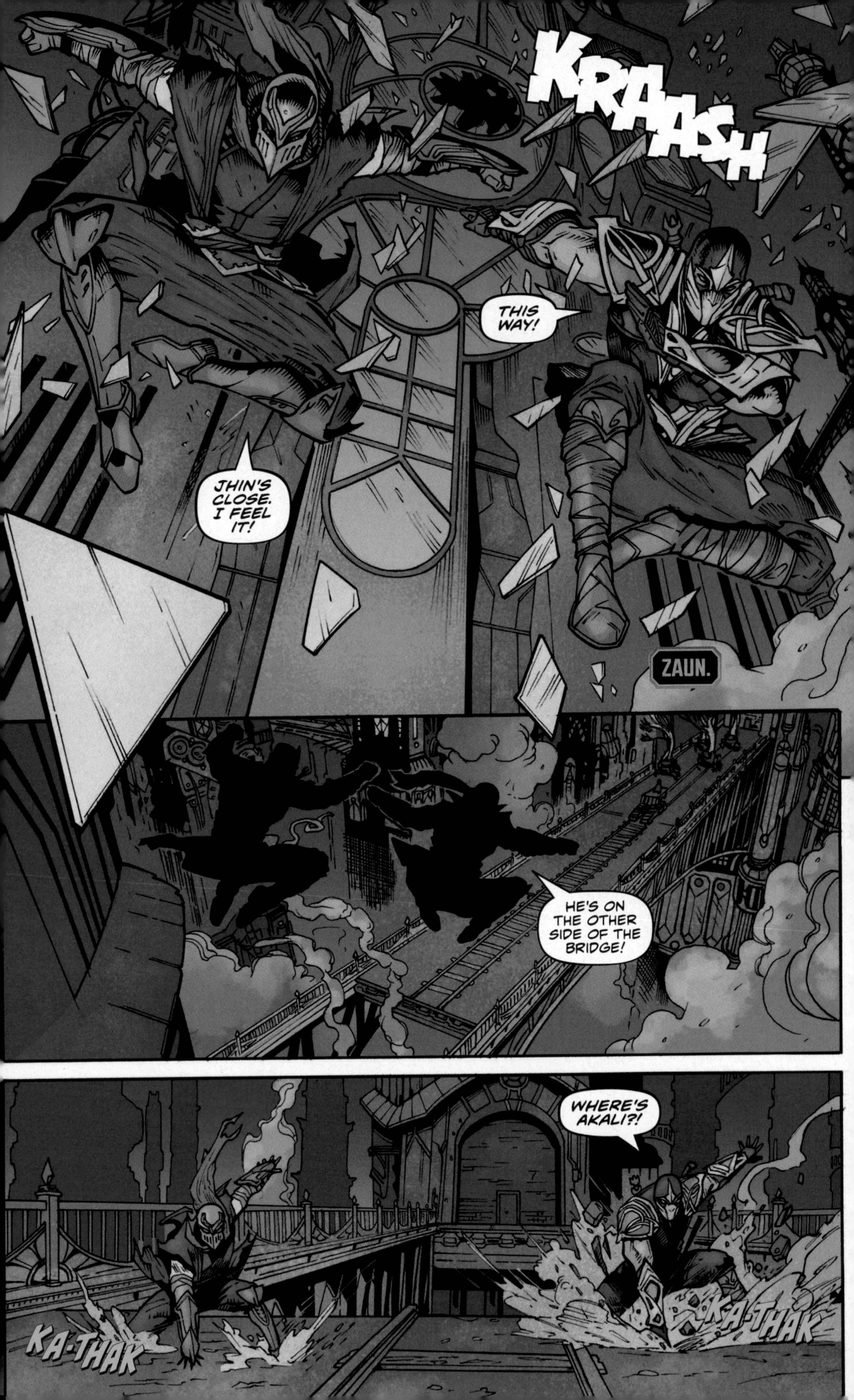
KRAAASH
THIS WAY!
JHIN'S CLOSE. I FEEL IT!
ZAUN.
HE'S ON THE OTHER SIDE OF THE BRIDGE!
WHERE'S AKALI?!
KA-THAK
KA-THAK

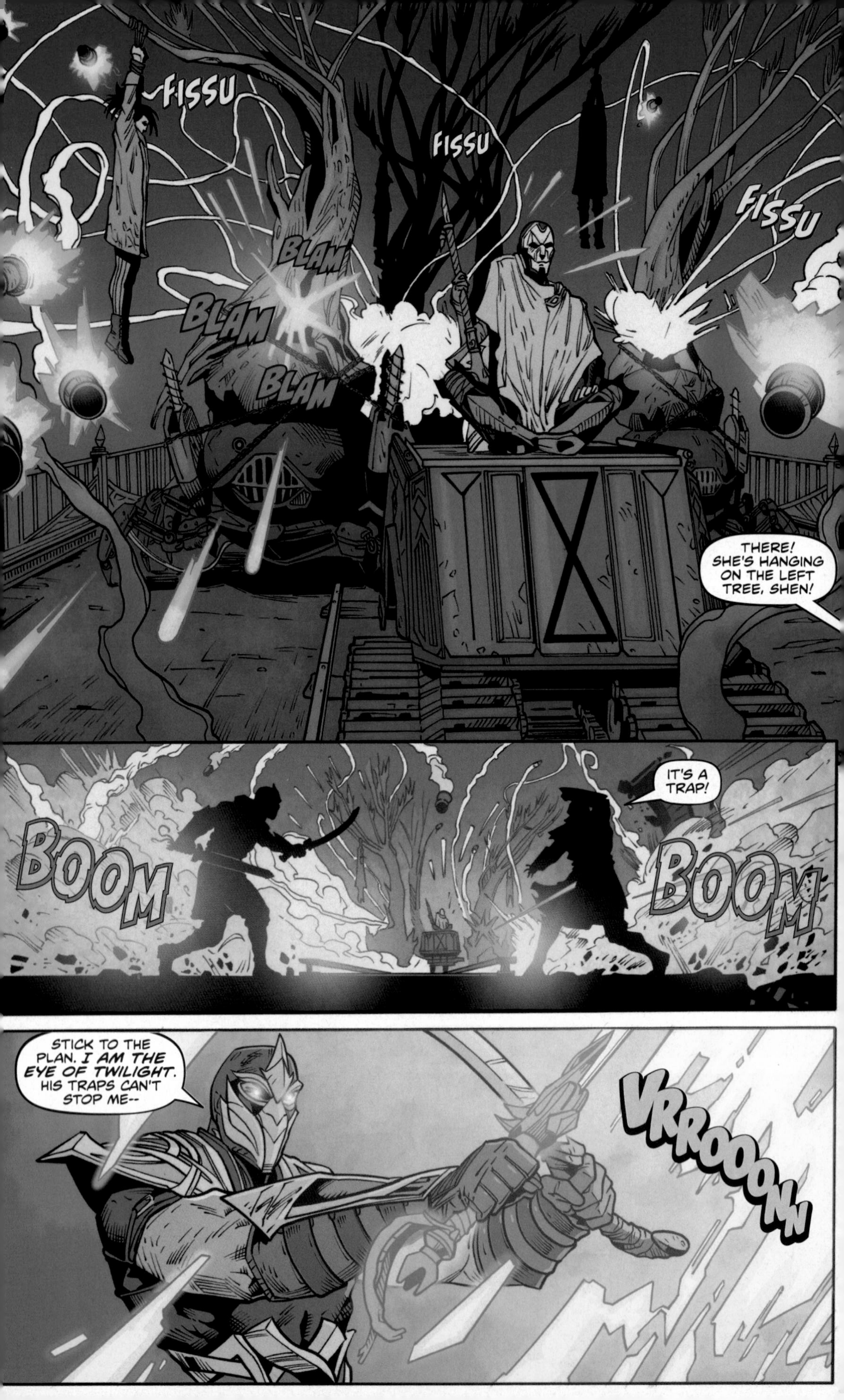
FISSU
FISSU
FISSU
BLAM
BLAM
BLAM
THERE! SHE'S HANGING ON THE LEFT TREE, SHEN!
IT'S A TRAP!
BOOM
BOOM
STICK TO THE PLAN. *I AM THE EYE OF TWILIGHT.* HIS TRAPS CAN'T STOP ME--
VRROOOONN

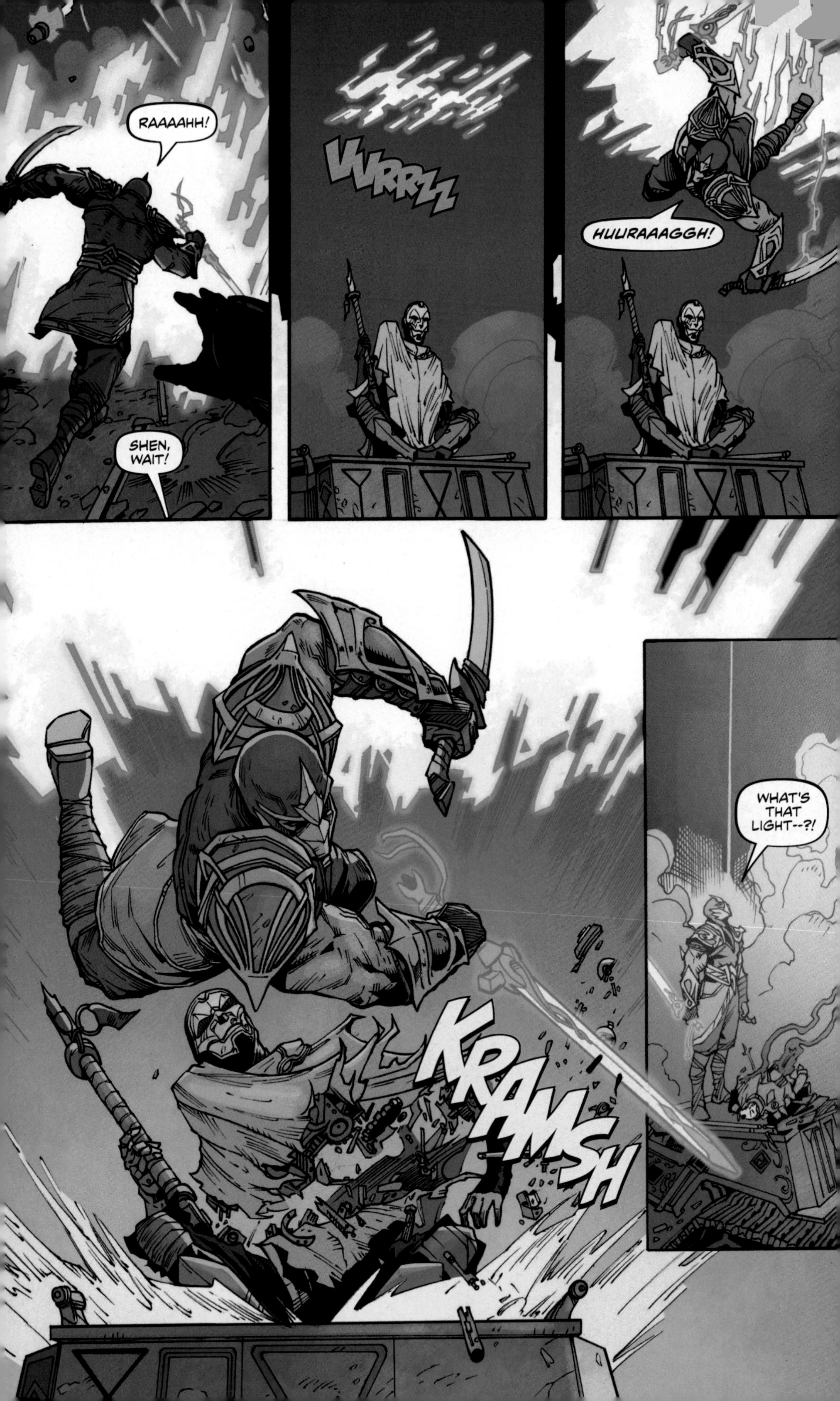
RAAAAHH!
SHEN, WAIT!
VVRRZZZ
HUURAAAGGH!
KRAMSH
WHAT'S THAT LIGHT--?!

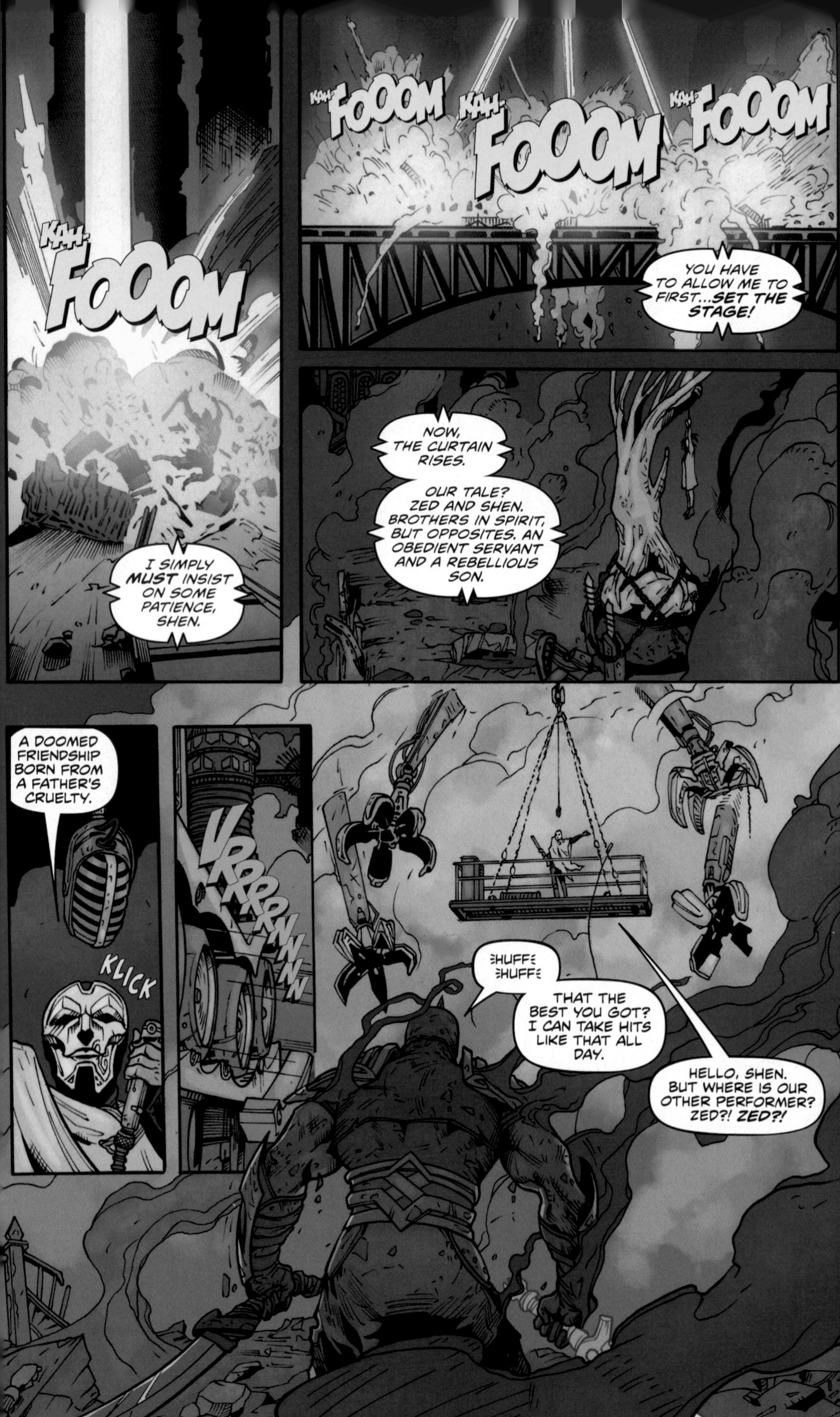
KAH-FOOOM
KAH-FOOOM
KAH-FOOOM
KAH-FOOOM
YOU HAVE TO ALLOW ME TO FIRST...SET THE STAGE!
I SIMPLY MUST INSIST ON SOME PATIENCE, SHEN.
NOW, THE CURTAIN RISES.
OUR TALE? ZED AND SHEN. BROTHERS IN SPIRIT, BUT OPPOSITES. AN OBEDIENT SERVANT AND A REBELLIOUS SON.
A DOOMED FRIENDSHIP BORN FROM A FATHER'S CRUELTY.
KLICK
VRRRRNNNN
HUFF HUFF
THAT THE BEST YOU GOT? I CAN TAKE HITS LIKE THAT ALL DAY.
HELLO, SHEN. BUT WHERE IS OUR OTHER PERFORMER? ZED?! ZED?!

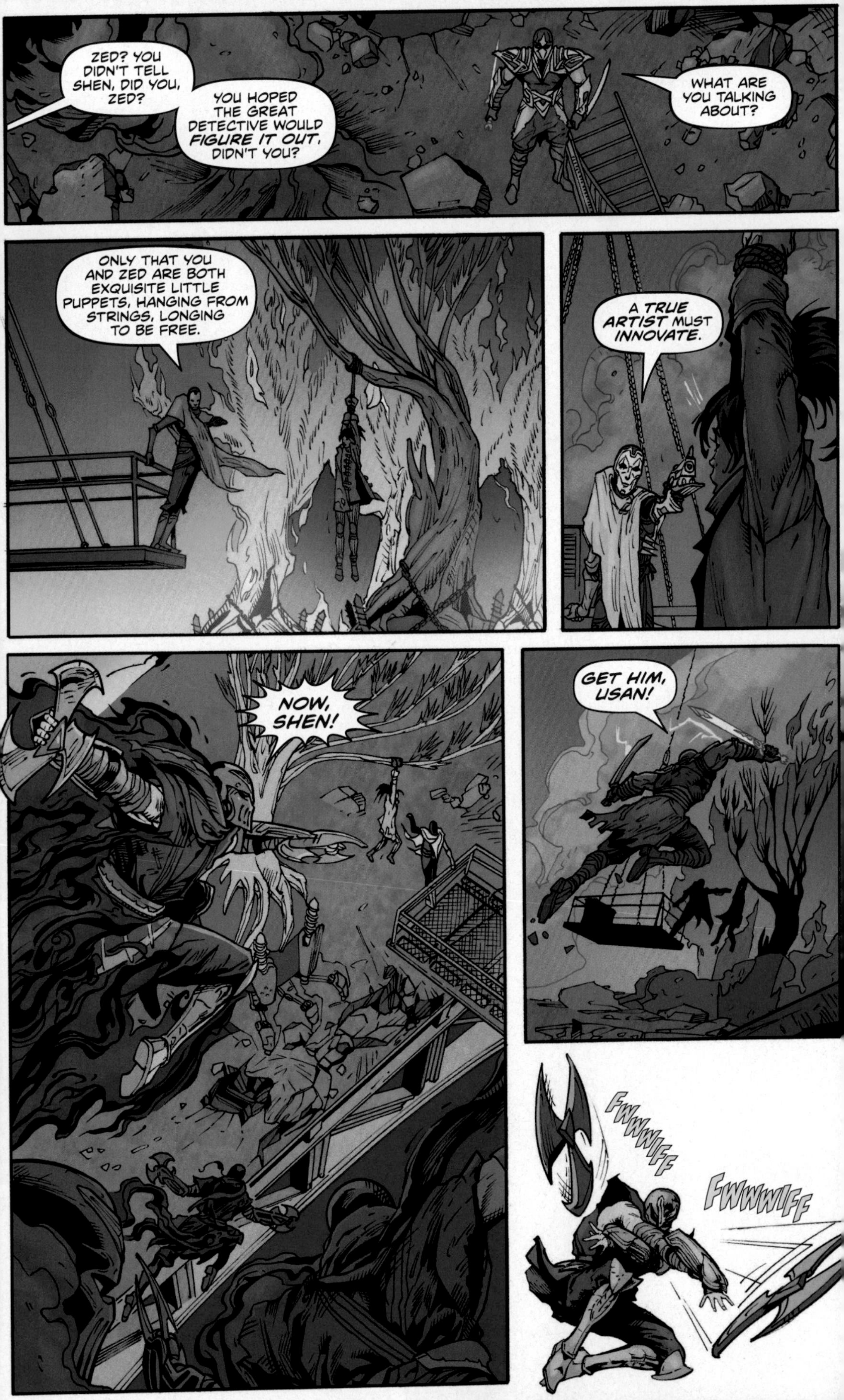
ZED? YOU DIDN'T TELL SHEN, DID YOU, ZED?
YOU HOPED THE GREAT DETECTIVE WOULD FIGURE IT OUT, DIDN'T YOU?
WHAT ARE YOU TALKING ABOUT?
ONLY THAT YOU AND ZED ARE BOTH EXQUISITE LITTLE PUPPETS, HANGING FROM STRINGS, LONGING TO BE FREE.
A TRUE ARTIST MUST INNOVATE.
NOW, SHEN!
GET HIM, USAN!
FWWWIFF
FWWWIFF

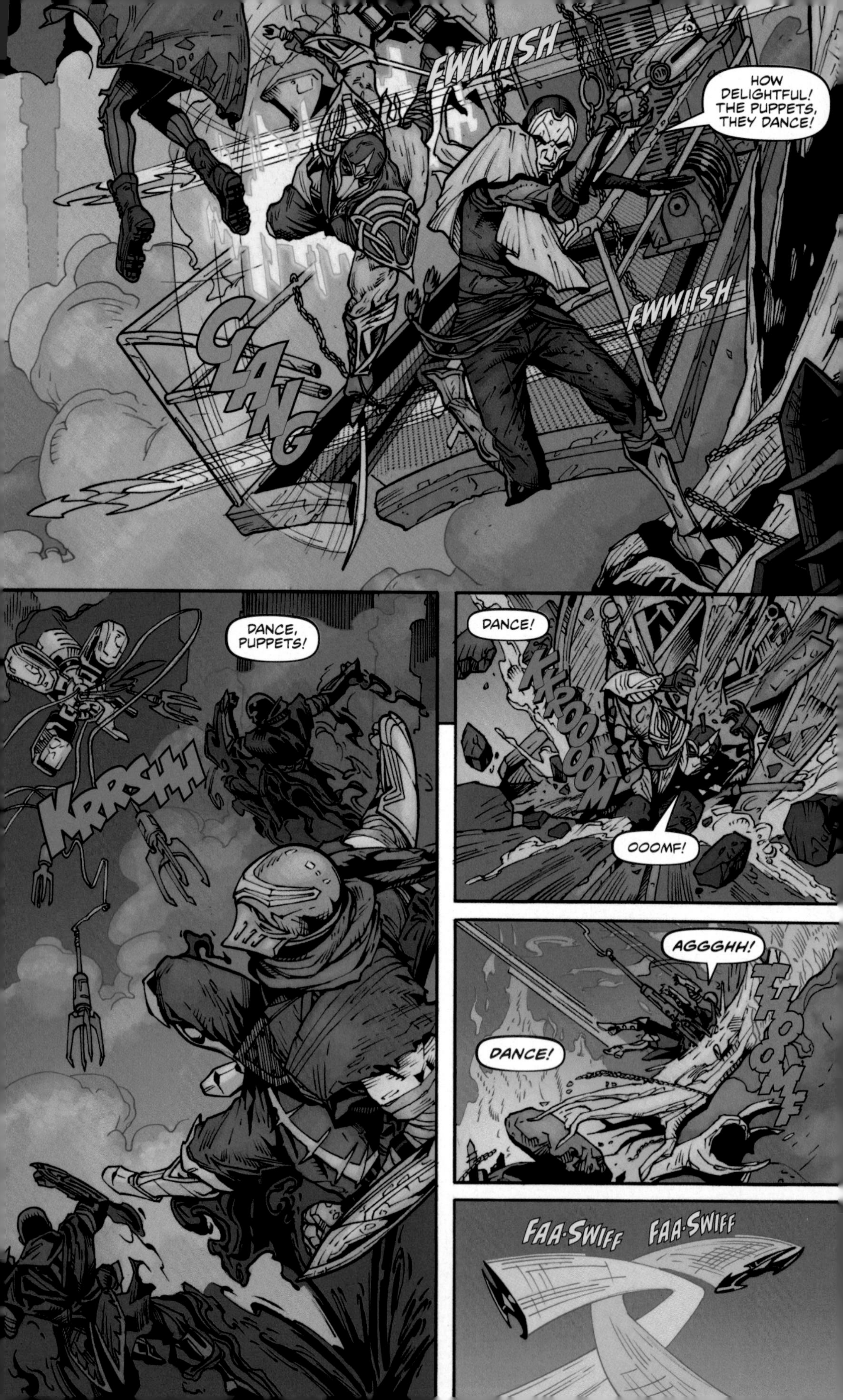
FWWIISH
HOW DELIGHTFUL! THE PUPPETS, THEY DANCE!
FWWIISH
CLANG
DANCE, PUPPETS!
KRRSHH
DANCE!
KKROOOOM
OOOMF!
AGGGHH!
THOOM
DANCE!
FAA-SWIFF
FAA-SWIFF

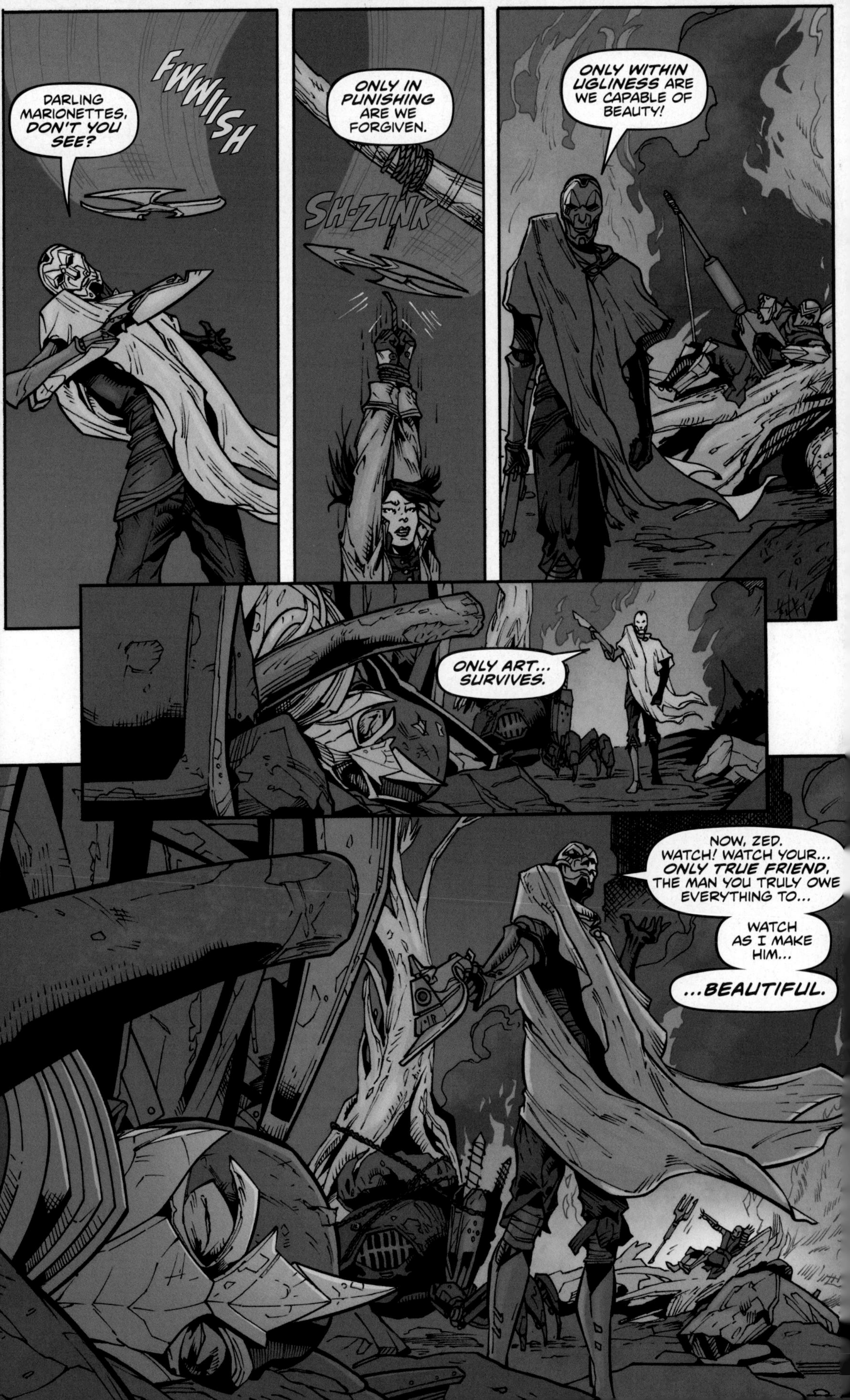
FWWIISH
DARLING MARIONETTES, DON'T YOU SEE?
ONLY IN PUNISHING ARE WE FORGIVEN.
SH-ZINK
ONLY WITHIN UGLINESS ARE WE CAPABLE OF BEAUTY!
ONLY ART... SURVIVES.
NOW, ZED. WATCH! WATCH YOUR... ONLY TRUE FRIEND, THE MAN YOU TRULY OWE EVERYTHING TO...
WATCH AS I MAKE HIM...
...BEAUTIFUL.

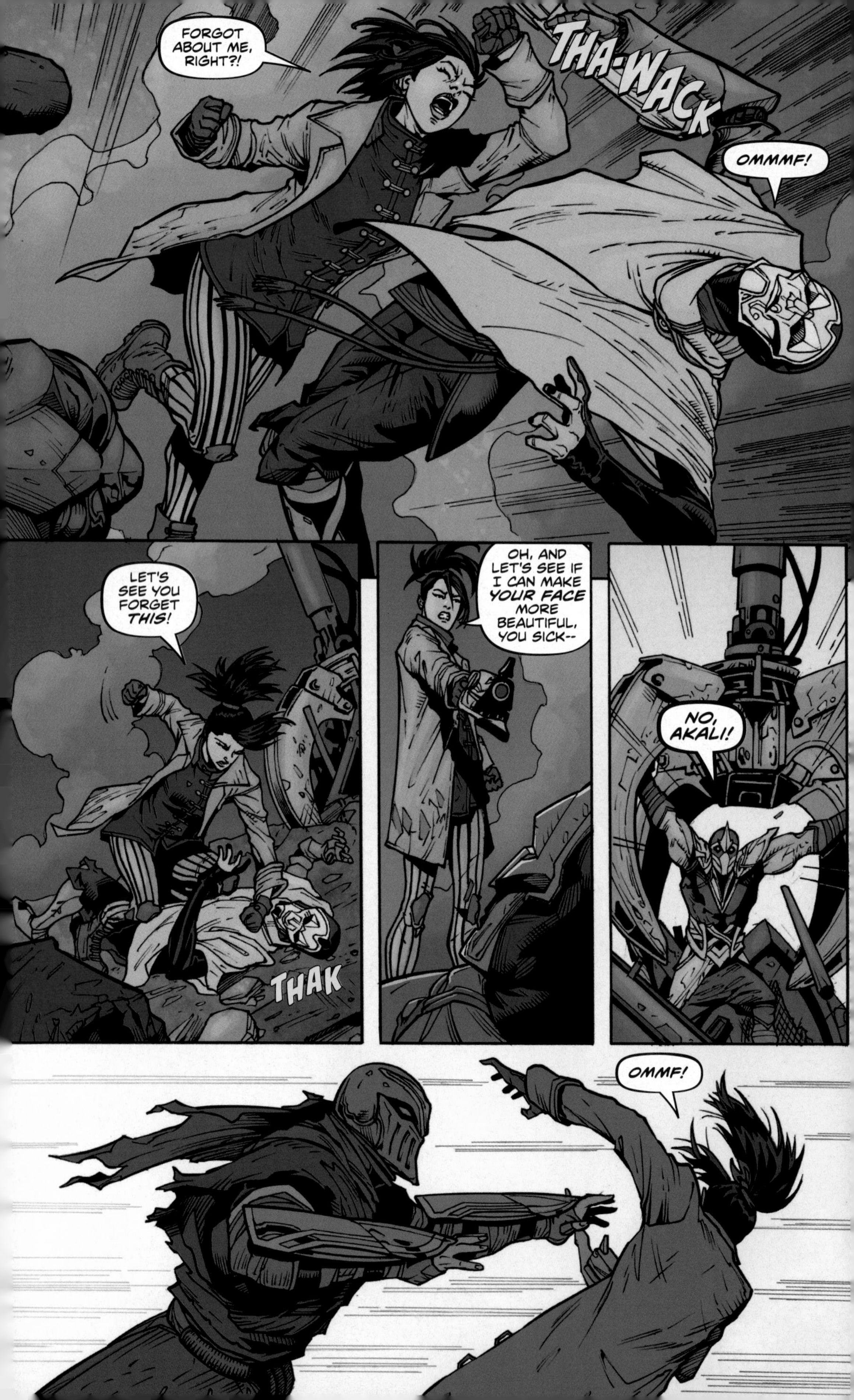
FORGOT ABOUT ME, RIGHT?!
THA-WACK
OMMMF!
LET'S SEE YOU FORGET THIS!
THAK
OH, AND LET'S SEE IF I CAN MAKE YOUR FACE MORE BEAUTIFUL, YOU SICK--
NO, AKALI!
OMMF!

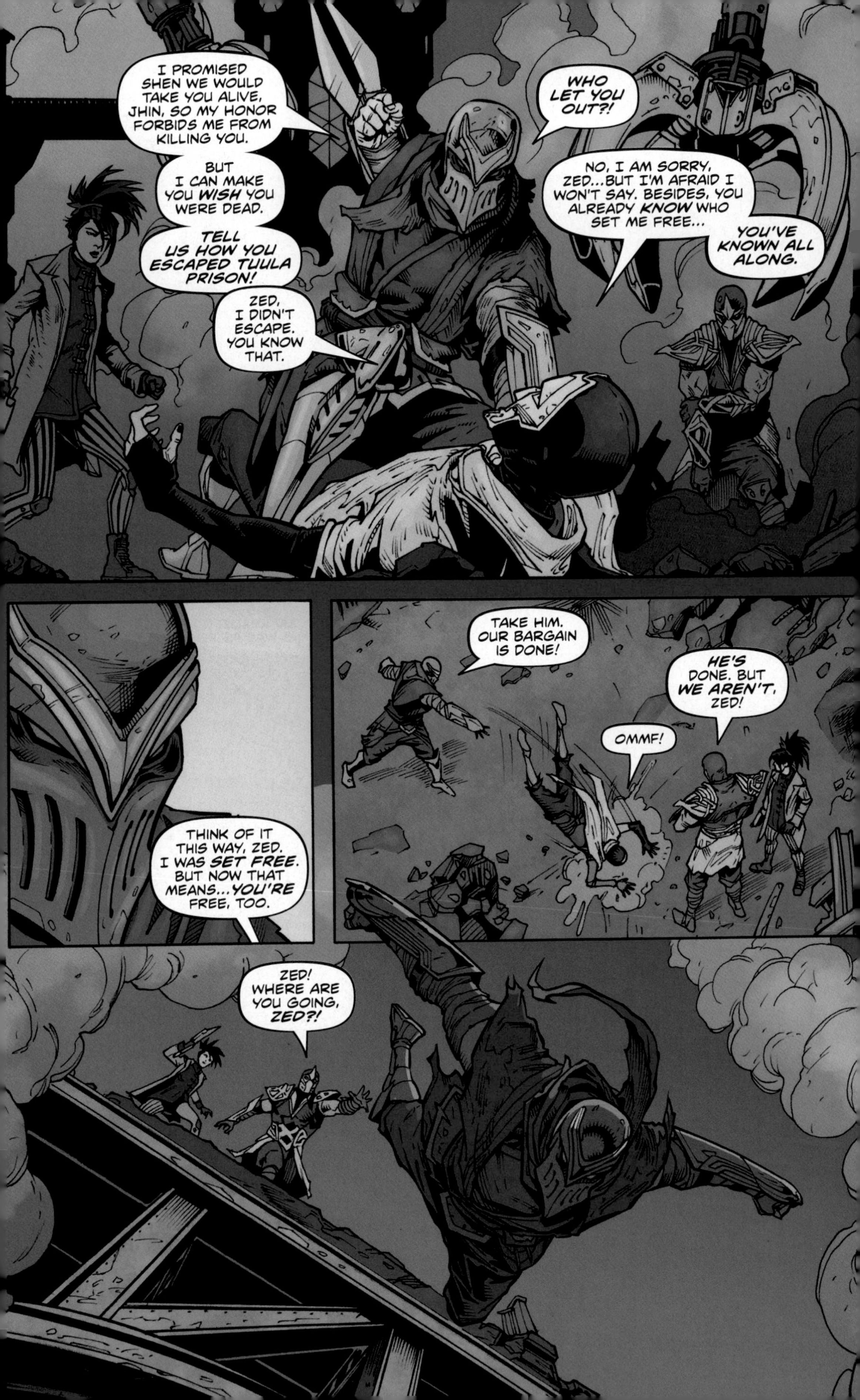
I PROMISED SHEN WE WOULD TAKE YOU ALIVE, JHIN, SO MY HONOR FORBIDS ME FROM KILLING YOU.
BUT I CAN MAKE YOU WISH YOU WERE DEAD.
TELL US HOW YOU ESCAPED TUULA PRISON!
WHO LET YOU OUT?!
ZED, I DIDN'T ESCAPE. YOU KNOW THAT.
NO, I AM SORRY, ZED...BUT I'M AFRAID I WON'T SAY. BESIDES, YOU ALREADY KNOW WHO SET ME FREE...
YOU'VE KNOWN ALL ALONG.
THINK OF IT THIS WAY, ZED. I WAS SET FREE. BUT NOW THAT MEANS...YOU'RE FREE, TOO.
TAKE HIM. OUR BARGAIN IS DONE!
HE'S DONE. BUT WE AREN'T, ZED!
OMMF!
ZED! WHERE ARE YOU GOING, ZED?!

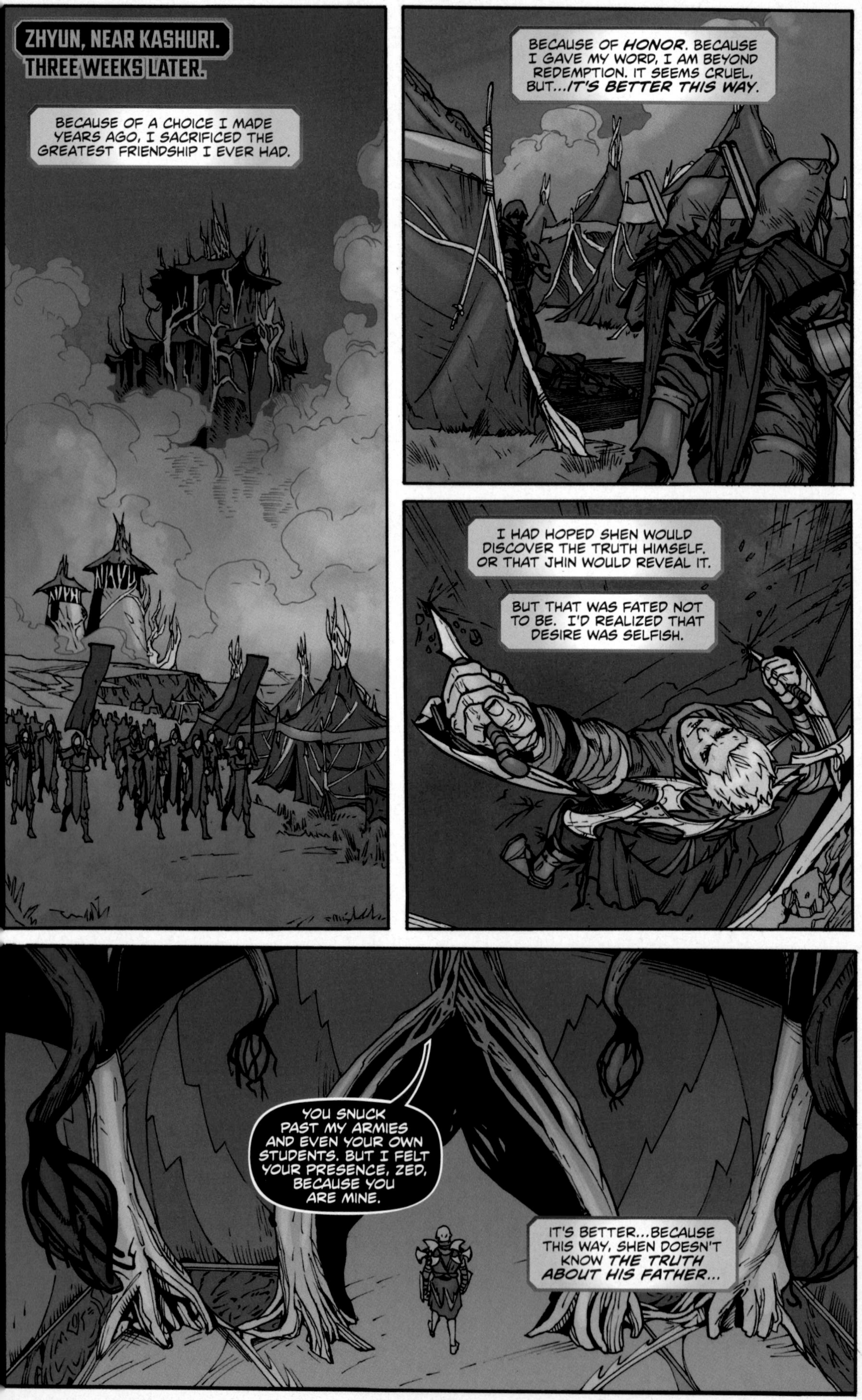
ZHYUN, NEAR KASHURI.
THREE WEEKS LATER.
BECAUSE OF A CHOICE I MADE YEARS AGO, I SACRIFICED THE GREATEST FRIENDSHIP I EVER HAD.
BECAUSE OF *HONOR*. BECAUSE I GAVE MY WORD, I AM BEYOND REDEMPTION. IT SEEMS CRUEL, BUT...*IT'S BETTER THIS WAY.*
I HAD HOPED SHEN WOULD DISCOVER THE TRUTH HIMSELF. OR THAT JHIN WOULD REVEAL IT.
BUT THAT WAS FATED NOT TO BE. I'D REALIZED THAT DESIRE WAS SELFISH.
YOU SNUCK PAST MY ARMIES AND EVEN YOUR OWN STUDENTS. BUT I FELT YOUR PRESENCE, ZED, BECAUSE YOU ARE MINE.
IT'S BETTER...BECAUSE THIS WAY, SHEN DOESN'T KNOW *THE TRUTH ABOUT HIS FATHER*...

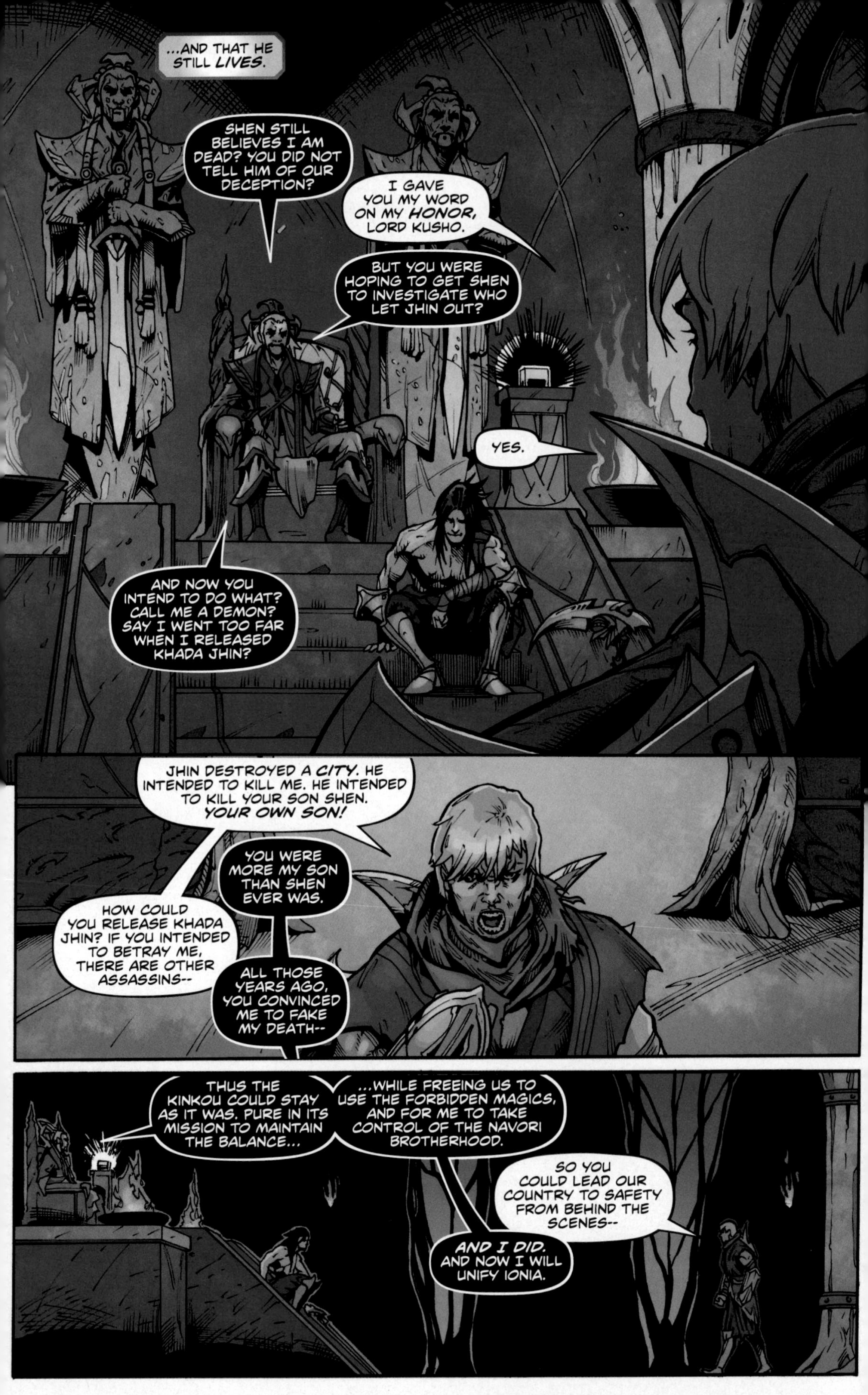

...AND THAT HE STILL *LIVES*.
SHEN STILL BELIEVES I AM DEAD? YOU DID NOT TELL HIM OF OUR DECEPTION?
I GAVE YOU MY WORD ON MY *HONOR*, LORD KUSHO.
BUT YOU WERE HOPING TO GET SHEN TO INVESTIGATE WHO LET JHIN OUT?
YES.
AND NOW YOU INTEND TO DO WHAT? CALL ME A DEMON? SAY I WENT TOO FAR WHEN I RELEASED KHADA JHIN?
JHIN DESTROYED A *CITY*. HE INTENDED TO KILL ME. HE INTENDED TO KILL YOUR SON SHEN. ***YOUR OWN SON!***
YOU WERE MORE MY SON THAN SHEN EVER WAS.
HOW COULD YOU RELEASE KHADA JHIN? IF YOU INTENDED TO BETRAY ME, THERE ARE OTHER ASSASSINS--
ALL THOSE YEARS AGO, YOU CONVINCED ME TO FAKE MY DEATH--
THUS THE KINKOU COULD STAY AS IT WAS. PURE IN ITS MISSION TO MAINTAIN THE BALANCE...
...WHILE FREEING US TO USE THE FORBIDDEN MAGICS, AND FOR ME TO TAKE CONTROL OF THE NAVORI BROTHERHOOD.
SO YOU COULD LEAD OUR COUNTRY TO SAFETY FROM BEHIND THE SCENES--
AND I DID. AND NOW I WILL UNIFY IONIA.

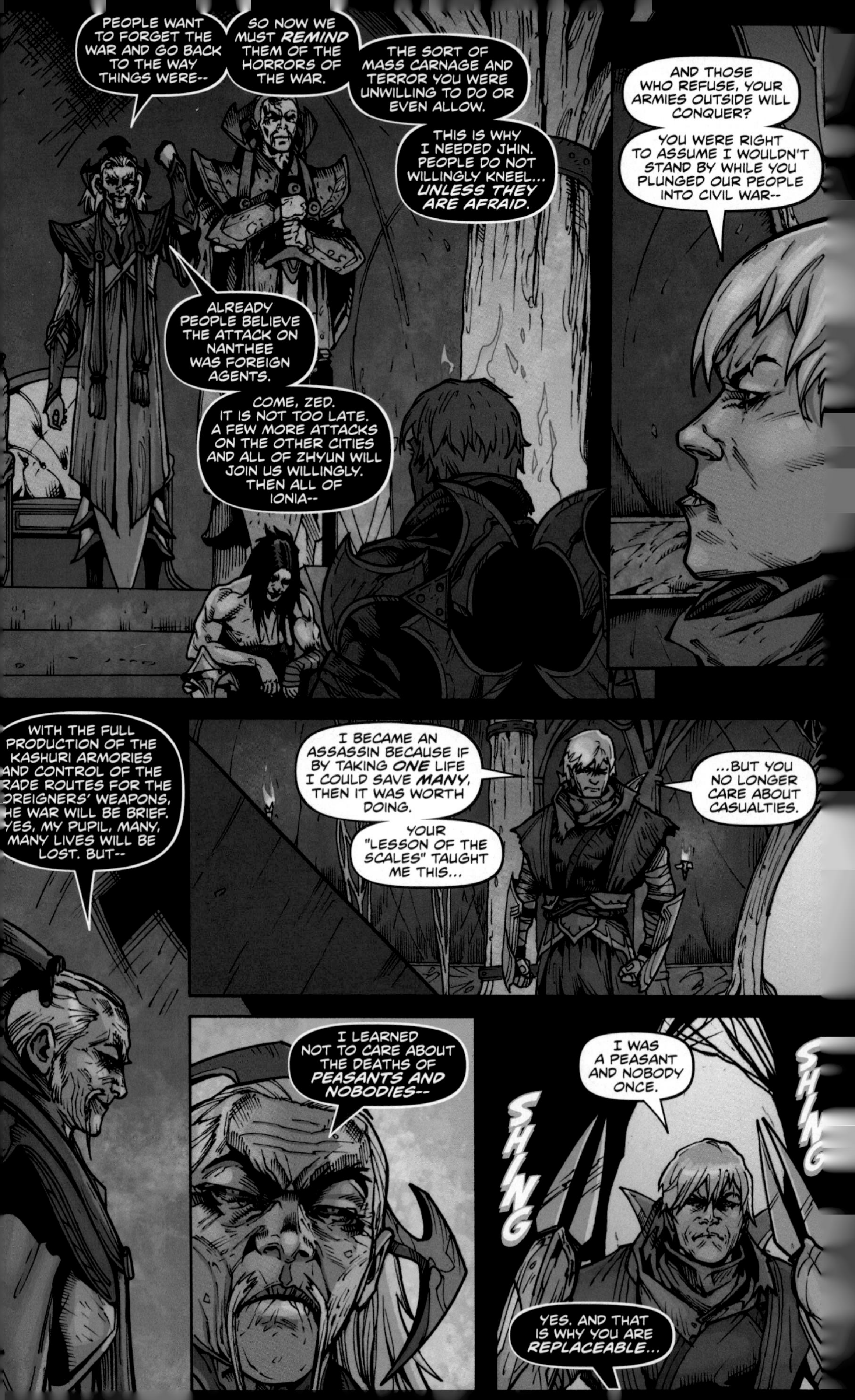
PEOPLE WANT TO FORGET THE WAR AND GO BACK TO THE WAY THINGS WERE--
SO NOW WE MUST REMIND THEM OF THE HORRORS OF THE WAR.
THE SORT OF MASS CARNAGE AND TERROR YOU WERE UNWILLING TO DO OR EVEN ALLOW.
THIS IS WHY I NEEDED JHIN. PEOPLE DO NOT WILLINGLY KNEEL... UNLESS THEY ARE AFRAID.
ALREADY PEOPLE BELIEVE THE ATTACK ON NANTHEE WAS FOREIGN AGENTS.
COME, ZED. IT IS NOT TOO LATE. A FEW MORE ATTACKS ON THE OTHER CITIES AND ALL OF ZHYUN WILL JOIN US WILLINGLY. THEN ALL OF IONIA--
AND THOSE WHO REFUSE, YOUR ARMIES OUTSIDE WILL CONQUER?
YOU WERE RIGHT TO ASSUME I WOULDN'T STAND BY WHILE YOU PLUNGED OUR PEOPLE INTO CIVIL WAR--
WITH THE FULL PRODUCTION OF THE KASHURI ARMORIES AND CONTROL OF THE RADE ROUTES FOR THE OREIGNERS' WEAPONS, HE WAR WILL BE BRIEF. YES, MY PUPIL, MANY, MANY LIVES WILL BE LOST. BUT--
I BECAME AN ASSASSIN BECAUSE IF BY TAKING ONE LIFE I COULD SAVE MANY, THEN IT WAS WORTH DOING.
YOUR "LESSON OF THE SCALES" TAUGHT ME THIS...
...BUT YOU NO LONGER CARE ABOUT CASUALTIES.
I LEARNED NOT TO CARE ABOUT THE DEATHS OF PEASANTS AND NOBODIES--
I WAS A PEASANT AND NOBODY ONCE.
SHING
SHING
YES. AND THAT IS WHY YOU ARE REPLACEABLE...

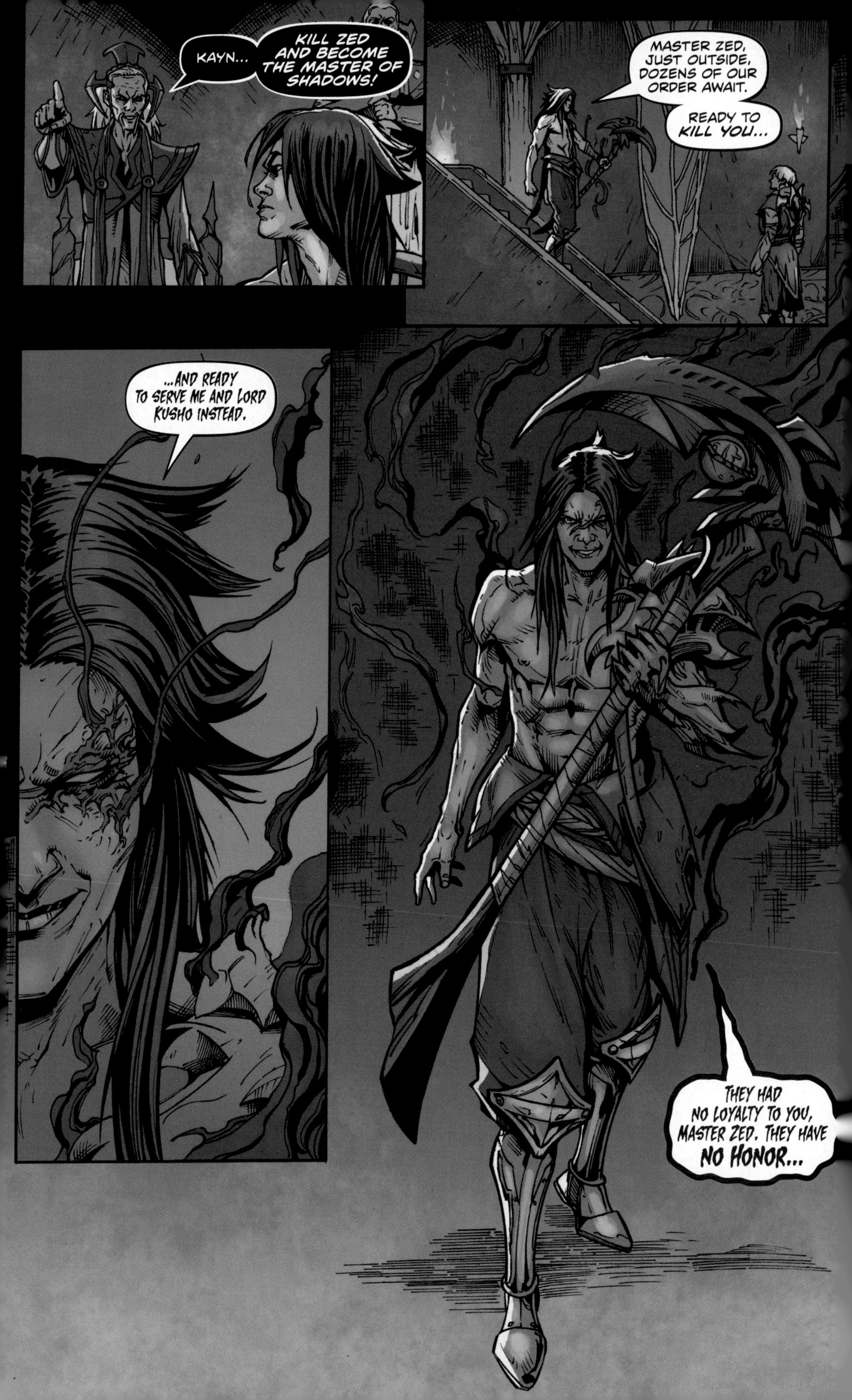
KAYN...
KILL ZED AND BECOME THE MASTER OF SHADOWS!
MASTER ZED, JUST OUTSIDE, DOZENS OF OUR ORDER AWAIT.
READY TO KILL YOU...
...AND READY TO SERVE ME AND LORD KUSHO INSTEAD.
THEY HAD NO LOYALTY TO YOU, MASTER ZED. THEY HAVE NO HONOR...

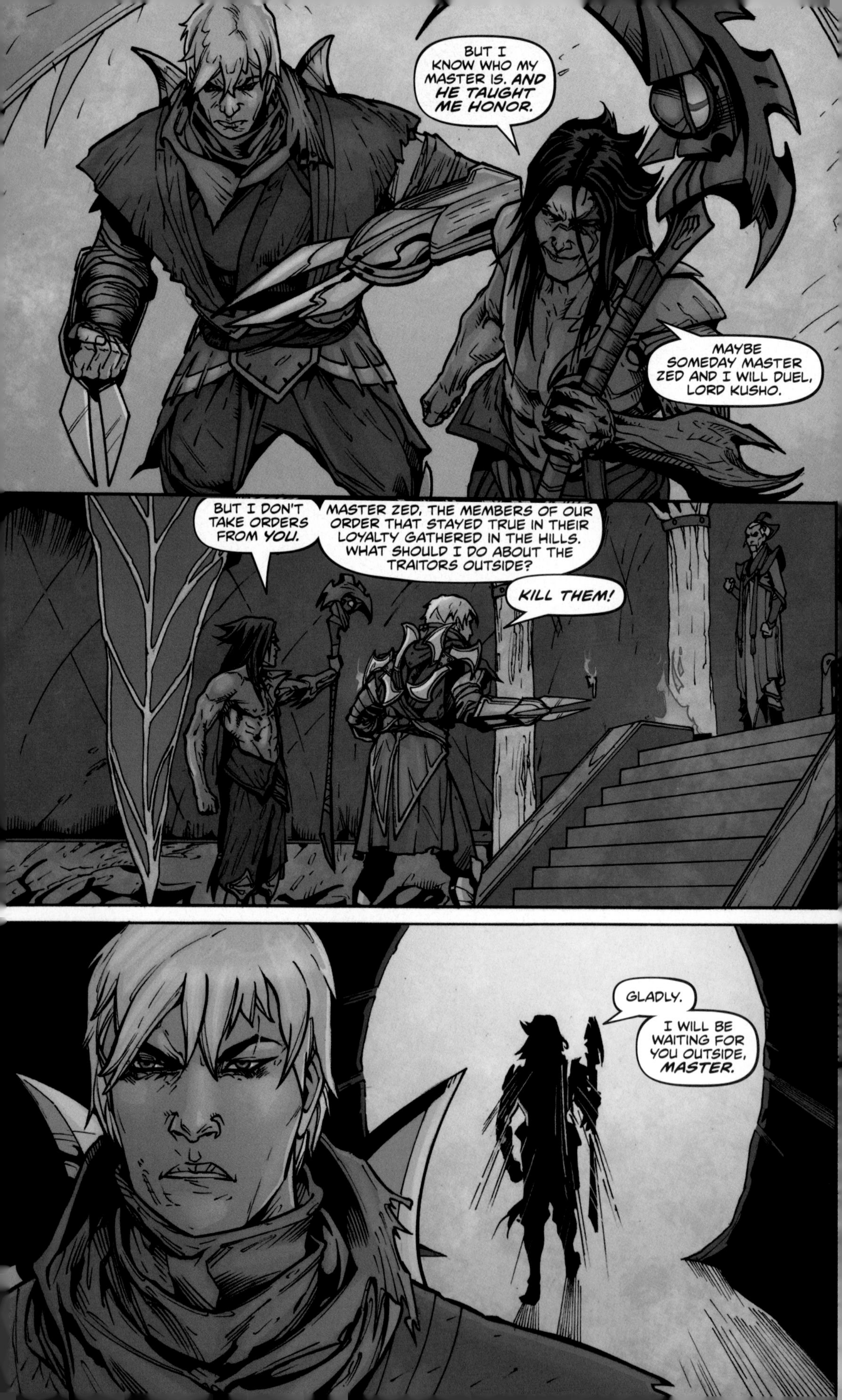
BUT I KNOW WHO MY MASTER IS. AND HE TAUGHT ME HONOR.
MAYBE SOMEDAY MASTER ZED AND I WILL DUEL, LORD KUSHO.
BUT I DON'T TAKE ORDERS FROM YOU.
MASTER ZED, THE MEMBERS OF OUR ORDER THAT STAYED TRUE IN THEIR LOYALTY GATHERED IN THE HILLS. WHAT SHOULD I DO ABOUT THE TRAITORS OUTSIDE?
KILL THEM!
GLADLY.
I WILL BE WAITING FOR YOU OUTSIDE, MASTER.

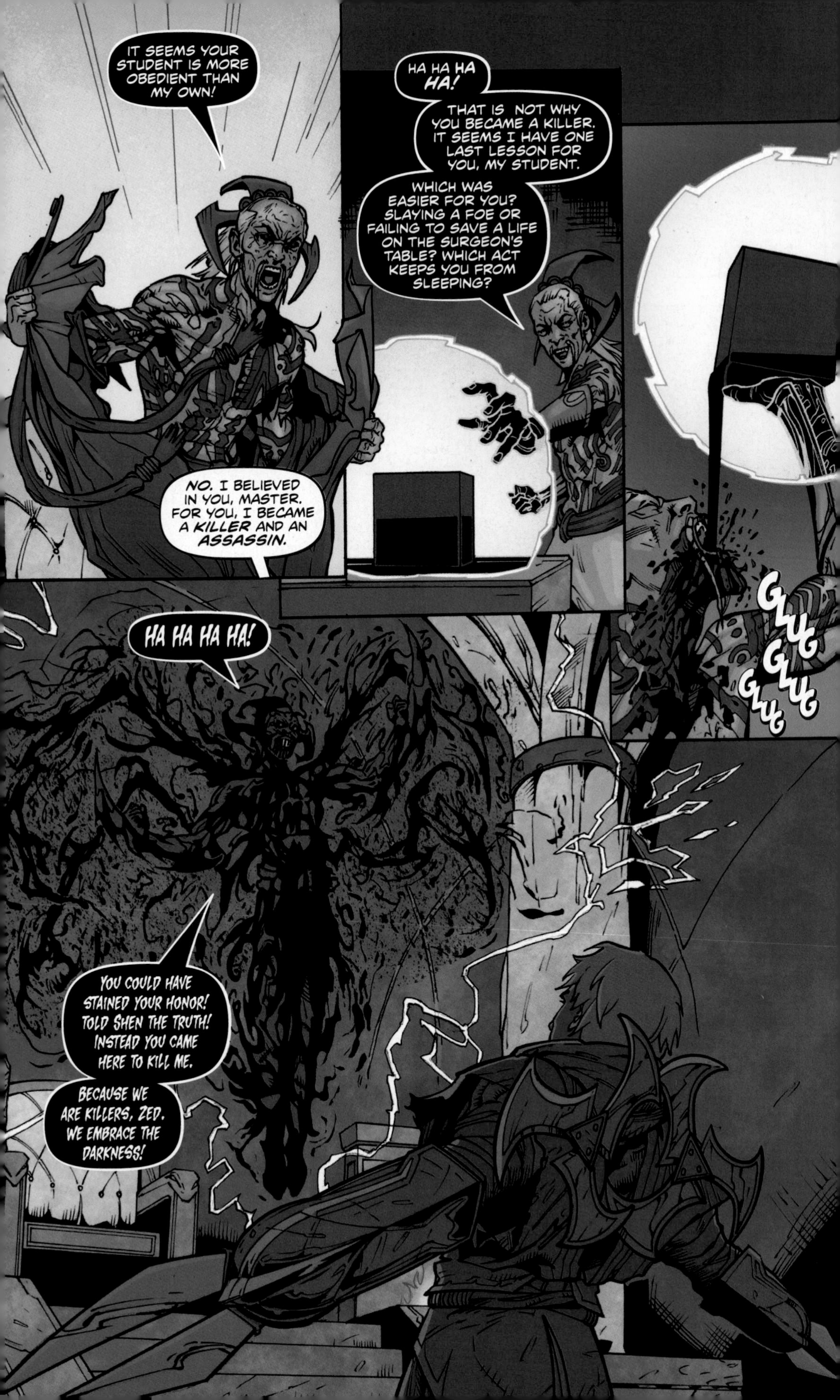
IT SEEMS YOUR STUDENT IS MORE OBEDIENT THAN MY OWN!
NO. I BELIEVED IN YOU, MASTER. FOR YOU, I BECAME A KILLER AND AN ASSASSIN.
HA HA HA HA!
THAT IS NOT WHY YOU BECAME A KILLER. IT SEEMS I HAVE ONE LAST LESSON FOR YOU, MY STUDENT.
WHICH WAS EASIER FOR YOU? SLAYING A FOE OR FAILING TO SAVE A LIFE ON THE SURGEON'S TABLE? WHICH ACT KEEPS YOU FROM SLEEPING?
GLUG GLUG GLUG
HA HA HA HA!
YOU COULD HAVE STAINED YOUR HONOR! TOLD SHEN THE TRUTH! INSTEAD YOU CAME HERE TO KILL ME.
BECAUSE WE ARE KILLERS, ZED. WE EMBRACE THE DARKNESS!

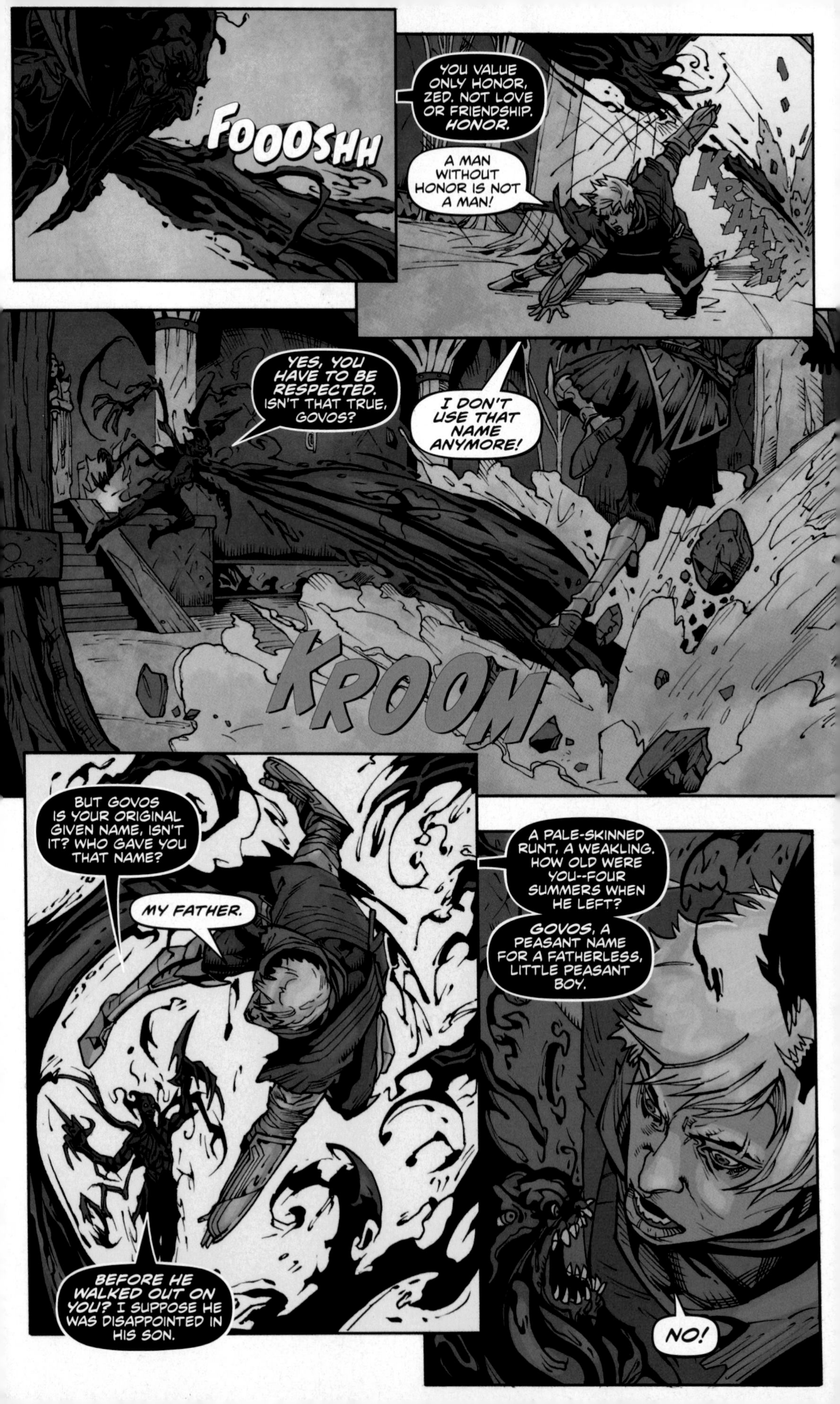
FOOOSHH
YOU VALUE ONLY HONOR, ZED. NOT LOVE OR FRIENDSHIP. HONOR.
A MAN WITHOUT HONOR IS NOT A MAN!
KRAAAASH
YES, YOU HAVE TO BE RESPECTED. ISN'T THAT TRUE, GOVOS?
I DON'T USE THAT NAME ANYMORE!
KROOM
BUT GOVOS IS YOUR ORIGINAL GIVEN NAME, ISN'T IT? WHO GAVE YOU THAT NAME?
MY FATHER.
BEFORE HE WALKED OUT ON YOU? I SUPPOSE HE WAS DISAPPOINTED IN HIS SON.
A PALE-SKINNED RUNT, A WEAKLING. HOW OLD WERE YOU--FOUR SUMMERS WHEN HE LEFT?
GOVOS, A PEASANT NAME FOR A FATHERLESS, LITTLE PEASANT BOY.
NO!

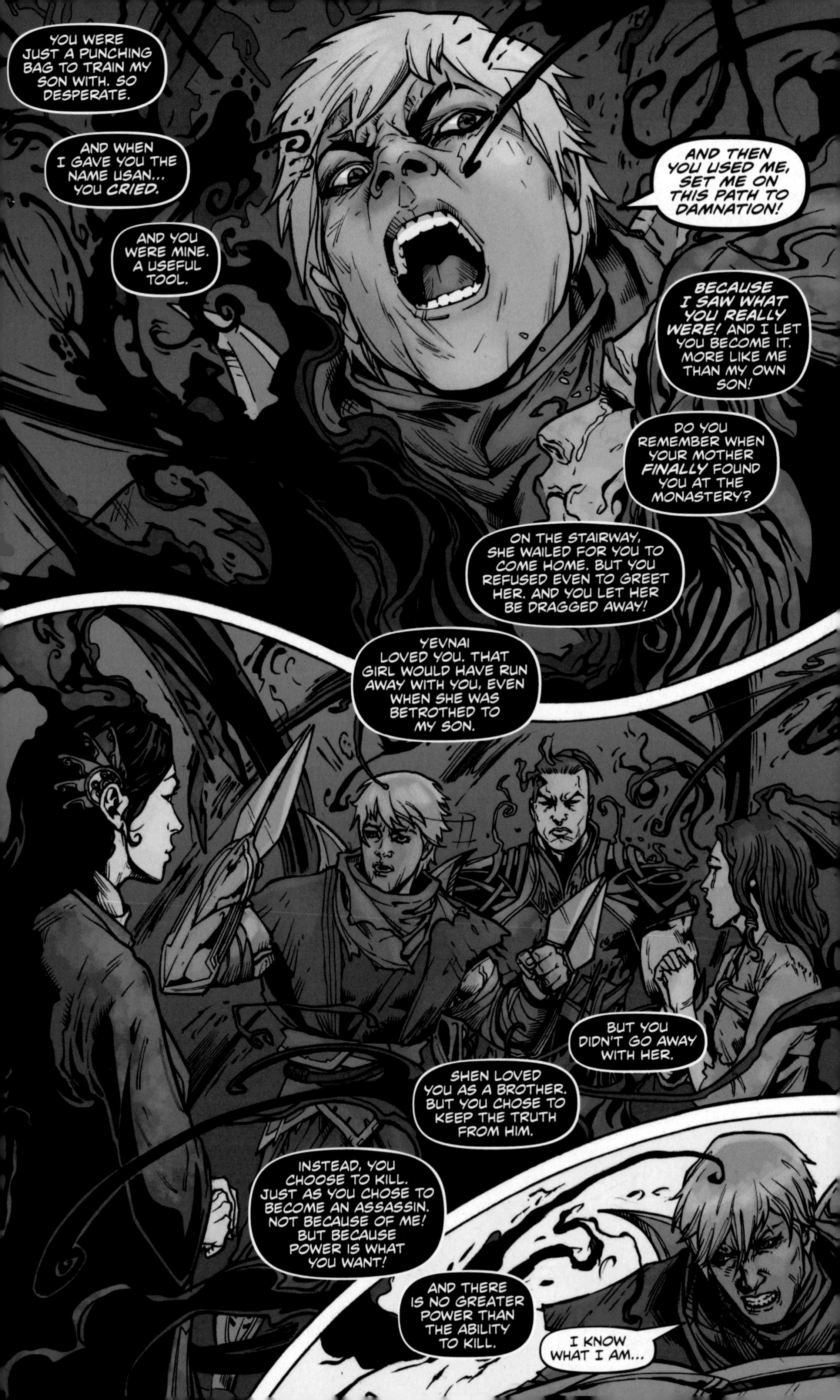

YOU WERE JUST A PUNCHING BAG TO TRAIN MY SON WITH. SO DESPERATE.
AND WHEN I GAVE YOU THE NAME USAN... YOU *CRIED.*
AND YOU WERE MINE. A USEFUL TOOL.
AND THEN YOU USED ME, SET ME ON THIS PATH TO DAMNATION!
BECAUSE I SAW WHAT YOU REALLY WERE! AND I LET YOU BECOME IT. MORE LIKE ME THAN MY OWN SON!
DO YOU REMEMBER WHEN YOUR MOTHER *FINALLY* FOUND YOU AT THE MONASTERY?
ON THE STAIRWAY, SHE WAILED FOR YOU TO COME HOME. BUT YOU REFUSED EVEN TO GREET HER. AND YOU LET HER BE DRAGGED AWAY!
YEVNAI LOVED YOU. THAT GIRL WOULD HAVE RUN AWAY WITH YOU, EVEN WHEN SHE WAS BETROTHED TO MY SON.
BUT YOU DIDN'T GO AWAY WITH HER.
SHEN LOVED YOU AS A BROTHER. BUT YOU CHOSE TO KEEP THE TRUTH FROM HIM.
INSTEAD, YOU CHOOSE TO KILL. JUST AS YOU CHOSE TO BECOME AN ASSASSIN. NOT BECAUSE OF ME! BUT BECAUSE POWER IS WHAT YOU WANT!
AND THERE IS NO GREATER POWER THAN THE ABILITY TO KILL.
I KNOW WHAT I AM...

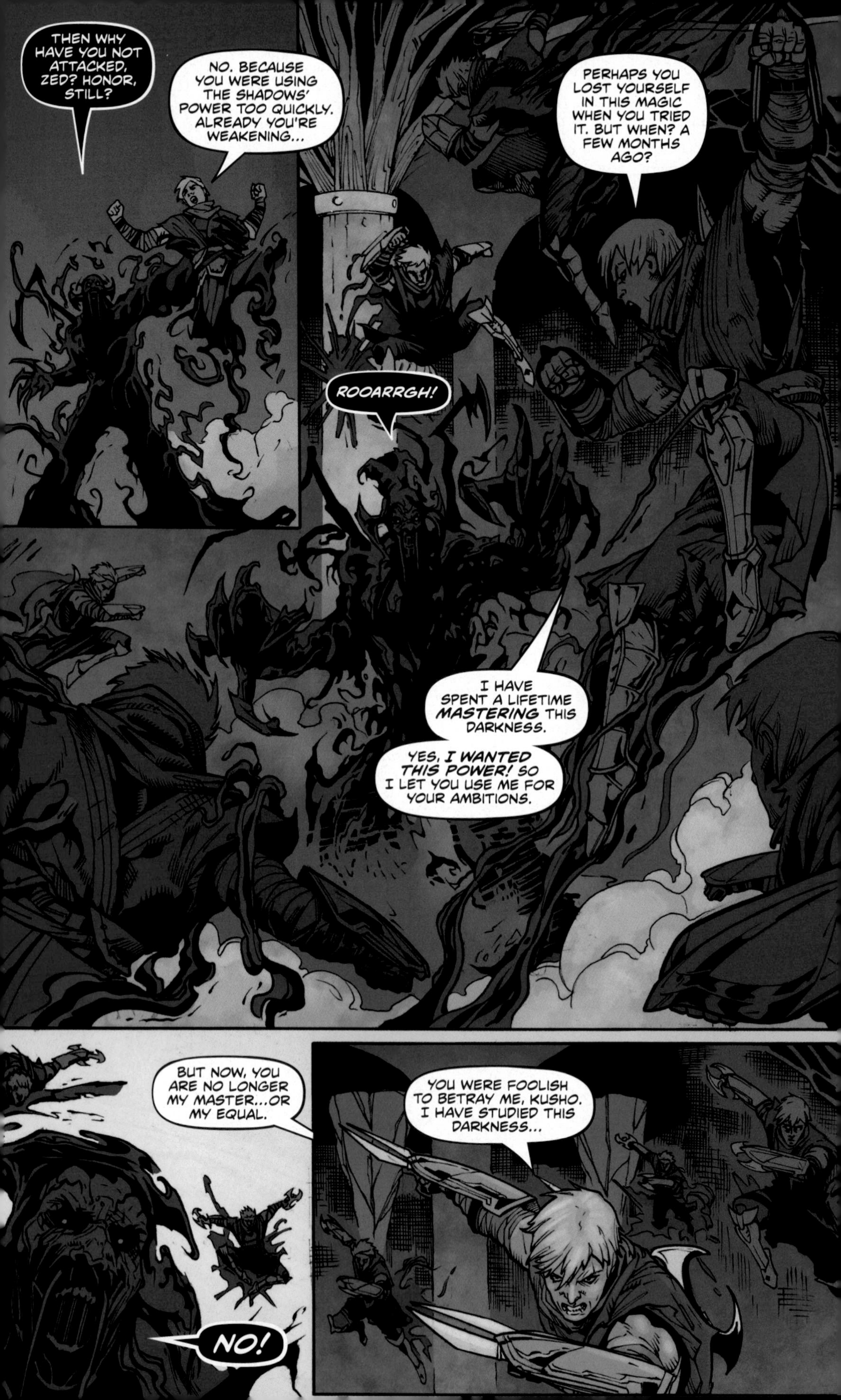
THEN WHY HAVE YOU NOT ATTACKED, ZED? HONOR, STILL?
NO. BECAUSE YOU WERE USING THE SHADOWS' POWER TOO QUICKLY. ALREADY YOU'RE WEAKENING...
PERHAPS YOU LOST YOURSELF IN THIS MAGIC WHEN YOU TRIED IT. BUT WHEN? A FEW MONTHS AGO?
ROOARRGH!
I HAVE SPENT A LIFETIME MASTERING THIS DARKNESS.
YES, I WANTED THIS POWER! SO I LET YOU USE ME FOR YOUR AMBITIONS.
BUT NOW, YOU ARE NO LONGER MY MASTER...OR MY EQUAL.
NO!
YOU WERE FOOLISH TO BETRAY ME, KUSHO. I HAVE STUDIED THIS DARKNESS...

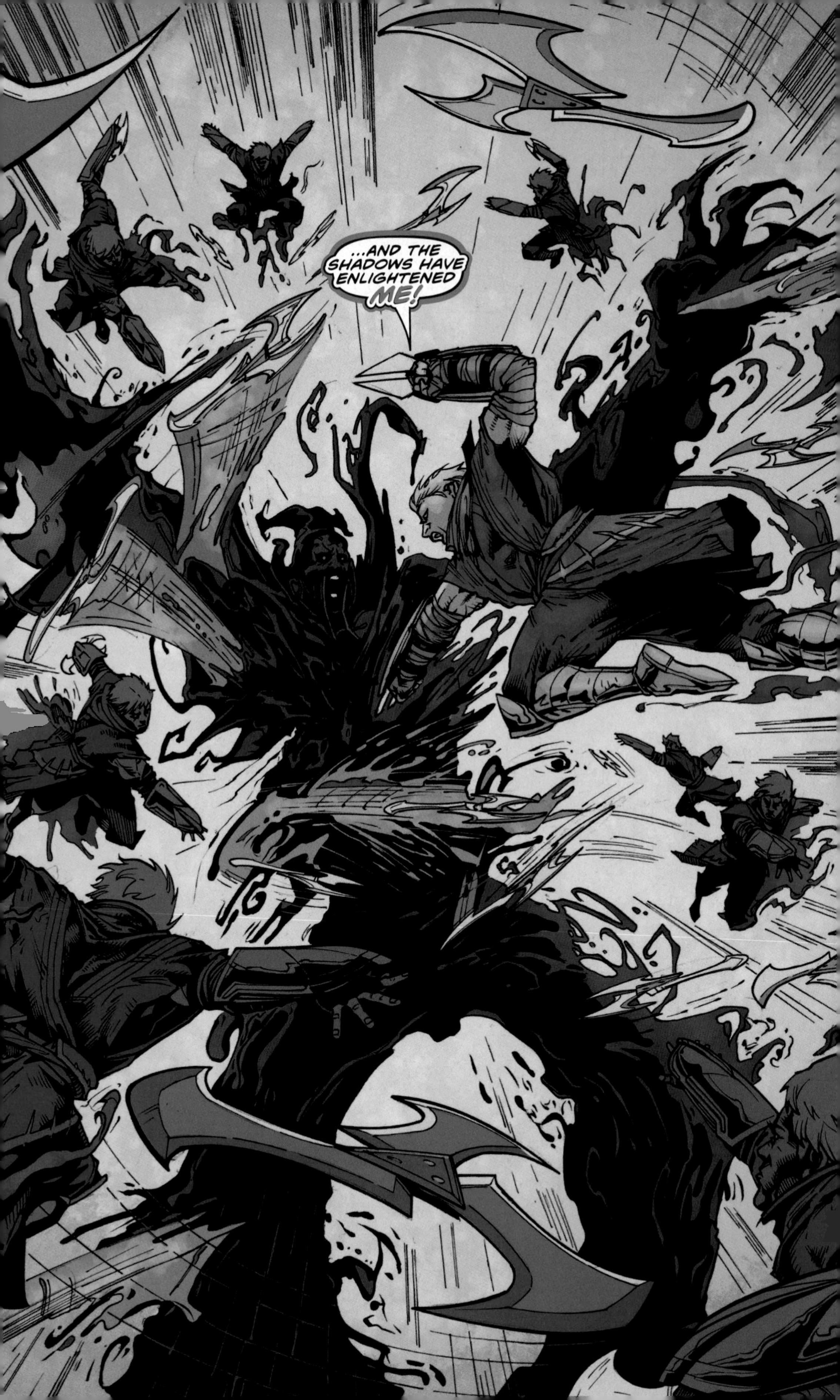
...AND THE SHADOWS HAVE ENLIGHTENED ME!

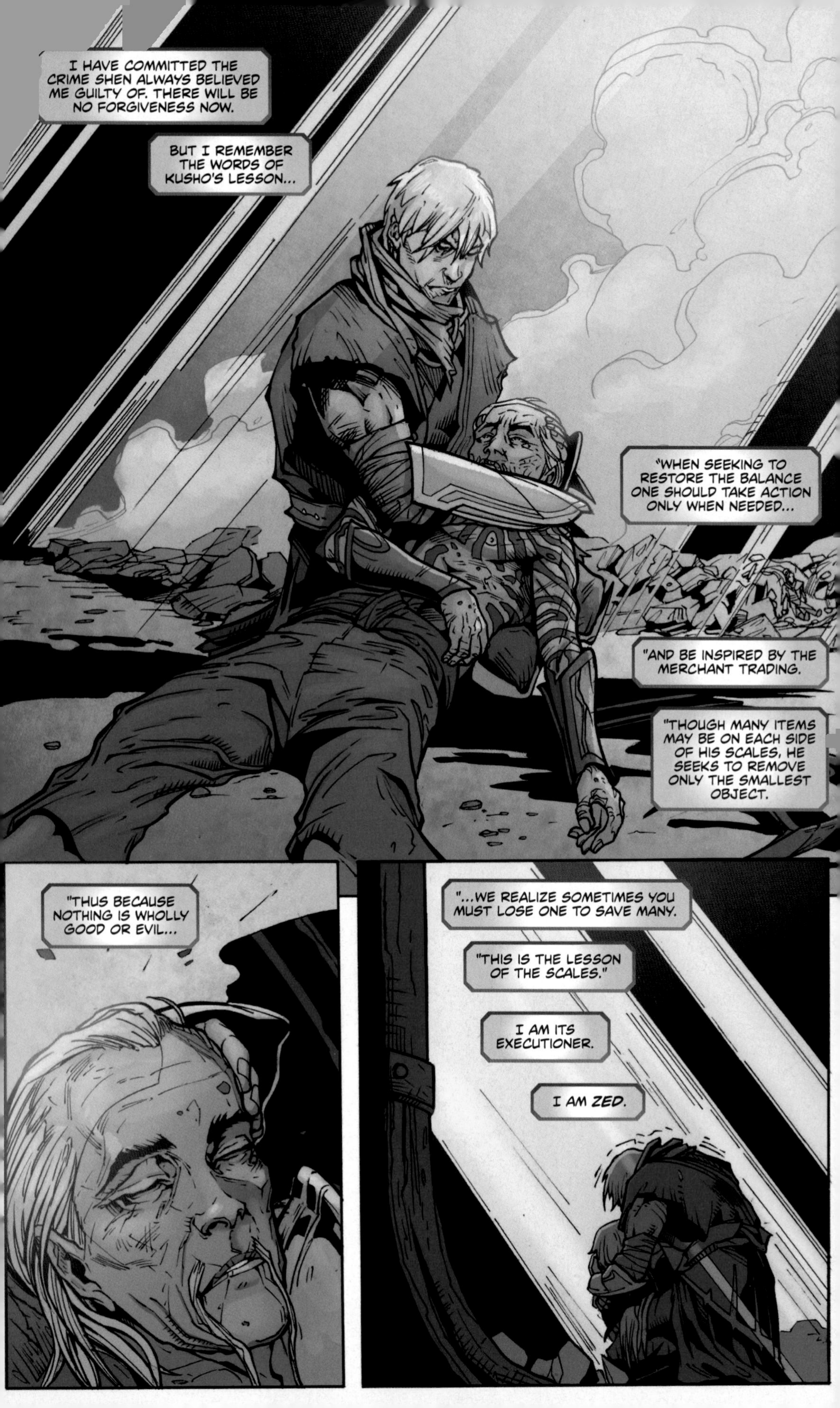

I HAVE COMMITTED THE CRIME SHEN ALWAYS BELIEVED ME GUILTY OF. THERE WILL BE NO FORGIVENESS NOW.
BUT I REMEMBER THE WORDS OF KUSHO'S LESSON...
"WHEN SEEKING TO RESTORE THE BALANCE ONE SHOULD TAKE ACTION ONLY WHEN NEEDED...
"AND BE INSPIRED BY THE MERCHANT TRADING.
"THOUGH MANY ITEMS MAY BE ON EACH SIDE OF HIS SCALES, HE SEEKS TO REMOVE ONLY THE SMALLEST OBJECT.
"THUS BECAUSE NOTHING IS WHOLLY GOOD OR EVIL...
"...WE REALIZE SOMETIMES YOU MUST LOSE ONE TO SAVE MANY.
"THIS IS THE LESSON OF THE SCALES."
I AM ITS EXECUTIONER.
I AM ZED.

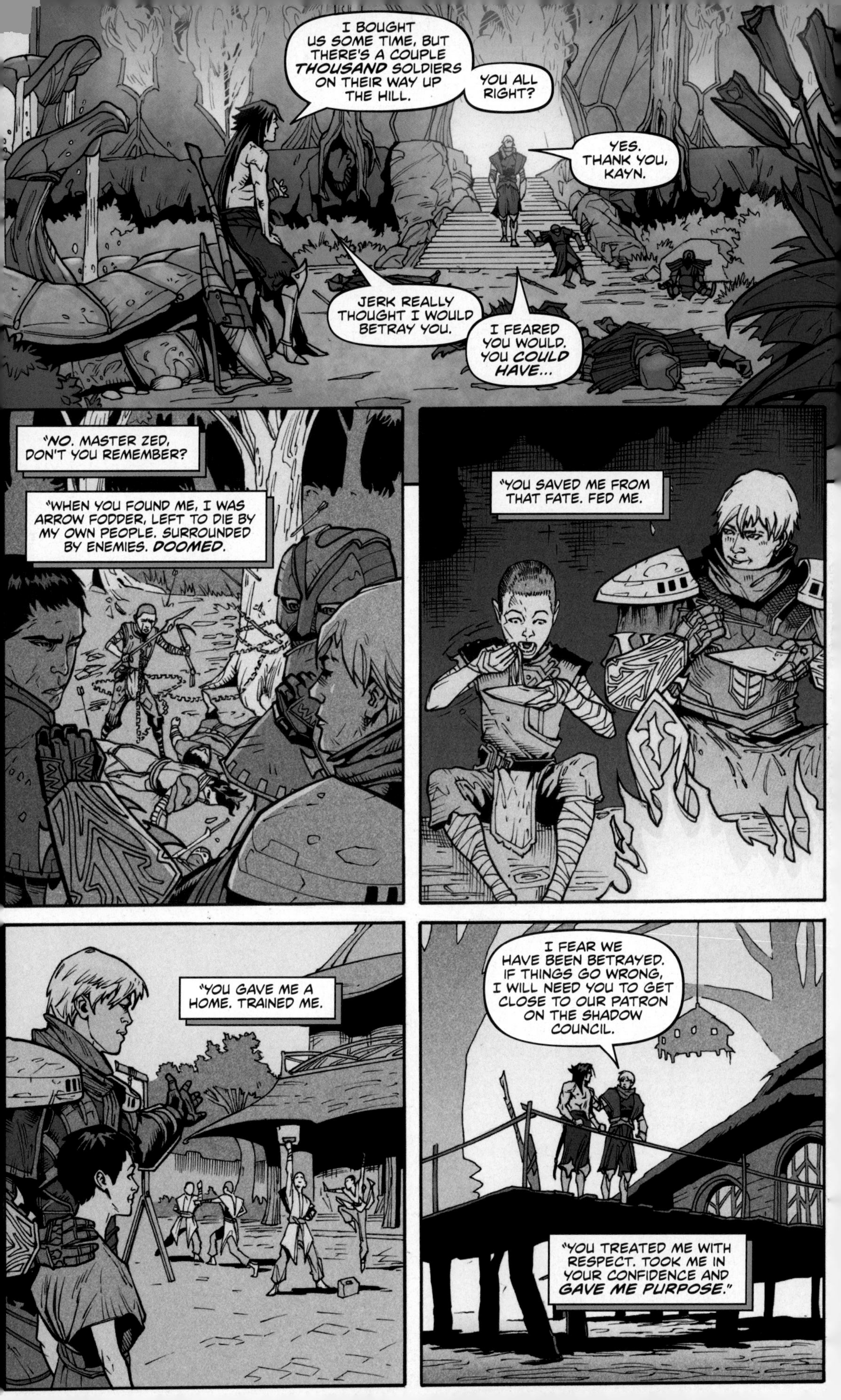
I BOUGHT US SOME TIME, BUT THERE'S A COUPLE ***THOUSAND*** SOLDIERS ON THEIR WAY UP THE HILL.
YOU ALL RIGHT?
YES. THANK YOU, KAYN.
JERK REALLY THOUGHT I WOULD BETRAY YOU.
I FEARED YOU WOULD. YOU ***COULD HAVE***...
"***NO***. MASTER ZED, DON'T YOU REMEMBER?
"WHEN YOU FOUND ME, I WAS ARROW FODDER, LEFT TO DIE BY MY OWN PEOPLE. SURROUNDED BY ENEMIES. ***DOOMED***.
"YOU SAVED ME FROM THAT FATE. FED ME.
"YOU GAVE ME A HOME. TRAINED ME.
I FEAR WE HAVE BEEN BETRAYED. IF THINGS GO WRONG, I WILL NEED YOU TO GET CLOSE TO OUR PATRON ON THE SHADOW COUNCIL.
"YOU TREATED ME WITH RESPECT. TOOK ME IN YOUR CONFIDENCE AND ***GAVE ME PURPOSE***."

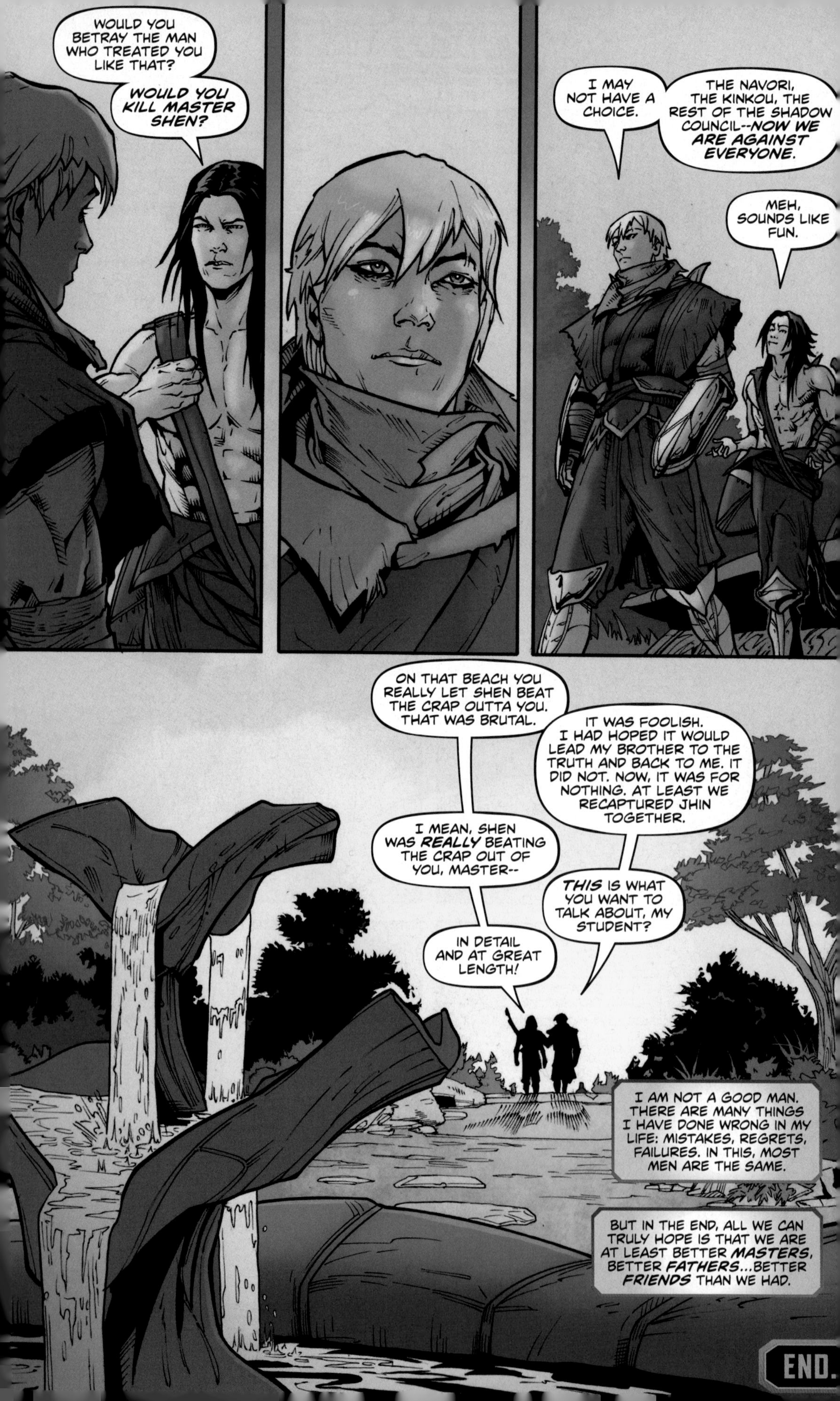

WOULD YOU BETRAY THE MAN WHO TREATED YOU LIKE THAT?
WOULD YOU KILL MASTER SHEN?
I MAY NOT HAVE A CHOICE.
THE NAVORI, THE KINKOU, THE REST OF THE SHADOW COUNCIL--NOW WE ARE AGAINST EVERYONE.
MEH, SOUNDS LIKE FUN.
ON THAT BEACH YOU REALLY LET SHEN BEAT THE CRAP OUTTA YOU. THAT WAS BRUTAL.
IT WAS FOOLISH. I HAD HOPED IT WOULD LEAD MY BROTHER TO THE TRUTH AND BACK TO ME. IT DID NOT. NOW, IT WAS FOR NOTHING. AT LEAST WE RECAPTURED JHIN TOGETHER.
I MEAN, SHEN WAS REALLY BEATING THE CRAP OUT OF YOU, MASTER--
THIS IS WHAT YOU WANT TO TALK ABOUT, MY STUDENT?
IN DETAIL AND AT GREAT LENGTH!
I AM NOT A GOOD MAN. THERE ARE MANY THINGS I HAVE DONE WRONG IN MY LIFE: MISTAKES, REGRETS, FAILURES. IN THIS, MOST MEN ARE THE SAME.
BUT IN THE END, ALL WE CAN TRULY HOPE IS THAT WE ARE AT LEAST BETTER MASTERS, BETTER FATHERS...BETTER FRIENDS THAN WE HAD.
END.

BAD DADS

A LONG, LONG TIME AGO—well, about six years ago—before Jhin existed, before Kayn existed. Waaaaaay back when I first joined Riot, about 80% of my time was pitching ideas to the story team and Riot's leadership. On the short list of characters they were interested in developing was Zed.

So, I wrote a bunch of pitches trying to figure out who he was and could be. I ended up writing a couple of animation and comics scripts featuring our red-clad assassin. They got some concept art, a lot of animation storyboards, and even a few pages of a very different Zed origin comic, but ...

None of it was ever released.

Nevertheless, from these prior executions, two central themes emerged: The psychological damage of witnessing violence when being unable to stop it and the desire to stay connected to, and honor, the people who made you who you are.

When I finally started writing this version of the Zed comic, I jokingly titled it, "Bad Dads." At the time, I was finishing the *Ashe: Warmother* comic—a story about how two girls' relationships with their mothers shaped them—and I realized for this book to work, I needed to address how Shen and Zed were messed up because of their jerk-dad, Kusho.

At one point, Ariel Lawrence, the head of Riot's Narrative, jokingly asked me, "What're you gonna write about, when you get over your family issues?" To which I replied, "I'm never gonna be that healthy." A joke, though certainly some of this book relates to my fears about being a good father.

Even so, I hope this book is about more than just bad dads and martial artists chasing a serial killer. Otherwise, I would have failed to learn anything from those previous versions of Zed's story. In my view, the Zed character is—ultimately—still a villain. He's a xenophobic national-ist, who prefers murder to conflict resolution. I suspect when you see him next he will be the antagonist in someone else's story and will be doing vile deeds.

But I hope when you see his figure covered up in armor and a mask you remember there's a boy named Govos and teenager named Usan hiding in there, too. Because nobody is just one thing. We exist in time. And though we may fall down sometimes, we also all have the capacity to learn from our experiences, to be better than our masters were, and to be better than we were yesterday.

Hoping you liked this book, and hoping that I'm better than yesterday. I hope you enjoy it.

Odin Austin Shafer
March 5, 2020

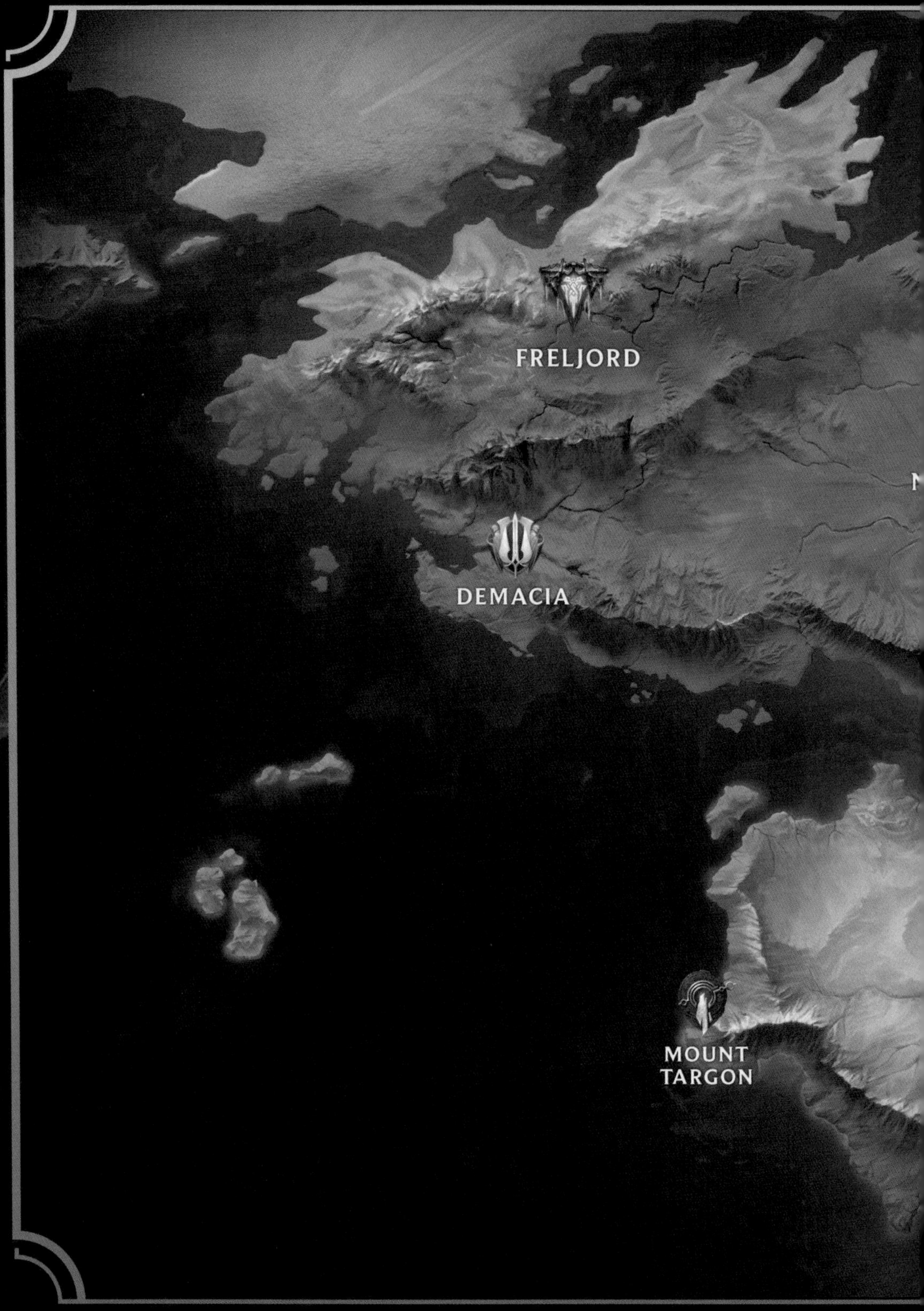
FRELJORD
DEMACIA
MOUNT
TARGON

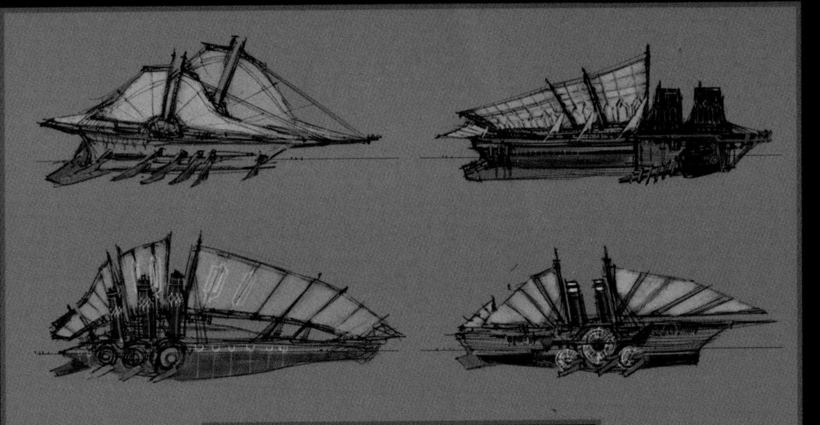

PILTOVER SHIPS BY ERIC CANETE

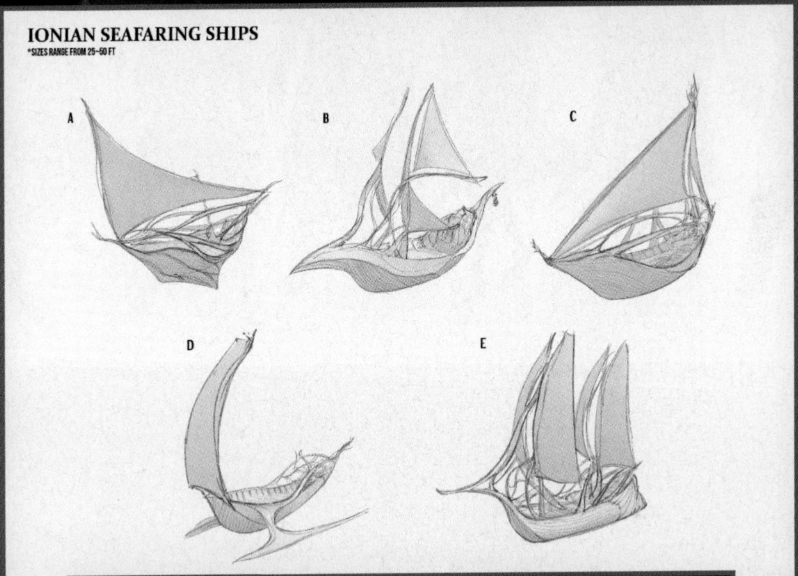
IONIAN SEAFARING SHIPS
*SIZES RANGE FROM 25–50 FT
A
B
C
D
E

IONIA SEAFARING SHIPS

The look of these ships were inspired by floating leaves on streams of water, but still needed to look substantial enough for the vast seas of the Runeterran Ocean. The challenge was to make these look unique and Ionian while still maintaining the look and feel of the seafaring ships that we know of.

BY SEAN YANG

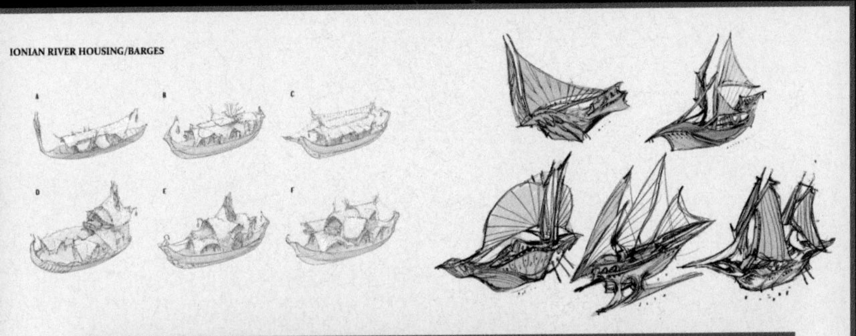
IONIAN RIVER HOUSING/BARGES

IONIA RIVER BARGES

These needed to look like they were of the working class, lived in, and not sleek like the Ionian temples. We also had it in the back of our minds that they were to be connected to other barges to create a larger town. Since we wanted a lively silhouette for the Floating City of Kotha, these needed to vary greatly in size to create an uneven silhouette that felt more spontaneous and not so planned.

BY SEAN YANG

CHARACTER DESIGNS

ACOLYTES BY MAX ZHANG

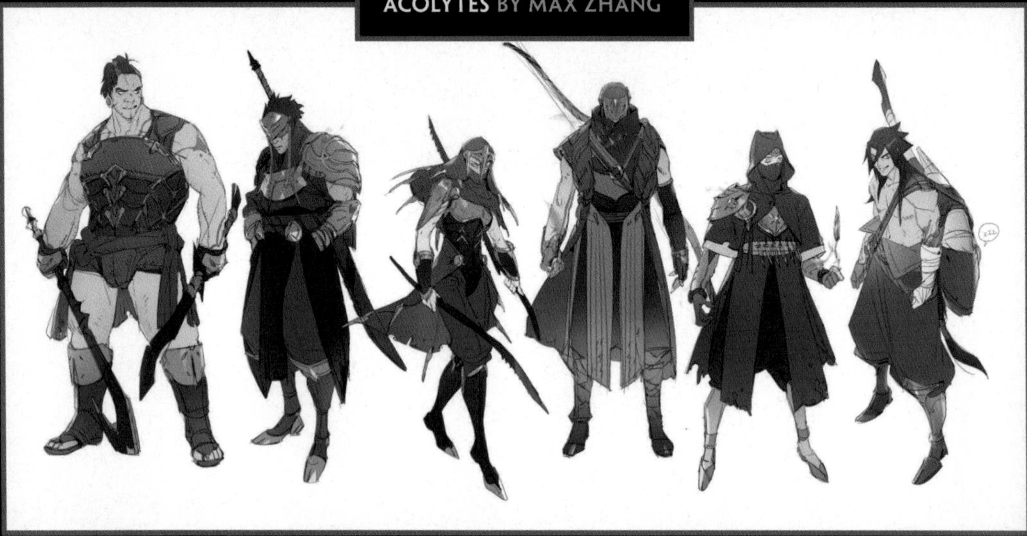

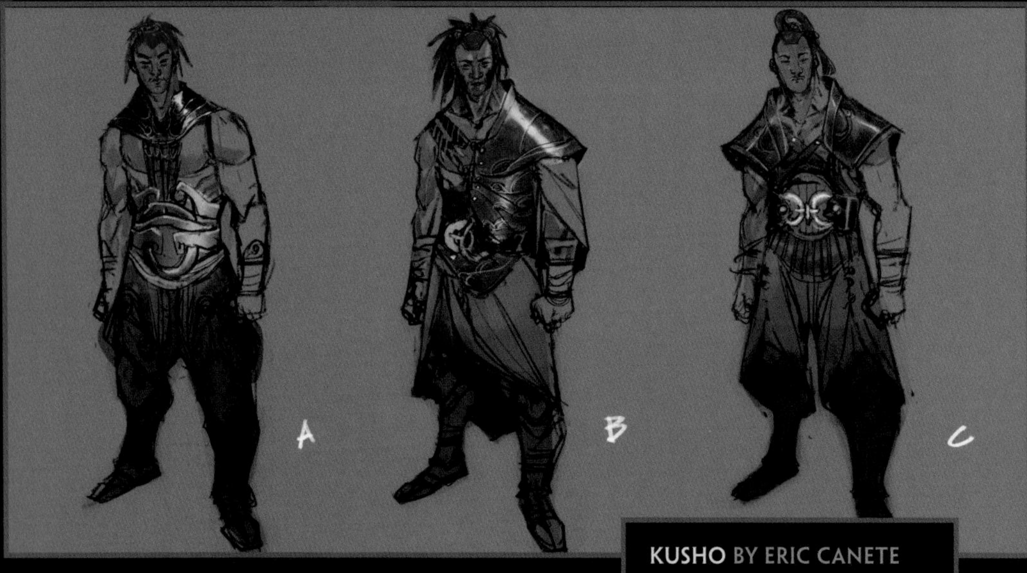
A
B
C

KUSHO BY ERIC CANETE

SHEN UNMASKED BY WILD BLUE STUDIOS

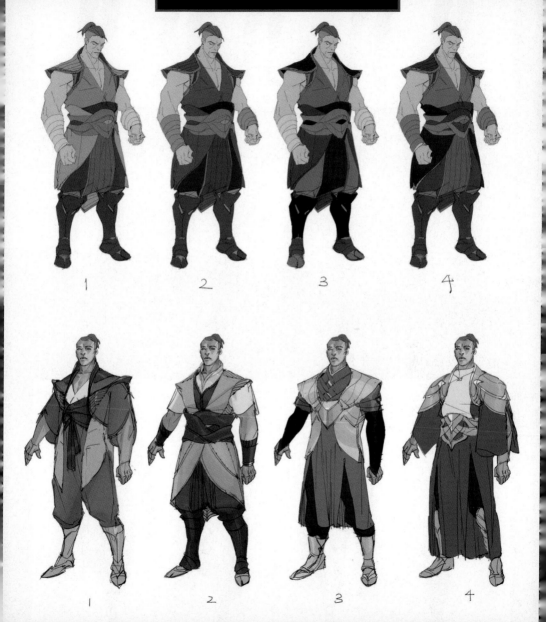

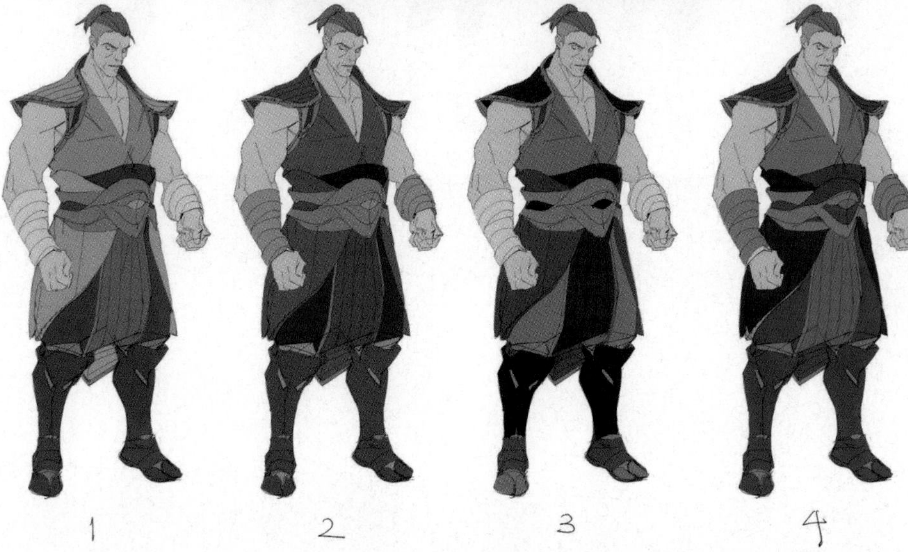
1
2
3
4

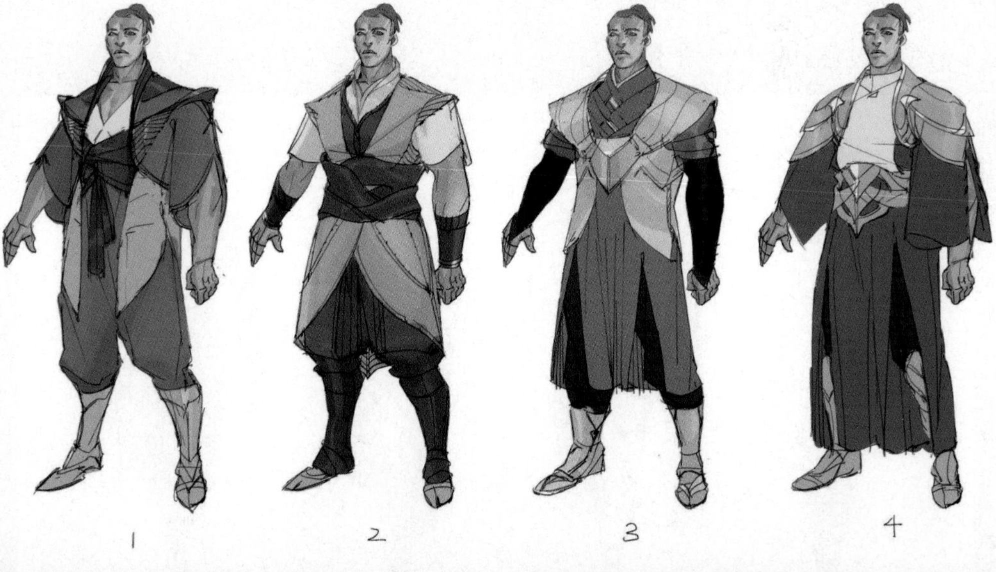
1
2
3
4

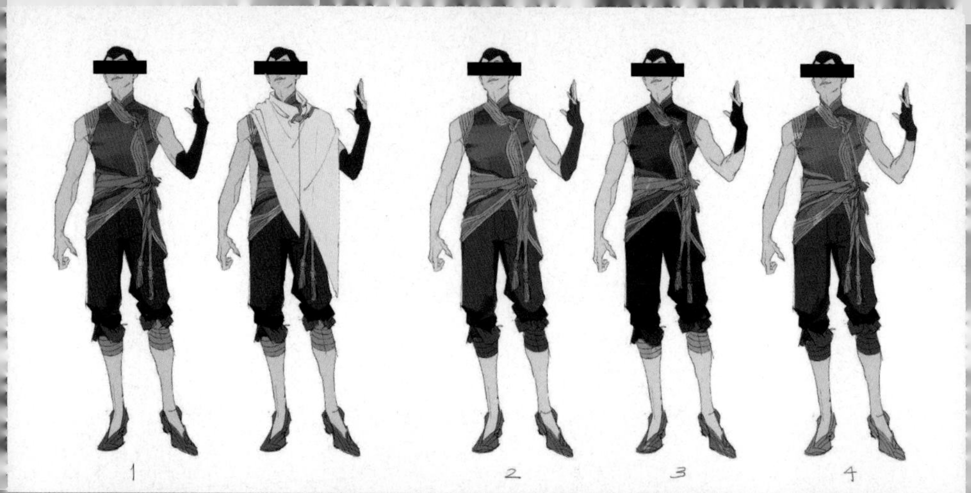
1
2
3
4

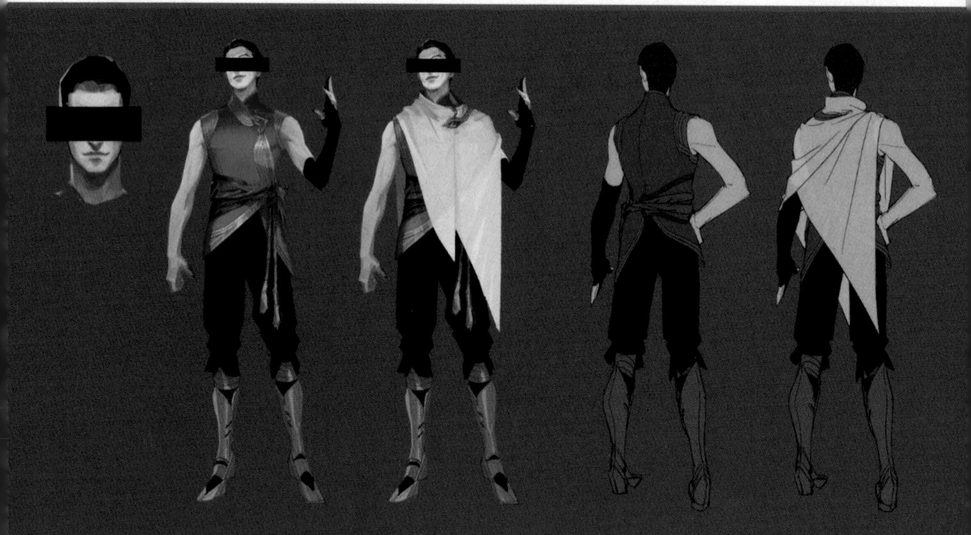

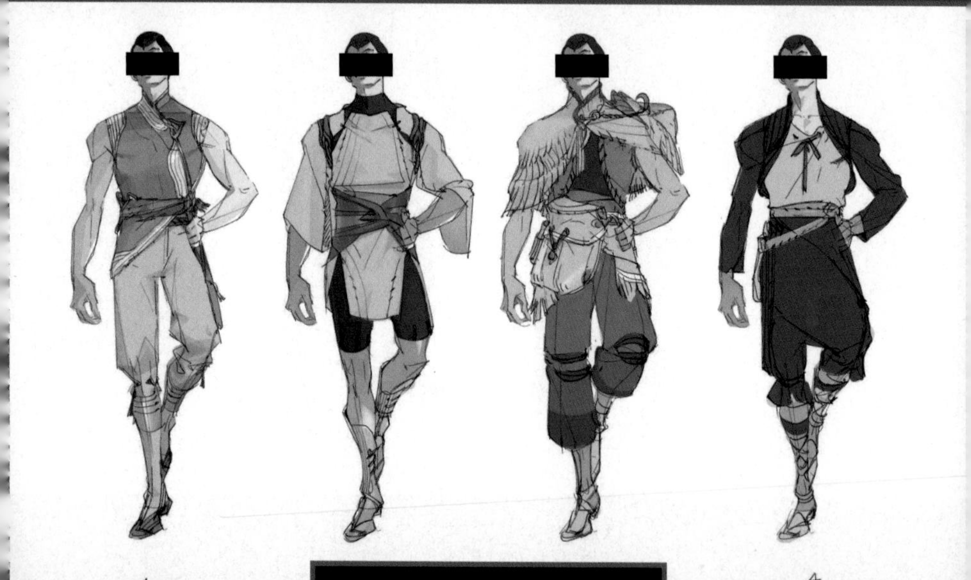
1
4

JHIN BY WILD BLUE STUDIOS

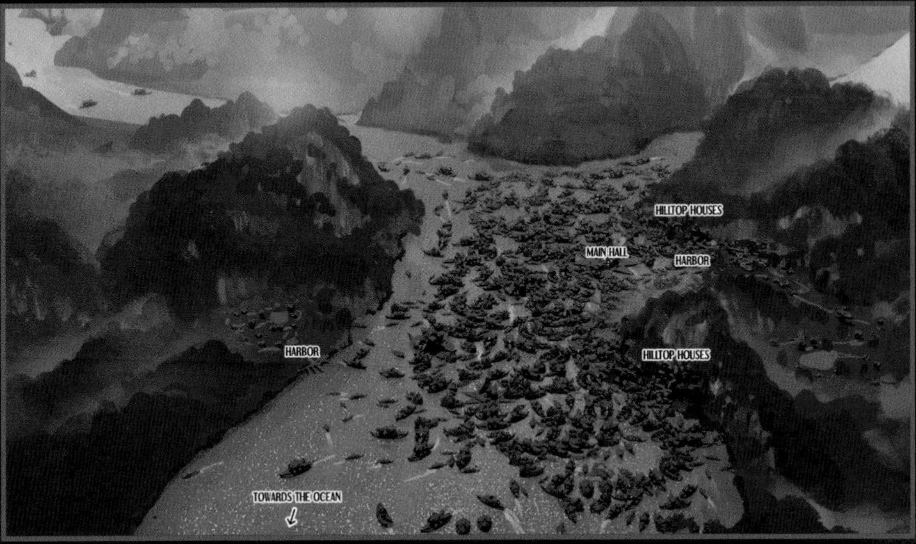
HILLTOP HOUSES
MAIN HALL
HARBOR
HARBOR
HILLTOP HOUSES
TOWARDS THE OCEAN

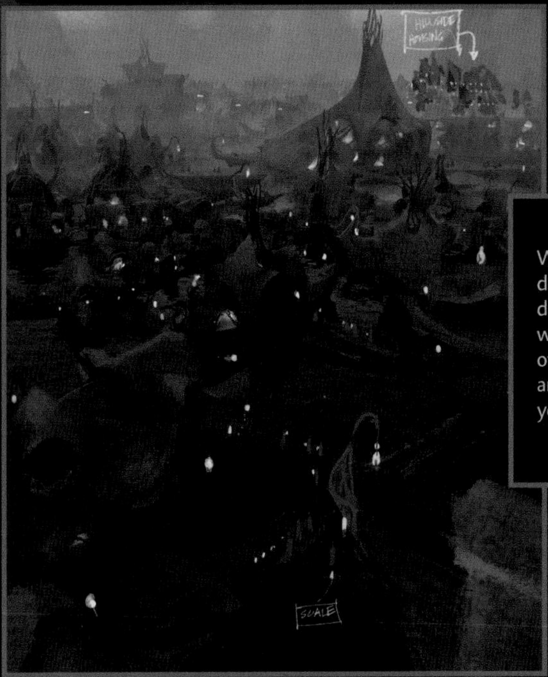
SCALE

FLOATING VILLAGE

We wanted something that looked quite dense. We had yet to delve into the more densely populated regions of Ionia so this was an exciting task. We looked at a lot of lotus leaves and how they scattered around the surfaces to create the organic, yet not chaotic, layout of the village.

BY SEAN YANG

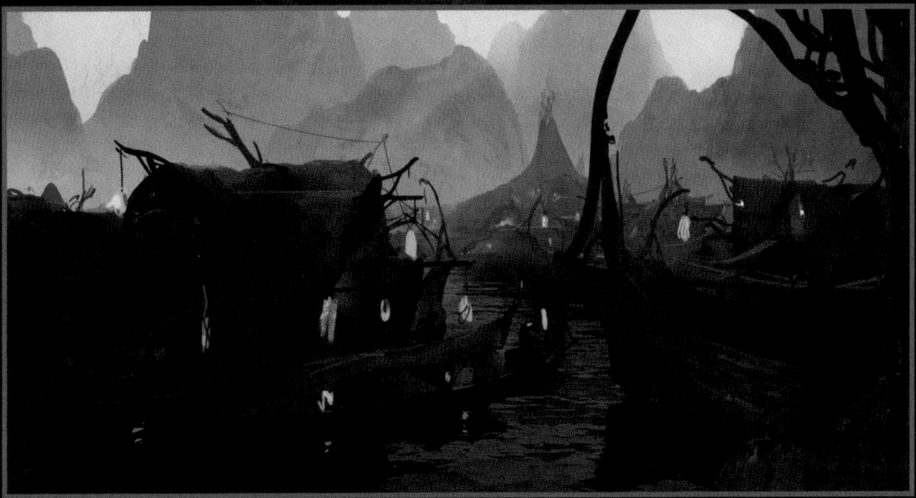

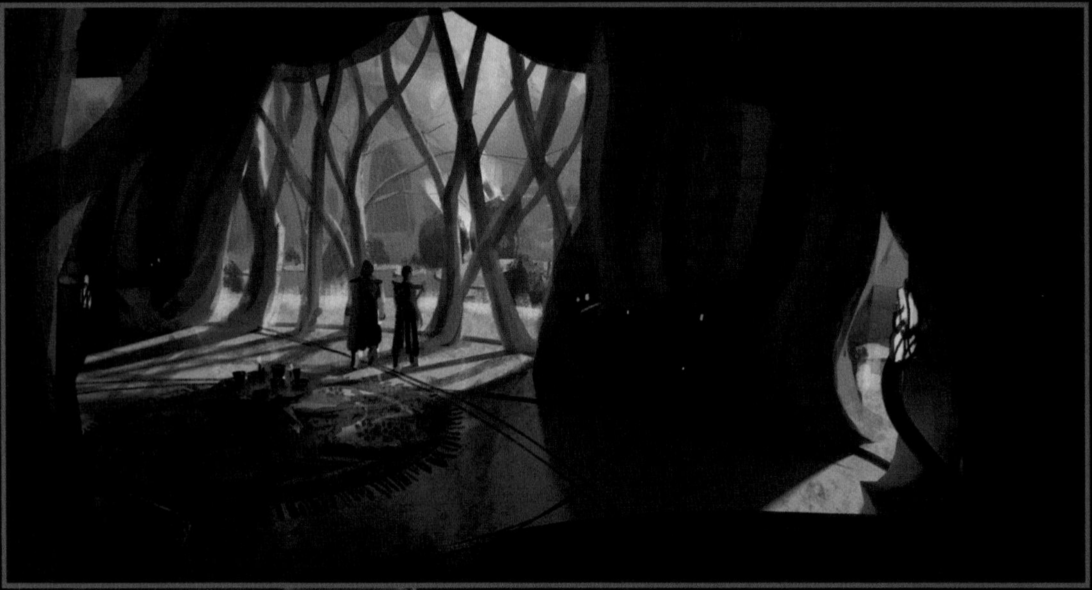

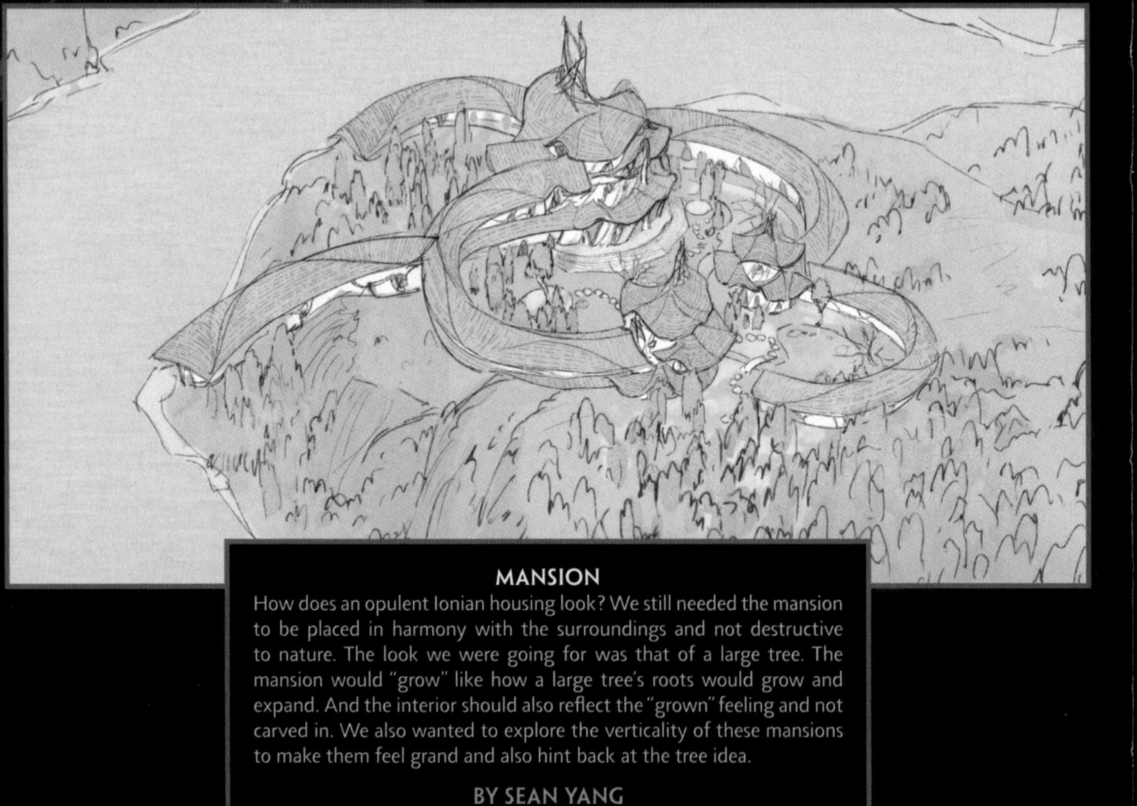

MANSION

How does an opulent Ionian housing look? We still needed the mansion to be placed in harmony with the surroundings and not destructive to nature. The look we were going for was that of a large tree. The mansion would "grow" like how a large tree's roots would grow and expand. And the interior should also reflect the "grown" feeling and not carved in. We also wanted to explore the verticality of these mansions to make them feel grand and also hint back at the tree idea.

BY SEAN YANG

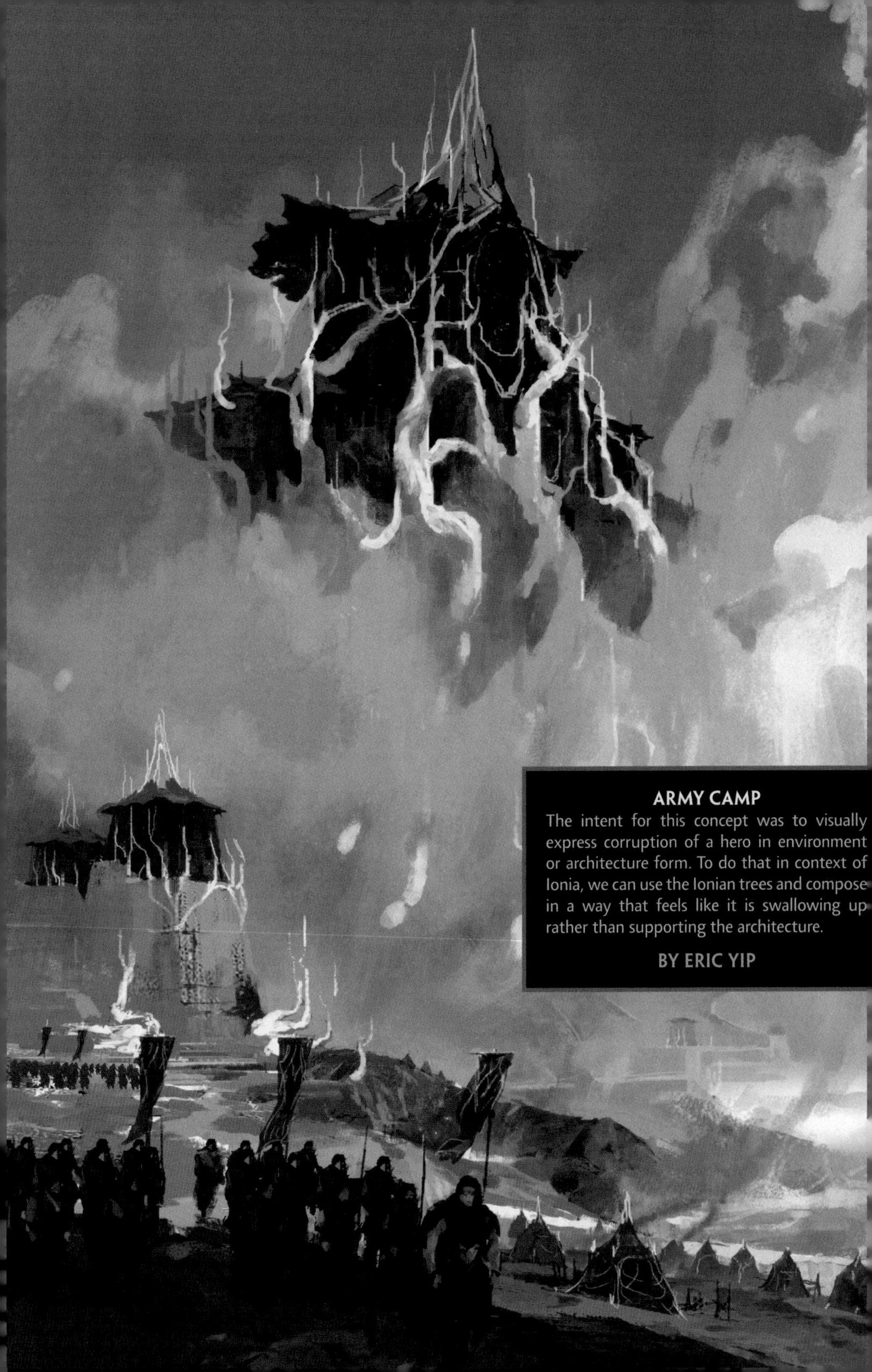

ARMY CAMP

The intent for this concept was to visually express corruption of a hero in environment or architecture form. To do that in context of Ionia, we can use the Ionian trees and compose in a way that feels like it is swallowing up rather than supporting the architecture.

BY ERIC YIP

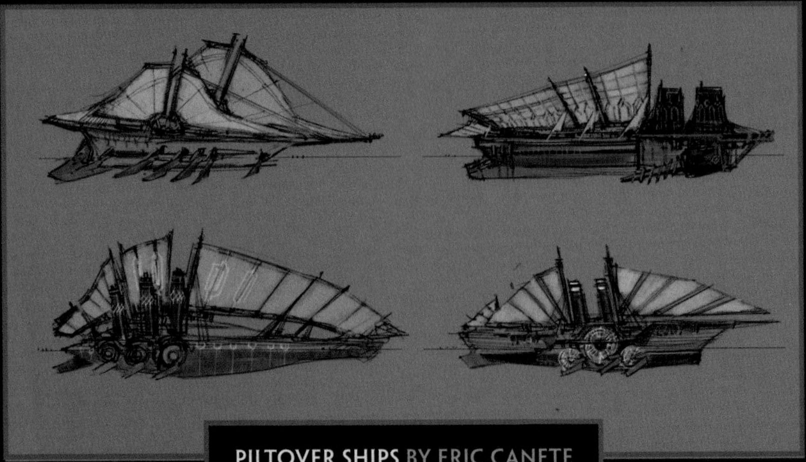

PILTOVER SHIPS BY ERIC CANETE

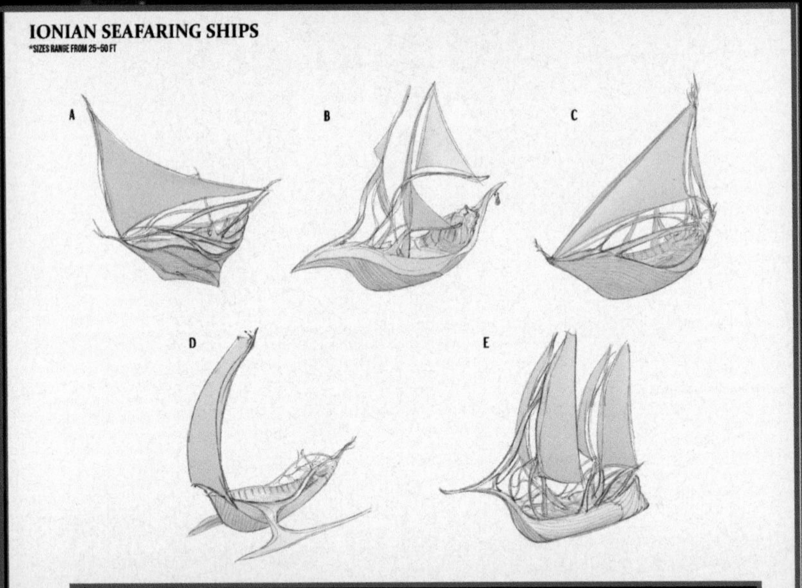
IONIAN SEAFARING SHIPS
*SIZES RANGE FROM 25–60 FT
A
B
C
D
E

IONIA RIVER BARGES

These needed to look like they were of the working class, lived in, and not sleek like the Ionian temples. We also had it in the back of our minds that they were to be connected to other barges to create a larger town. Since we wanted a lively silhouette for the Floating City of Kotha, these needed to vary greatly in size to create an uneven silhouette that felt more spontaneous and not so planned.

BY SEAN YANG

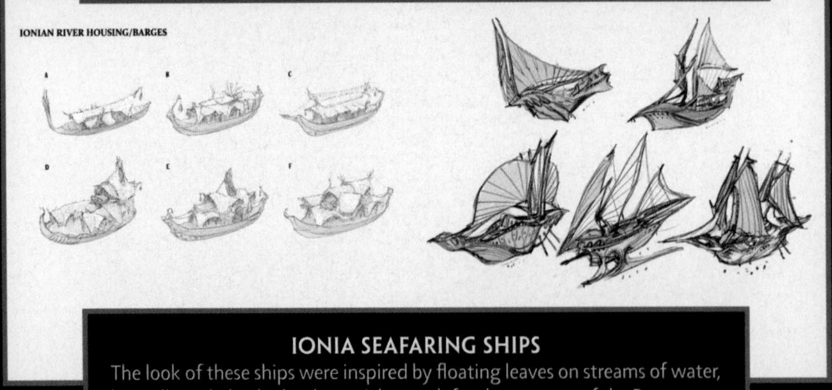
IONIAN RIVER HOUSING/BARGES

IONIA SEAFARING SHIPS

The look of these ships were inspired by floating leaves on streams of water, but still needed to look substantial enough for the vast seas of the Runeterran Ocean. The challenge was to make these look unique and Ionian while still maintaining the look and feel of the seafaring ships that we know of.

BY SEAN YANG

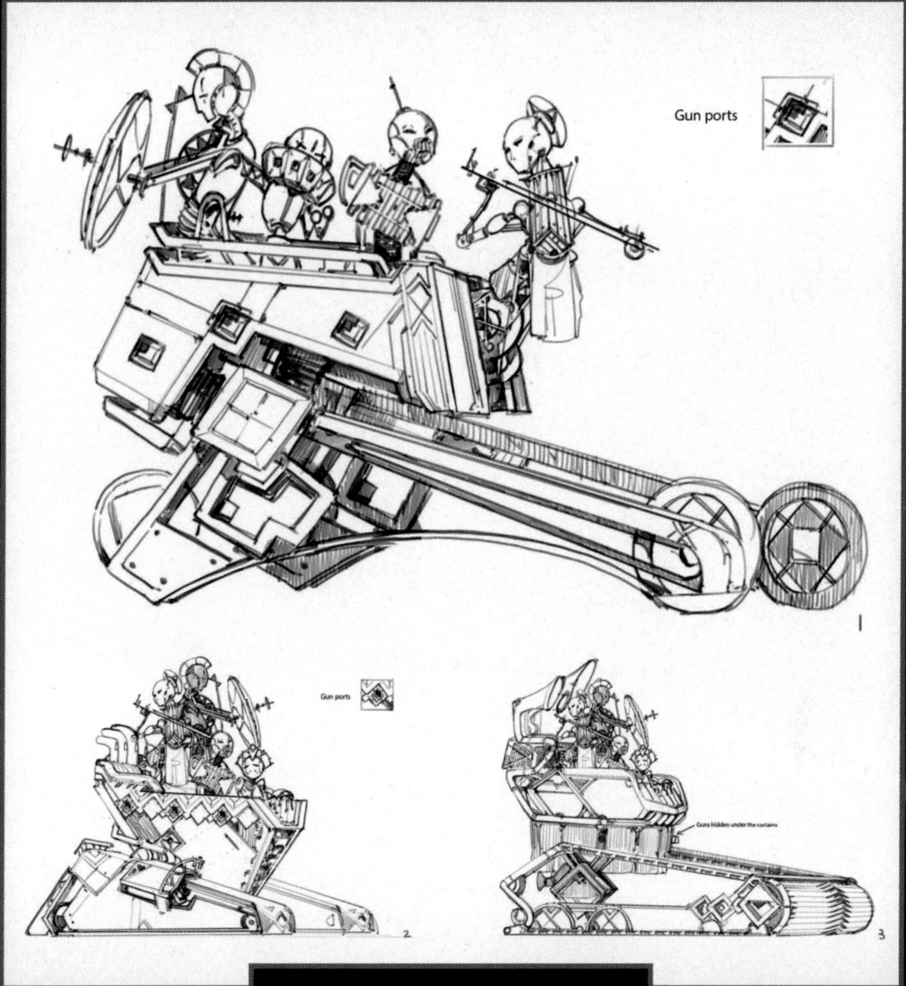
Gun ports
1
Gun ports
2
Guns hidden under the curtains
3

PILTOVER TANK BY QUY HO

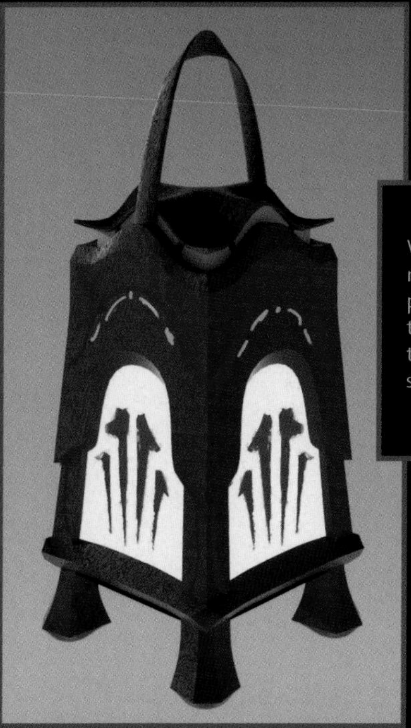

RED JHIN LANTERN

We needed something quite bold and graphic to be noticeable right away in the action-packed comic pages. We tried a couple of different variations that had symbols to represent Jhin, and it seemed that the most obvious one read the best — a more simpler lantern with four marks on it.

BY SEAN YANG

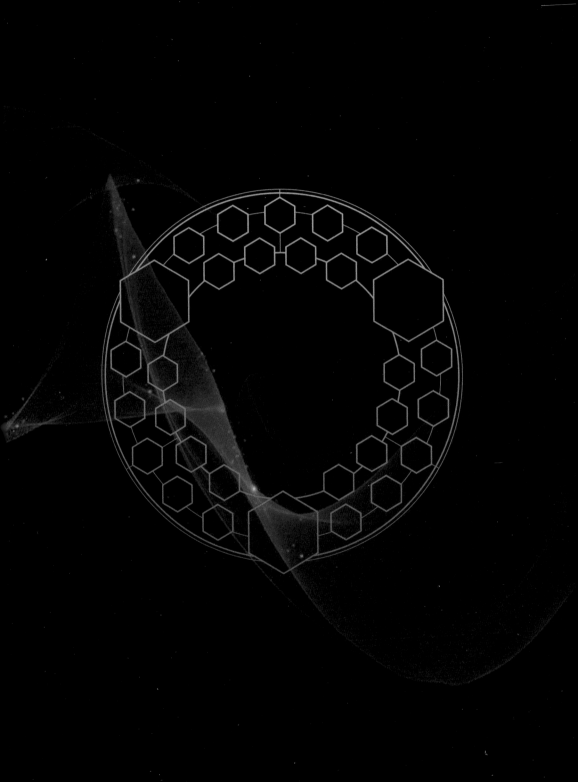